Getting and Spending

A Primer in Economic Morality

Peter L. Danner

Sheed & Ward

Sheed & Ward™ is a service of The National Catholic Reporter Publishing Company.

Library of Congress Cataloguing in Publication Data

Danner, Peter L.
Getting and spending : a primer in economic morality / Peter L. Danner.
p. cm.
Includes bibliographical references and index.
ISBN 1-55612-552-6 (pbk. : alk. paper)
1. Economics--Moral and ethical aspects. I. Title.
HB72.D233 1994
174--dc20 93-40686
CIP

Published by: Sheed & Ward
115 E. Armour Blvd.
P.O. Box 419492
Kansas City, MO 64141

To order, call: (800) 333-7373

DEDICATION

To a generation of students
of economics as a behavioral science
from whom I got as much as I gave.

Contents

PREFACE

To admit to one dominant idea throughout one's academic life may be to confess to a meager intellectual achievement. So be it. But in my case the conviction, that economic principles derived from the universal fact and condition of scarcity must somehow mesh with moral principles based on the dignity of human personality, was the inevitable result of my course of studies. Starting my economics program while I was working toward a licentiate in philosophy at St. Louis University, I, willy-nilly, had to hold simultaneously the validity of two diverse sets of behavioral principles, the economic and the moral.

This general and somewhat amorphous attitude was brought to focus while reading Adam Smith's *Wealth of Nations* for my dissertation on Smith's Social Philosophy. I still remember the Syracuse University Library setting as I spotted this almost passionate paragraph by the usually genial and bland Scots economist.

> Servants, labourers, and workmen of different kinds, make up the far greater part of every great political society. But what improves the circumstances of the greater part can never be regarded as an inconveniency to the whole. No society can surely be flourishing and happy, of which the far greater part of the members are poor and miserable. It is but equity, besides, that they who feed, clothe and lodge the whole body of the people, should have such a share of the produce of their own labour as to be themselves tolerably well fed, clothed and lodged.[1]

The quote had such a familiar ring that I knew I had seen

something similar before and in a quite different course. In fact, I recalled it from an undergraduate course in the Papal Social Encyclicals and specifically from the first of them, Leo XIII's *Rerum Novarum.*

> In the provision of material well-being, the labor of the poor . . . is most efficacious and altogether indispensable. Indeed, their cooperation in this respect is so important that it may truly be said that it is only by the labor of the working man that States grow rich. Justice, therefore, demands that the interests of the poorer population be carefully watched over by the administration so that they who contribute so largely to the advantage of the community may themselves share in the benefits they create—that being housed, clothed and enabled to support life, they may find their existence less hard and more endurable.[2]

That Leo XIII repeated substantially the thought a century old of the acknowledged Father of Economics may owe somewhat to Matteo Liberatore who knew the Classical economists and contributed importantly to the first stage draft of the Encyclical.[3] Granted that, the really remarkable fact is that the scholar-Pope used the same common sense argument to illustrated how people can and should implement God's providential care of human well-being as did the Scots humanist—only mildly Christian—who wished to demonstrate that such sharing was not only just but beneficial for the whole economy. For me it was sufficient to set an agenda for an academic career.

This modest work, therefore, is the fruit of a half-century of study and teaching in the spirit of the conviction that economic rationality and moral convictions can be blended into a consistent set of guides for making decisions and acting in contemporary economic settings.

This conviction sets the tone of the book. It is frankly personalist, not only in the sense of taking the human person as the fundamental fact but even more so in addressing the moral needs of the individual person, rather than attempting to redress society's ills. This also implies, first of all, that it will stress the development of that moral attitude which is fundamental to ethical conduct rather than discuss ethical issues which more frequently than not are so complex as to require professional elucidation.

Second, it starts with the world as it is, which for most of its readers is a world lavish of material well-being and very complex. It makes no apology for economic abundance and affluence. Rather it implies that, all things being equal, it is better to be affluent than not, while at the same time it acknowledges that affluence produces its own complex of moral problems.

Finally, it warns that forming a consistent economic morality is not a pollyannish affair. Shying away from trying to remake the world, it will point to the more discomfiting task of reforming one's self. That, it will imply, is not simply a matter of good will, a once-and-for-all moral conversion. The concepts, fundamental to an economic morality, require study and contemplation, as is illustrated by the efforts of scholars of centuries past to fashion them up to contemporary stages of understanding. Indeed, the study of economic morality will require the humble recognition that people of good will and moralists of acknowledged competence may and will disagree with much presented here and that many issues therein have no definitive answer. Yet, despite this, the book will urge putting its principles into practice, that the intention is all important and that the effort, despite repeated failures, blesses the enterprise.

The thesis of *Getting and Spending* may be summarized as follows. It is not the usual book on business ethics, analyzing the axiological principles pertinent to business and economics and using them to address ethical issues. Rather it formulates the more fundamental attitude of economic morality, a consistent and coherent guide of economic and business conduct, blended from both moral and economic principles of action.

The study starts from a personalist conception of men and women and views the economy and economic acts as essentially social. After a frank look at the benefits and perils of economic abundance, it deduces from the universal and inevitable condition of economic scarcity (the problem of making ends meet) to the need to use material resources and human effort efficiently. This process economics analyzes and guides by developing a galaxy of quantitative ratios, the most familiar of which are price, wealth and gain. These constructs, while wanted for themselves, are instrumental toward producing and getting the commodities and services by which personal and social values are realized.

Thus the crucial analysis of the book centers on the understanding of gain-seeking as a human drive essential for the economy to function and as a distinctive human appetite which, being prone to sensuality, self-glorification, greed and love of power, must be kept in hand especially by the virtues of justice, moderation and spiritual poverty.

All of this brought together produces the conclusion that the moral and economic enterprises, while operating at different levels of human endeavor, are compatible and indeed mutually confirming.

While founded on the nature of the human person and tried in the crucible of controversy, the key concepts of this work have filtered through and been colored by my experiences and convictions, giving them a singularity which is not matched by anyone else's. Every reader, therefore, must try to make them his or her own and apply them to his/her own life and circumstances.

Given the singularity of the book's arguments and my sole responsibility for them, I am beholden, nevertheless, to many, more than I can acknowledge here or even remember. But one association must be singled out from a lifetime of study. The Association for Social Economics, to which I belonged for forty years and was an officer for over twenty, is little known among the larger academic groups in economics, but it is a lively community of scholars, united in conviction that economic science is more than a set of techniques for solving technical problems but is fundamentally a behavioral science which relates to people's larger concerns in life, personal, social, political, moral and religious. Coming from many ideological perspectives, its members provide a forum for writing about and discussing economics in this larger context. They have been a consistent source of inspiration and enlightenment.

To mention here all who have contributed to my understanding of economic morality would be impossible. On the other hand and even at the risk of not mentioning some whom I should, my debt is too great to a few to pass them by without a sincere expression of gratitude. Lowell Dunlap, Ed O'Boyle, Steve Worland, Jonathan Boswell, George Rohrlich, Rupert Ederer, Arnold McKee, Henry Briefs among the living and Thomas Divine, S.J., Bernard Dempsey, S.J., Josef Solterer and Joseph Grau who have passed away. Among these must be included in a special way, William Waters and John Davis, both for their personal influence, and for their splendid editorial work in maintaining the high quality of the *Review of Social Economy* as the intellectual focus of the Association for Social Economics.

The Marquette community, on the other hand, has provided continuous encouragement and material support. This applies to the two excellent deans under whom I served, Bob Martin and Tom Bausch, my colleagues in the economics department, Brian Brush, Masatoshi Abe, Peter Toumanoff, Gene Smiley, indeed all the rest. A general thanks to Marquette's library staff for their unfailing courtesy and help. A special thanks to my competent copyreaders, Susan Gardner, Joan Miller, and to Jim Petr, Dol Rewolinski, Susan Gannon and Marianne Schulz and Nick Schroeder for guiding this novice through the complexities of bringing my thought into print. Much of this work's good is owing to all these Marquette colleagues, its failings are my own.

This acknowledges with thanks permission from Sheed & Ward to reproduce two quotations from Karl Rahner's *Christian in the Market Place.* These appear respectively on pp. 46-7 and 167-7.

1. Smith, Adam, *Wealth of Nations*, (Cannon Edition) Chicago: Encyclopedia Britannica, p. 33.
2. Leo XIII, *Rerum Novarum*, para. 27, *Seven Great Encyclicals*, Glen Rock, NJ: Paulist Press, 1963.
3. Misner, Paul, "The Predecessors of *Rerum Novarum* Within Catholicism," *Review of Social Economy*, (Winter, 1992), p. 450.

Wauwatosa, Wisconsin
March 28, 1993.

CHAPTER ONE

PERSON, COMMUNITY AND SOCIAL ECONOMY

This book is about economic morality. While some people may find 'economic' and 'morality', if not contradictory, incompatible, in fact, the two are found related every day as when a person argues that a labor contract is unjust or a tax bill is unfair. Economic morality, therefore, is concerned with ideas and concepts drawn from both economic and the moral sciences, demonstrating how the principles from both interact in ordinary industrial, market and governmental economic activity. More importantly it helps form a healthy and moral attitude to a side of life which is fraught with material cares and generally subject to the downward pull of secular and often selfish goals.

Economic morality, to be sure, takes its place within a range of behavioral disciplines. In particular it relates to both economic ethics and policy-making but differs from both. Economic ethics attempts to formulate criteria for judging economic and business decisions, actions and policies as morally good or bad. Economic morality is less judgmental and more concerned with promoting and developing an attitude of mind which not only comprehends more and more clearly how the economic and moral dimensions of behavior interact and collaborate, **but puts this understanding into practice.** Ethical judgments, therefore, must be nourished by moral insights lest they become mechanical and legalistic. Moral perceptions, on the other hand, must be tried and judged in the crucible of action and decision-making, lest they become simply idealistic and undoable.

Economic morality is even further removed, but not divorced, from the formation of business and public economic policy. While practical considerations of feasibility, given the actual mores and common practices of a given people at a given time, may dictate policy specifications, nevertheless, policies offensive to the moral convictions of even a minority who are articulate will eventually be modified and even repealed. Conversely, the economic climate generated by current business and public policies will influence, if not people's moral convictions, the relative weight they attach to particular ones. Indeed, the very effort to live up to moral convictions against the pull of social conformity will change their configuration. People mired in poverty, for example, will differ in their moral emphases from those lapped in affluence.

These then are the convictions which motivate presenting this book on economic morality. 1) The hard judgments economic ethics must at times make will go easier if drawing upon a lively sense of economic morality. 2) Similarly, people who can articulate an economic morality are better able to mold business and public policies consistent with rational moral convictions. 3) Whatever the issues, even those requiring an unsatisfactory and unstable compromise, and however adverse the social climate, people, who have a firm grasp on the principles of economic morality, will find that their business and economic concerns can further their development and purposes as human beings.

In other words, people in their everyday economic settings, on shop floors, in offices, boardrooms, banks and supermarkets, engage in moral actions. This, in turn, implies that all economic relations are social relations, persons dealing with persons; that as such they require mutual respect between the parties; and that honest dealing, restraining cupidity and concern for others soften the harsh edges of economic acts by generating a kind of community of shared benefits. Indeed, a sense of economic morality, honed to a fine point, will go beyond being fair in one's daily business dealings to the higher goal of sharing one's material well-being with others.

Economic morality obviously, therefore, is not economic analysis with a dollop of moral principles, nor moral science with a thin veneer of economics. Rather it is an attitude and practice which blends the principles of the two sciences, economics and ethics, neither of which is derived from the other nor denies the other's validity. Obviously also, economic morality only encompasses those principles of each which bear on transacting business and making economic decisions. **In sum, economic morality blends economic understanding into moral convictions so as to form an integrated and consistent guide and goal for business and economic behavior.**

Thus it illustrates once again that cross-fertilization of opposing principles and potencies from which human life begins and human culture develops. The paradigm of this, of course, is human gender: men cannot exist or achieve full development without women, nor women without men. The creativity of the interplay between opposing polarities is illustrated throughout life: male/female, divine/human, adult/child, artist/audience, faith/reason, mind/heart, logic/feeling, action/contemplation, day/night, summer/winter. Neither denies the other, neither absorbs the other. Each modifies and enriches the other in action. So too, economics and morality clarify each other in pertaining to economic and business issues.

During the course of examining the constituents of that attitude called economic morality, the reader may well have discerned three key concepts: **person, community and social economy.** The first is obvious, since every economic actor, whatever his or her role as worker, manager, consumer, banker, borrower, broker or tax-collector, is a person and must be treated as such. Second, persons develop and find their happiness in community with others—in marriages, families and neighborhoods; in classes, clubs and teams; in religious, charitable and social associations; in military squads and work gangs—in any grouping which shares common values and provides mutual support. For economic associations to be truly human they too must foster in some way the spirit of community. Finally, the possibility of economic community lies in this that, since all economic actions and transactions involve others, they are social and all economics is social economics. **Person, Community and Social Economy,** as key themes running through the book, it will be necessary to examine each of them in turn.

PERSON AND PERSONALITY

Of the three the really key concept is *person*. If economic agents are persons, then, as the chapter will explain, they are moral beings and their actions, and of special interest here, their economic actions, are subject to moral criteria. It is necessary, therefore, to lay out a clear and complete definition of what a person is.

This task will draw from a Personalist view of humans and especially that formulated by the French philosopher and Vichy dissident, Emmanuel Mounier (1905-50).[1] Personalism starts from the assumption that the human person is the most appropriate subject of human contemplation. Though not a philosophic system itself, it mines all systems, classic, medieval and modern, for insights into human personality. It is especially owing to the Judeo-Christian conception of men and woman as free and immortal beings, each the unique creation of a loving God who unites all to himself as their beginning and ultimate end. For the purpose here, sorting out the contributions of particular philosophies to Personalism can be left to historians of philosophies.

Instead it is necessary to examine in a common sense way the essential features of human personality. A look at one's self and at the men and women met everyday reveals that people come in all shapes and sizes from midgets to all-pro tackles; colors, from off-white to blue-black; cultures, Amazonian villagers to Manhattan socialites; moral convictions, Mother Teresas to Josef Stalins. Despite this diversity, all are persons. What then is the essential trait which constitutes each as person?

Self-Awareness

Asking the question answers it. A person is alone of all earthly beings able to ask: Who or What am I? Persons can be conscious of their being here and now, can remember themselves as the same from infancy to old age and can imagine themselves in other circumstances and times, and yet maintain their integrity of being. **In short, persons possess not only sight but insight, hindsight and foresight and know themselves as the same, past, present and future.**

While part of the chain of material being from rocks to plants, to animals, to humans and sharing with them materiality, vitality, instinct and sensibility and often being surpassed by them in these abilities, humans are a class apart in possessing self-consciousness. The Genesis story says it well that Adam named all the plants and animals, that is, knew their natures, but found none like himself. This ability to differentiate other species bestows command over them: people can not only learn from them but can domesticate and use them. As a consequence we humans are responsible for the other species' care and survival. (To emphasize the self-analysis here the text shifts to the first person.)

Self-awareness distinguishes how we know ourselves. Unlike the way we know other people and things from the outside by weighing and measuring them and by observing their actions and functions, we see ourselves from within as we think, will, feel and the rest. Of course, we cannot know all our physical conditions; often misinterpret our thoughts, wishes, impulses and addictions; and can never fathom the innermost mystery of our personality. Nevertheless, knowing ourselves is of endless fascination to us humans as the millions of diaries, letters, poems, biographies and the endless talk about what we think and feel attest. All of this is unique to humankind. No chimpanzee as yet has told us what being a monkey means. Until one does, the gap between us and them is impassable.

Self-awareness is also self-judgment. We can not only know what but why we do what we do. We can know our motives and purposes. While we may not do this always and some people seldom if ever, nevertheless, we can examine our reasons for acting and judge them and the act right or wrong. This is the basis of our moral responsibility. We need not rely on the reaction of other people to critique our conduct. Indeed, we can criticize ourselves when others praise us and justify our conduct when others condemn it.

Self-awareness, therefore, is the essential trait, distinguishing the human person from all other species. Any other definition, for example, the Aristotelian 'rational animal,' presupposes it, since we cannot describe or define ourselves unless we are first aware of ourselves. The self-awareness of this creature, who is bound to matter like other earthlings, is both humanity's grace and glory and the source of human tragedy. Constrained yet free. Bound to others yet individual. Material yet spiritual. Mortal yet seeking immortality. This fascinating and complex being calls for more than the brief examination we can give to this **free, material, social and transcendental human person.**

Free and Responsible

The ability to appraise and evaluate who we are and what we do is essential to human freedom. For freedom consists in knowing one's own good, being able to do it and taking responsibility for it. The human person, alone in all material creation, possesses this power. All material creatures are programmed to do what they do and to become what they become. What they want is driven by instinct or dictated by another. Our lives are also in some sense programmed in that we are born, flourish, decline and die, largely regardless of our will in these events. But within this framework we enjoy wide latitude of action, making choices which will have consequences for our future conduct and well-being. Such a wonderful power needs some looking into.

First and foremost, freedom and responsibility go together like heads and tails of coins. An act for which I am not responsible is not really mine and is not, therefore, a free act. Denying or ignoring my responsibility for actions produces a sham freedom called licence. In short, freedom must meet two tests: accountability and acting for one's own good, however mistaken that might be. So freedom, this awesome power persons possess, is not an absolute good and end in itself, but only the means required by self-knowledge and self-judgement for humans to realize their good and achieve their purposes.

Second, human freedom is not unlimited. Obviously, we are not free to do what is physically impossible. Personal freedom is violated by others' imposing through force or fear their good on us at the expense of our own. Nor are we acting truly freely, when through habit, passion, ignorance or wilfulness we do what we think is good but really bad for us. Thus freedom, the very glory of humankind, is at the same time a source of frustration, of bitter quarrels and a cause of physical and moral self-destruction. It brings a terrible responsibility which most of us at some time in our lives, in major matters or small, are tempted to relinquish. **Freedom is not for the faint-hearted. Slavery, political, economic or moral, has an appeal to which many succumb.**

Freedom, therefore, is a second theme which will run through this study. Sketchy though this presentation, these considerations should be kept in mind: freedom distinguishes humans from all other species; freedom imposes responsibility; freedom, therefore, is the way, unique to human persons, by which they achieve their good and ultimate fulfillment.

Limited and Constrained

Freedom's limitations point to a fundamental feature of our nature as human persons: as material beings we are limited in time and space but as spiritual beings we are not so restricted to the here and now. We can in thought communicate with peoples across the world or long dead. We can in memory roam throughout our past or in imagination throughout the universe. We are free in will and hope to aspire to goals, now seemingly impossible. In short, spirit is *the* source of our freedom, while as bodies we are restricted to the here and now.

My being here now results from a long series of events: conception, birth, family moves, schooling, jobs, marriage, purchase of homes, and more immediately getting out of bed to come to the office. With some of these events, I had no choice;

others I freely chose but now regret; others I resisted but now approve. However, they occurred, they did and I am *here now and cannot be elsewhere.* This conclusion, to which a moment's reflection will concur, means that to be body is to be **confined to a specific place at a specific time.** Where and when are determined by all the past events in one's life.

Body is indeed restricting: physically, biologically and socially. Like all matter body is subject to physical laws: gravity, space, entropy. Bodily movements, however graceful and agile, are limited to one's musculature and skeleton. As biological, the body must breath, eat, exercise and sleep; as mammalian, it must reproduce sexually; as material and mobile, its travel and possessions must be governed by law; as living it is subject to disease, decline and death. As embodied beings, we are limited by others' property, space and rights to move about and to express their minds and feelings. In all this body confines and limits freedom.

Body is, however, the means by which we act. We learn only through our senses; we communicate only by sound, gesture, facial expression or by operating machines. Every act, even the most spiritual, requires physical effort. The concentration study, for example, requires is physically tiring. When the body malfunctions or the mind is weary, intellectual effort suffers. Lacking sleep or in shock, a person becomes incoherent. Old age can reduce the most brilliant mind to idiocy. On the positive side, however, our bodies are operational marvels, every organ and system wondrously complex in design yet functionally simple, responsive to change yet resilient to damage. The records of athletes, the accomplishments of geniuses and the endurance of heroes attest to the lengths to which spirit can push the body. Nevertheless, the free play of spirit is confined to the range of the physically possible, which limitations, however, permit some predictability in human behavior.

All of this is relevant to understanding ourselves as persons. We can view ourselves as bodies so marvelous that they invade the realm of spirit or as spirits so low on the scale they need bodies to function. Realism, however, demands knowing and accepting ourselves as both body and spirit, and counters the simplifying tendency to see the human person as just one or the other. Let philosophers argue, as they have and will, whether we are spiritualized bodies or embodied spirits. For this study we need but accept that our physical state conditions our mental and spiritual functions and that our spiritual well being, a sense of purpose and meaning in life, helps to husband bodily powers, to maintain health, and to give zest to life. **A fundamental realism about ourselves as persons argues for keeping in balance our bodily needs and spiritual aspirations.**

Singular but Social

A further function of body is to individualize us. We can neither reduplicate another nor be reduplicated. Even identical twins have subtle differences which distinguish them. For all others, one's genetic code is specific to each of us. There is, finally, an inner sanctum solely our own which we in this life cannot entirely penetrate and certainly is unutterable to others. We are each a unique historical event. But our singularity and individuality need little stressing in the contemporary emphasis on being one's self and doing one's thing. What is slighted is our social nature.

We are social beings, being related by existence and nature to other persons. We are conceived and born related to a man and woman as natural parents and through them to their other children and to their parents, brothers and sisters. From conception, therefore, we are suspended in this web of personal ties—parents, siblings, grandparents, aunts, uncles, cousins and so on from generation to generation. Traced to its beginning this network unites us by blood to all people. **We come into existence so related or we never exist at all.**

If then we are all related to each other, then other people are as much person as I am. Hence, persons must be infinitely reproducible, each unique but an authentic person. As such no person manifests the totality of human personality, the quality of being person. And so from everyone we can learn something about being a person.

Experience testifies that we learn best about being human from loving relationships, from a warm family life, from school and neighborhood friendships, from joining in a common effort and sharing common values, and especially from an affectionate marriage. But every newscast, book, picture or performance can tell us something of human aspirations, creativity and tragedy. Even passing contacts or events across the world can bring home to us what being human means. Enemies and those who dislike us are particularly beneficial because, though they may exaggerate our faults, they are embarrassingly accurate in spotting them. **All of life involves learning more about ourselves by and in knowing others.**

At the same time, our knowledge of our own thoughts, feelings and motives allows us to achieve a certain objectivity regarding others's psychic states. All those ministering functions of advising, counselling and mentoring in an on-going way, or serving as confessor, judge or jury in grave singular matters presuppose that in knowing our own inner states we can help others to know theirs. Without this constant interplay between others' reaction to us and ours to them, our self-awareness becomes in-grown, distorted and often festering. **Self-knowledge must be social knowledge.**

Personality indeed grows and flowers only in a social setting by using the cultural institutions available. We obtain knowledge from parents, teachers, schoolmates and authors. We absorb beauty from poets, painters, sculptors, actors and musicians. We practice cooperation in earning a living by producing the commodities others desire. We acquire civility and tolerance in democratic relations and political interaction. We learn to respect property and life in the processes of justice. We grow in love of God through the word and example of moral leaders. Social interaction is, indeed, the very matrix for growth in personality. **We cannot exist, know, or develop except as a social person.**

The Transcendence Dimension

Implicit in the other facets of human personality is a dynamic, an urge to grow, a striving to fulfill one's possibilities as an individual and as a person. In some this is so low key as to be almost non-existent; in others it is a compelling and consuming drive; for most it translates into a sense of never being completely satisfied with what one is or has. This is what can be called a person's transcendence dimension.

Transcendence has several meanings, most rather esoteric. Here is meant the desire to achieve a better state of being than the present. Children play at being grown-up. Teen-agers anticipate college or a first job. A company, earning its first million of profits, sets its sights on 10. Scholars strive to write that definitive article or book; artists to recapture the vision of absolute beauty; saints to achieve perfect union with God. The discouraged, the traumatized and victimized express negatively the universal desire to be better off. Defenders of the status quo will take improvements for themselves which they might deny to others. Even the complacent, if pushed, can envisage changes which would better their lives.

This dynamic, therefore, is not only universal but incorporates all the other aspects of personality. It goes beyond the notion that we are accountable for what we are and have done to the further idea that persons, utilizing their freedom, can and do change from what they are now, fashioning themselves from within. In striving for fulfillment persons must be aware and critical of themselves and their actions. Knowing others as different, though authentic, manifestations of personality provides object lessons on what we can do and become. Yet such striving must be realistic, taking into account what we are and what goals are possible. We are what we are even in striving to be better than we are.

Most importantly, this transcendental drive is the crowning thrust of human freedom. For each of us, regardless of our initial disadvantages or social circumstances, is ultimately responsible for what we become. This dynamic, therefore, encapsulates the very essence of personality. Each person's unique destiny, expressed in human sociality, implies a role to play in relation to others, a vocation which the person should fulfill. Ontologically, transcendence means that every person is not only a seeker of values but an **absolute and unique value. This is the basic dignity of each of us, the common denominator of all human beings. No matter how lovable or execrable, each of us is sacred. The greatest crime against anyone is to destroy this dignity. The greatest crime against ourselves is to lose this self-respect.**

So this is the human person, the one being I know from within. Contemplating myself and, by analogy, others, I see this marvelously simple—the unique "I" through all its transformations from infancy to now—and yet bewilderingly complex individual person as part of material creation, yet transcending it. Physical: like a rock, subject to the laws of physics and chemistry; biological: like all animals, self-moving, sexual, alimentary, governed by an inner principle of growth, senescence and death; like the higher animals, sensitive, learning by feeling, seeing, hearing and smelling, responsive to pain and pleasure; social, involved with others personally, politically and economically. Yet at the same time spiritual and free, apprehending the natures of people and things and desiring them as good; and transcendental, striving for some only hoped-for ultimate end and purpose, which for many is union somehow with infinite reality. (With that the text reverts to third person.)

Human Action

Just as persons are complex, so their actions are multifaceted, simultaneously physical, biological, social, economic, political, transcendental and so forth. Consider the many features of the every day act of buying a loaf of bread: the bread is material; it is nourishing and shared by others; it is an economic good and as property protected by law. Even so the act is transcendental: the bread as means toward some goals beyond the present. This simple act, therefore, can become the subject of many sciences and disciplines, attesting once more to the paradox of a **complex system and a simple function.**

The many characteristics of human acts, which may be called *principles of action*, obviously proceed from and correspond to the many aspects of human personality. Some elements of action, like the physical and biological, are instinctive. Some, like the aesthetic and moral, must be cultivated. Some, like the hope for a better life, respond to deep ontological yearnings. Whatever their genesis, the principles of action are hierarchically ordered: the highest relate to a person's highest good, the next to relations with others, and the lowest to the material conditions of life. While each principle is distinct, they so blend together in action that a change in one changes the entire act. To steal the bread, for example, would make the act illegal and the thief might end up in a lock-up instead of at the family table. **If any element of an act is permanently modified, the entire act is changed.**

Most frequently what changes the proportions of the ingredients and thus differentiates an act from others is the person's *purpose* for acting, the good or goal he or she seeks. The act of voting, for example, is called a political act because the person purposes to make a political statement and thus emphasizes that particular aspect. Indeed some purposes may be so intense, like the rush out of a burning building, that all other principles may be swamped by the biological desire for survival. **Purpose, motive and intention, therefore, as the reasons for acting are primary bases for assessing an act's morality.**

While brief, the foregoing emphasis on human personality and action indicates that the study will try to avoid the current fashion of talking in abstractions, labor, management, society, government and the like, for the more concrete and flesh and blood realities of workers, managers, politicians, bureaucrats and householders who actually do aspire, form policy and act, and are, therefore, in real life the economic and moral actors. With that, the chapter turns to its second theme, community.

THE SPIRIT OF COMMUNITY

Persons, because they are dynamic, will always be in process of change. Of all the ways people can develop as persons and enhance their endowed qualities what is of interest here is that they can foster their innate sociality by **forming community.**

Community here does not mean neighborhood, although such can become one, but it refers to the close relation which develops among mutually caring people who share common values and a sense of belonging. Community, therefore, besides fostering mutual friendship and love, provides support in holding the values the group and its members espouse.

The family unit is often cited as the paradigm of community, since ideally each spouse cherishes the other's good as his or her own and the children begotten of their mutual love become the common good of both. But just as family unity can range from the closely knit to the severally estranged, so the spirit of community can animate a group more or less intensely. Secondly, the many reasons for people associating together will change the kind of community it is as, for examples, a church, school, social club, athletic team, political party and, of interest here, a work-place. Finally, a bogus community can also take many shapes and forms. It can be aped in an ephemeral group organized for a particular purpose who will disperse once the campaign is over. It can be perverted in the violence and hatreds of street gangs. It can be counterfeited by demagogues playing on class, racial and religious bigotry.

Given the great variety of bogus and partial community, it is important to examine briefly the three essentials which define **true** community. 1) True community is a fellowship of *individual persons,* 2) who share *common purposes and values* and 3) whose grouping has some *structure* and promises some *continuity.*

A Fellowship of Persons

Only persons can generate community. Only persons can commit themselves freely to others. Only persons can voluntarily enter into association with others as individuals, bringing their particular abilities and talents along with their physical, social and spiritual limitations. Only persons can responsibly seek their own good in the common good of the group, always remaining answerable for their own actions, even those performed for the good of and in the name of the group. Conversely, what a member seeks and what the association offers will never match perfectly. But the tension between group and individual may be good for both: for the group in stretching its goals to accommodate the needs of the member and for the individual by refining his or her expectations to within the scope of a more comprehensive common goal. Where no fit of goals or values is possible the person should depart as freely as he or she entered the association.

Sharing Cultural Values

This concern for personality and individuality is the paramount value sought in community. It implies as values all those features of personality already discussed. Thus community meets the need for human sociality, it accepts differences in talents and limitations, and safeguards personal freedom and transcendental aspirations. Obviously, members cannot be cut from the same cloth, brain-washed to fit a preconceived pattern, nor dragooned into lock-step behavior. By the same token members must respect each other's individuality and personality, affirming that **the strength of community arises from combining diverse talents and limitations, aspirations and contributions.**

While the spirit of community and of commitment to a common good is impossible without this fundamental respect of each in the group for the *unique value* that is every person, the individual must affirm the purpose and values for which the group is formed and which differentiate it as a community. Families are founded for the values of shared and intimate love; churches for worship, good works and moral growth; schools for acquiring knowledge, understanding and intellectual development; athletic teams for exercise, sportsmanship and winning; and so for other varieties of true community. Among the shared values each member's priorities will differ. Achieving collaboration, therefore, will require consensus, reached through a process of compromise and the blending of opinions in which no one dominates and to which all contribute.

A third set of values would be assumed but perhaps not

articulated. These would be such social values as love of country, respect for law and public institutions, welfare of families, moral convictions, concern for the disadvantaged, social justice and the like. Ignoring these values poses the danger of the group's turning in upon itself, selfishly putting group interests ahead of and at the expense of the public good. Every such association is part of society and cannot like a cancer destroy the social organism from which it draws its members.

The sharing of values, it is obvious, is the very spirit of community, not an equal sharing, not even a conscious sharing for some, but sharing nevertheless. For community is generated by mutual respect for each other and for each's aspirations. It happens spontaneously when some members, maybe not all, realize they share a common set of values and want to contribute to the good of the group holding the values. From this conviction they proceed to that rapport which tells them they belong.

Belonging

In a group united in the spirit of community each member belongs as an individual. With this group a person is at home. It is, writes the psychologist Rollo May, "where I share my innermost thoughts, bring out the depth of my feelings, and know they will be understood . . . [It] is the group in which I can depend upon my fellows to support me." Here I have status, a role. I am somebody, not just one of the crowd, not just a statistic. I may not be liked, even thought obnoxious, but I am accepted and have a voice. "It is where," continues May, "my moral courage, consisting of standing against members of my own community, is supported even by those I stand against."[2]

The spirit of community is, therefore, a new dimension of human sociality. It cannot be forced or legislated: it simply happens and seldom in a dramatic way. But for those for whom it does, life in a subtle way takes on new meaning. More than relating to others, people become committed to each other so that everyone can rely on everyone else. Community spirit both enhances personal freedom and restrains it. It constrains by requiring the sacrifice of lesser individual goods of time, money and effort to support the larger community good. It enhances freedom by sharing in the communal good, enriching not supplanting each individual's good. As with freedom itself, community is a way by which people fulfill their vocations in society and realize their destinies in life. But this larger scope for freedom is not without it own perils.

Tension, of course, can arise between the group's good and the individual's good, in that each can be, and often is, a means to achieve the other: the member using the group for his or her own benefit; the association exploiting the member to its advantage. But this tension should not be eased in such a way as to favor either because the tension itself can energize the spirit of community, whose essence consists in the members' contributing to the community good and thereby simultaneously and reciprocally helped to reach their own goals and good. These two movements, therefore, the members contributing to group goals and the group supporting members' aspirations both sustain the spirit of community and threaten its demise. Once community ceases to further its members' goals it dies. Once it becomes a cockpit of competing personal interests, it disintegrates.

Continuity: Authority and Structure

The tension inherent in any association suggests that, while community is essentially a matter of spirit, some authority and structure is necessary for a community to survive as an institution. Members must fit into their roles or be encouraged to adapt to new ones. Their different talents and commitments, weaknesses and needs require coordination. Survival means replacing old members with new, meeting their different needs and responding to changed circumstances. Policy must authorize an executive or executive committee to interpret or restate the values and purposes of the community to new members and staff. Methods must be available by which the community responds to new demands, undertakes new activities and effects the transition to new leaders.

In families this occurs naturally in a cycle of formation, growth, decline and death, one generation giving way to the next. The same is true of other informal groups like "the old high-school crowd." Leadership here is natural as with families or casual with spontaneous fellowships. In more formal associations the executive may be appointed by a higher body or elected by the members. Authority, the obligation to articulate the goals and values of the group, is usually vested in the leadership but it may be shared by a cabinet of advisors or arise out of group consensus. This diversity in structure and authority from the highly formalized to the nearly inchoate reflects the variety of purposes which initially generates community.

Summing Up

Community, briefly put, is the spirit which animates a group of people who know they belong and in which they are at home. Essential to it is sharing values and mutual support. Accepted as individuals, members possess status and perform roles according to each's talents and commitment. No one can decree community to exist: when the psychic chemistry is right it happens. People may enjoy community without knowing it, realizing only after losing it that their lives and relations with others were richer and fuller. Community, although more a matter of feeling and perception than constitution and organization, nevertheless, for continuity needs structure and authority. These, in turn, will vary widely according to the nature and function of the association.

While an overall spirit of community may not be manifest in a large organization, it may flourish in coteries within it: for example, in a production department or research laboratory. Thus, if only in the minimal sense of respecting customers, colleagues and bosses as fellow human beings, the spirit of community can germinate in a sales, office or work setting. This study, in fact, will demonstrate that economic morality is not only necessary for but will tend to generate at least an embryonic condition of community. At the same time, the study will acknowledge that community in a business milieu, in being consistent with the nature of such institutions, will not be suffused with the warm love of a family circle or the easy camaraderie of a social club. In showing that some degree of community is possible, it will argue that any is better than none. **Where community, however embryonic and incomplete, abides, the business and—extrapolating—the economy will run better and people will live fuller and more integrated lives.[3]**

Having examined what the human person and the spirit of community are, the chapter turns to the third of its basic entities, the social economy.

THE SOCIAL ECONOMY

Most economists would not typically stress the view insisted here of the social nature of economic relations. They would, if asked, tend to group around the two extremes of the minimal restrictions of Individualistic Capitalism or the freedom-smothering control of State Collectivism. Social Economics steers a third way between the two, conceiving the economy as a vast network of people, both individually motivated and inescapably social in their actions, who are, therefore, subject to moral judgment and who may seek community in their business and economic dealings.

There are, of course, valid and useful ways of analyzing the economy in which its social nature is not so glaringly apparent: as streams of money and credit from banks and the financial market into the economy and back again; as vast flows of goods and services produced, sold and consumed; as the power relations among businesses, government agencies, labor unions and financial institutions; or even as an abstract mathematical matrix of inputs and outgoes. Each of these captures an aspect of the economy and has its analytic usefulness. But each glosses over the basic reality of people acting, making decisions and dealing with each other: bankers-depositors, buyers-sellers, lenders-borrowers, producers-consumers, employers-workers. **An economy, in short, is an infinitely complex and changing web of social actions, people producing goods and services**

for and exchanging them with each other.

To validate these assertions that the economy is a social system and that economic action is, therefore, subject to moral judgment requires showing at least in a preliminary way how sociality permeates the entire economic process.

Scarcity and Competition

How the world economy grew is a long and fascinating story, the warp of human history whose weft is political and cultural history. Basic to this story is a condition which is a problem for everyone, individually and collectively, and also a spur to economic action. After taking it for granted for centuries, as most people still do, economists now perceive it as the fundamental problem their science addresses and call it the problem of *scarcity.* **People generally experience it as the problem of *making ends meet, of never having enough income to buy all they want.* Scarcity in economic science does not ordinarily suggest a dearth but rather that what is available (and this may be most abundant) is less than what is wanted and that people will give up something (usually money) to have.** In other words, everything with a price, be it commodity or service, is scarce. Scarcity, therefore, is universal, inevitable and social.

That almost everything people want, whether necessity, convenience or luxury, has a price is fundamental to why trying to make ends meet is a **universal** problem: for the rich as well as the poor. In a sense the rich may have a greater problem, as witness the failure of the United States, the richest government in the world, to keep its spending within its astronomical and increasing income. Scarcity is **inevitable**. The alternative would be that everyone would have at hand everything he or she would or could want. Even if possible, there would not be enough space on poor little earth to keep all this in inventory. Nor will increased production eliminate scarcity. More production generates more income which simply increases more spending. Finally, scarcity is **social**, a problem facing all humankind and one to which all contribute. For what one wants and gets deprives another who wanted it, and vice versa.

All this considered, scarcity is clearly part of the human condition, the consequence of humans being spiritually free to aspire however they would and yet physically limited to the material means needed to achieve their aspirations. Consequently, people's realizations are always less than their hopes. Even the most spiritually minded, therefore, cannot envisage a world in which prices do not ration practically every material good and most human services. Neither can they devise a world in which people do not have to compete for what they need and want.

People pay lip-service to economic competition but find it a most galling feature of modern living and try to escape it if possible. Surprisingly, economic competition is less harsh than other kinds of competition accepted as normal. In sports, games and the pursuit of office or honors only one is winner and all others are losers. Economic competition differs in that there are always two winners and really no losers. Sellers win by offering more or better product or a lower price, all which benefit buyers. Buyers win over others by offering more money. In both cases, some buyers and sellers win, while the disappointed ones do not really lose, since they have the commodities or money with which they started and can try their luck at another, perhaps more opportune time. **Economic competition, therefore, whether in the commodity, job, capital or financial market, must be called *social* because one party's good is locked into another's realizing his or hers.**

This demonstrates the benefit of scarcity itself. Because competition responds to scarcity by offering more to get more, it tends to reward competence, to prod complacency and to weed out inefficiency. Throughout history, cultures, where competition was keen in coping with scarcity, developed the most dynamic economics. Where scarcity was little felt and/or competition tepid, economies stagnated. **Competition in responding to scarcity energizes economic activity by kindling self-interest.**

Self-Interest

Many, of course, will claim that the motive of self-interest argues against the social nature of economics. Many economists will concur in this, some even equating economic self-interest with selfishness. Both ignore the most ancient and basic moral principle, that everyone acts for his or her own good. While one may be deluded as to what that might be in particular situations and actually choose what is morally and even physically harmful, the bad is still chosen in the guise of the good. The more recondite aspects of this issue can be left to moral philosophers. Here it is only necessary to assume that people in economic matters will act rationally: buying what they hope will do them good, seeking jobs that will be better than what they have, starting businesses, anticipating success not failure.

But as with every act a person perceives as good, as of his or her interest to do, economic self-interest is not necessarily self-benefit. Such is a commonplace of life, as when a mother sees it in her interest to get a job to finance her children's college careers or a foundation contributes to a drug rehabilitation program. Sticking to the tenets of Radical Individualism that self-interest means self-benefit simply flies in the face of every day life. Even harder to understand is not perceiving the sociality implicit in the most fundamental and time-honored economic principles. This is illustrated by examining briefly three of them: the principles of substitution, comparative advantage and profit maximization.

The **principle of substitution** simply states that in choosing between two or more possible purchases a person weighs the benefit anticipated from each against their prices and chooses the best ratio of benefit to price. The result: both seller and buyer are better off, while the disappointed sellers are no worse off, still able to sell their stock to others. Like this, the **principle of comparative advantage** applies to choosing between alternative lines of production or employment. In comparing two job offers a person should contrast the gain in income and benefits from one against what would be surrendered at the other, and choose the better. Thus employer and employee are better off and the unfilled job is available to another. Here again one person's gain becomes a benefit to another. Similar logic applies to choosing lines of production. **The self-interest inherent in both principles is not only applied common sense but socially beneficial.**

The **gain- or profit-maximizing principle** presents more difficulty. For profits, as the difference between selling price and costs, are increased by raising the former and decreasing the latter. Both actions harm others: consumers by raising prices and employees and suppliers by cutting costs. But such policies are both limited and short-run. The seller who raises prices too high loses sales and thus profits. Bosses who work their people longer and harder while decreasing wages, will like the farmer, who worked his mule longer and fed him less and less, destroy their workers incentive and in time their profits. Also such tactics can continue only with monopoly control or in a static market, both of which invite competition.

The best hope for increasing profits occurs with business growth, selling more and thus needing more workers, buying more supplies and investing in more plant. In short, growth means that more customers benefit from the product and more income is generated for workers, suppliers, investors and tax-collectors. **Maximizing profits is a social principle, not only in involving others but by linking business success to customer satisfaction and constituents' incomes.**

These brief comments leave many questions and issues about economic self-interest, even hinting that this powerful economic drive needs the moderation of moral principles. At the same time, the text has demonstrated the social nature of the economy, of its basic problem of scarcity as well as the forces of self-interest and competition by which people cope with scarcity. The presentation is rounded out by showing that the economic process, means and results are also social.

Market, Money and Property

Exchange is obviously a social act, and its two sides, wanting and providing, are also social. Most things people want involve others. Public goods, like parks, roads and government services, are by definition social. Much a person buys is for family, relatives and friends. Almost every want is stimulated by advertising or by what others have. On the other side, everything is socially produced. Professional and personal services are provided directly, but behind the contact person is usually a team of co-workers. Most commodities are produced in a complex process, coordinating the skills, knowledge and effort of thousands who will never know the final buyer. Behind the check-out counter clerk is a huge network of delivery people, machine operators, managers, accountants and the like, bringing the fabricated produce from farm, forest or mine to final sale. In every stage of this complex process the final customer is the ultimate, if unknown, beneficiary.

A market, therefore, is not a mechanism (however useful for economic analysis so conceiving it may be) but a social process, relating the many who offer a commodity for sale to the many more who want to buy. Further, no individual market exists isolated from other markets, because suppliers can shift from one product line to another and customers to spend their money on one good and less on another. All the problems of estimating how buying will respond to changes in income, supply and prices, estimations upon which millions of sales, jobs and investments depend, boil down to gauging how people's decisions to buy affect decisions to produce. However mechanized a market, predicting their progress requires understanding human behavior and social interaction. **Markets are social institutions.**

Money is the means by which exchange takes place. It is truly the economy's life blood. How the modern money and credit system developed is also a fascinating story. Here it can only be noted that almost everything bought is with pieces of paper which were issued by government central banks, checks written against private banks or numbers raised on pieces of plastic. There is a law requiring people to take central bank money but none to take checks or credit card credit, by far the most popular forms of exchange for everything from carrots to corporations.

But people take them because they trust the credit of governments, banks and credit companies which guarantee these purchases. **In fact, therefore, modern money is simply credit and as such it is preeminently social.**

Property itself, the reward of economic activity, is social. A person's claim to things from the common pool of natural or produced goods is based on moral and legal rights, sanctioned by the general public and usually expressed in law. The material goods themselves are social in that they can be used and enjoyed by many others. This fact is, of course, the basis of all transfers of property, whether by barter, purchase, loan or gift. **Thus property, as also its use and transfer, is social.**

More certainly, wealth, the economic value of property, is social. This runs counter to people's usual perception of wealth as being very proprietary: 'my wealth and your wealth.' But wealth is not one's property or its usefulness to the owner but its economic value. In fact, wealth is not the owner's estimate of the value of his or her property but the market's assessment, what other people would pay for it or something comparable. In sum, there are three distinct but related phenomena, the thing owned, its usefulness and its market value and **each is social. Property is sanctioned by generally accepted moral and legal principles. How it is used is limited by law and conditioned by one's obligations to others. Its worth as wealth is entirely determined by the market and, as reward for business and economic effort, it is social.**

Thus what was to be demonstrated can be restated. The economic process in all its elements is social: the problem is social; the response to the problem is social; the motive for acting is social; the resolution through exchange is social; the monetary means is social; and the wealth generated is social. Economics is a social science: economics is social economics and economic behavior, therefore, is subject to moral principles.

Preliminary to exploring the elements and implications of economic morality, the chapter analyzed three realities which will run as themes through this study: the essential features of the human person, the genesis and meaning of community, and the economy as first and foremost a social phenomena. The next two chapters will examine economic abundance, its origin and social problems and then the principles by which the economy runs. Chapter 4 will establish the key relationship between moral values and economic value and the next three chapters will show how the moral virtues of justice, moderation and spiritual poverty relate to economic goals and activity. Finally, chapter 8 will demonstrate how the two life-long enterprises, the moral and economic, can blend together.

ENDNOTES

1. Mounier, Emmanuel, *Personalism,* University of Notre Dame, Notre Dame, 1952.
2. May, Rollo, *Power and Innocence*, W.W. Norton & Co., New York, 1922, pp. 247-8.
3. A most persuasive case is made for generating economic community by Jonathan Boswell, *Community and the Economy: The Theory of Public Cooperation*, Routledge, New York and London, 1990. The first three chapters and the final one are particularly recommended as relevant to this section.

GLOSSARY

capitalism—An economic system in which people and institutions are generally free to contract their efforts and property to produce goods and service for private gain.

collaboration—An action by two or more people of combining work and resources to achieve a common purpose as in industrial production.

community—A sense of belonging to a group, which treats members as persons and blends their respective contributions to and sharing in a common interest or endeavor.

economic morality—A personal attitude which blends understanding the operations of economic processes with those moral principles applicable to business and economic behavior.

economic process—A progressive series of operations by which human effort, techniques and materials are combined to produce useful goods and services to be distributed by a complex system of exchange prices and incomes.

economic scarcity—The universal human condition, that the wants of individuals, families, businesses and nations always tend to exceed the income needed to satisfy them.

mammalian—Pertains to those species of animals and humans whose females suckle their young. This usually implies sexual reproduction.
principles of action—The necessary characteristics or features of human actions, derived from the necessary features of the human person.
ontological—Pertains to one's essential being or nature.
radical individualism—The doctrine or philosophy which denies the social nature of persons and affirms that the individual's being and purpose is unique to each and distinct from all others.
social economics—Economic science with emphasis on its nature as a social science in that all economic relations, actions and institutions are social.
state collectivism—An economic system in which the principal economic decisions are made by government or a government agent and most productive property is owned socially.
transcendence—A state surpassing a previous mode of being. It here implies an urge or aspiration to go beyond one's present condition or state.

QUESTIONS FOR FURTHER DISCUSSION OR RESEARCH

1. Demonstrate by a concrete example how and to what extent a change in the purpose of a particular action will highlight certain principles of action and downplay others.
2. As the text suggests show in what sense voting is a religious act.
3. Recall, if you can, a period in your life when you experienced community—in family, in marriage, in school, in athletics or otherwise. Analyze that experience of belonging: Was your growth as a person enhanced or retarded? Did you feel accepted, tolerated or ignored?
4. Trace from *The Wall Street Journal, Forbes, Business Week* or other journal the rise and fall of some business celebrity, like Robert G. (Bobby) Baker, Robert Vesco, Ivan Boesky or other example of a spectacular business career. Show how self-interest, turned to greed and selfishness, propelled both the person's rise and fall.

ADDITIONAL SUGGESTED READING

1. *Economic Justice for All: Catholic Social Teaching and the U.S. Economy*, National Conference of Catholic Bishops, 1989.
2. Emmanuel Mounier, *Personalism*, Notre Dame: University of Notre Dame Press, 1952.
3. Rollo May, *Power and Innocence*, New York: W.W. Norton & Co., 1972, esp. chs. 1, 2, 3 and 12.
4. Jonathan Boswell, *Community and the Economy: The Theory of Public Cooperation*, Routledge, New York and London, 1990. Chapters 1-3 and the final one are especially recommended.

CHAPTER TWO

THE ABUNDANT ECONOMY

No one can dispute that people in the United States live in an economy which is highly technical, heavily industrialized, pervasively financial and thoroughly institutionalized, in other words, in a modern, abundant economy. Indeed, people here take for granted that most command a plane and standard of living much higher than what the vast majority of people in the world have today and have had throughout human history. Paradoxically, however, they are dismayed that any segment of the population fails to achieve this standard and tend to panic at any change which might in any way jeopardize it.

Two reasons help explain this paradoxical attitude. Americans, while not isolated because of their global leadership, are an insulated people. Most have little sense of history and by and large little appreciation of cultural diversity, not in the limited sense of knowing and living with people of differing ethnic origins—because as a matter of fact the U.S. presents a marvelous rainbow of people multiformity—but by way of experiencing radically different patterns of living. Consequently, few appreciate in a practical way that they and the peoples of other affluent countries enjoy amenities which the wealthiest of earlier ages could not even imagine and which the poor of the world today, even if they knew about them, could only long for.

Secondly, Americans are an adversarial and competitive people in sports, business, legal and political issues, in matters they consider important for living and even in their moral and religious attitudes. This is accentuated by communication and entertainment industries which trumpet the immediate, the current, the "news", not events and ideas of lasting importance but what is different and startling. Thus media practices playing on social contentiousness sharpen ideological and political discord to the harm of understanding, consensus and compromise.

Addressing changing economic conditions, this contentious insularity, therefore, tends to divide sharply along pessimistic or optimistic lines, one group seeing every change as a threat to some sector of the economy, the other as evidence of economic dynamism. Whichever, the state of the economy becomes critically important politically, inspiring conflicting political agendas. Minuscule statistical changes are read by economists as the Roman high priest used to read the entrails of birds, the media and the public veering from anxiety to euphoria in response. All of this reveals considerable economic naivete often from the top of government down, people and press ignoring the overall context of abundance and forgetting that change is inherent in a complex economic system.

At the risk of being attacked from both sides, this book is premised on the fact that a large percentage of the world's population—not the majority by any means—enjoys a goodly measure of economic well-being, which can be called and is economic abundance. This stance, on the other hand, in no way denies that the process by which abundance is achieved produces a gamut of problems from threats to the very planet humankind inhabits to great disparities, both worldwide and domestic, in sharing in this abundance and thus to moral issues which is the main interest here. It, nevertheless, urges especially American readers, who are daily bombarded with worries about the government debt, trade imbalances, the homeless, the unemployed, world competition—all legitimate concerns—to keep in mind that the U.S. economy, while it does not dominate as it did the poorer world of the '50s and '60s, has over the last 50 years produced unprecedented changes in the nation's physical living.

Transcontinental and transoceanic air travel, a national expressway grid, long-distance, international and domestic, telephoning, space flight; pervasive computerization and faxing, robotization and laser technology; micro-wave ovens, oil and gas heating, air-conditioning, insulation, the ubiquitous use of plastic, VCRs and television; open-heart surgery and organ transplants, therapeutics, antibiotics and the elimination of tuberculosis, scarlet fever and polio. The listing could go on and on of changes in the way a people, who already enjoyed in the years immediately after World War II the highest plane of living in human history, were able to live longer, travel farther and faster, produce more with less effort, and acquire and transmit knowledge more accurately and easier. **However disenchanted and fearful Americans, who have experienced these changes, may be about them, the fact is that wave after wave of peoples from impoverished economies have risked the most terrible sufferings and dangers to share in them.**

This chapter, therefore, sets before itself three tasks: 1) to describe the elements of economic abundance by reviewing the stages in the Abundance Revolution of the last 250 years; 2) to examine the effect of these changes on how affluent people live; and 3) to analyze in turn the effects of these changes on their thinking and expectations, hence, on the moral context of their lives.

THE ABUNDANCE REVOLUTION

Gauging what the Revolution in Economic Abundance of the last 250 years has meant for the developed industrial nations can best be seen by comparing the U.S. to India's economy. India is chosen because she is not a primitive society, to the contrary, boasting a culture, literature, learning and philosophic and religious traditions which predate much of Western culture, but because, despite this, hundreds of millions of Indians subsist on the verge of destitution, lacking adequate housing, clothing, food and medical care. Despite the Green Revolution, extensive irrigation, industrialization and tremendous expenditures on the economy's infrastructure, 80% of her population struggle all their lives just to produce enough food to survive. **India for all its advances since independence is still what may be called a survival economy.**

India is not singled out to point a finger of scorn. Rather she exemplifies the condition of today's affluent countries 250 years ago: England, France, Germany and so forth were largely agricultural economies in which the livelihoods of the vast majority of their peoples were constantly threatened by famine, plague, fire and war. The trade, nascent industrialization, cultural and educational achievements were all based on the work of the overwhelming majority who lived out their lives in economic hopelessness.

By contrast one farmer in the U.S. today can on average produce enough to feed 70-75 people and still generate an exportable net surplus. And blue-collar workers, making up but 14% of the total population, manufacture the machines, generate the energy, build the houses, produce the automobiles, make the clothes and shoes, slaughter the meat and package the food, and deliver all of these for the other 86%. In other words less than 20% of the work force provides for the physical needs of the country; the other 80% provide professional, personal, managerial, financial and clerical services. Many of the latter, of course, are needed to coordinate the work of the 20% and to get their product to the ultimate consumer, but more of them are devoted to the cultural, spiritual, political, social and medical wants of the nation. Such is the labor force profile of an abundant economy in which most of its human effort is devoted to producing goods and services not necessary for survival. Such a picture is far different from that of a prosperous economy 250 years ago. The stages and factors in that revolution are worth reviewing to round out the understanding of what an **abundant economy** is.

There were, of course, other periods in human history of extended material prosperity. All great civilizations recall golden ages, some of which lasted for centuries like that in Egypt (1500-1200 B.C.) or the first centuries of Imperial Rome or China during the Ch'in and Han dynasties. But the Western Abundance Revolution of the last 250 years differs from others in its world-wide extension, in totally changing how people live and in surviving (indeed contributing to) two centuries of the most devastating wars and some of the most dramatic social, political and demographic changes in human history.

Its beginning, while disputed, can be set in the second half of 18th Century England when steam power began to be used in the cotton textile industry, starting to flourish in the Yorkshire moors around modern Leeds. From England it spread to France, the Lowlands and Germany, and was smuggled into the States. British colonials introduced industrialization into all parts of their Empire, and the Dutch, French, Germans in theirs, often disastrously for native populations. Communism imposed socialized mass production on formerly backward economies, war sparked industrialization in some countries and Islamic nations began to awake to the benefits of modern technology. **In sum, the economies of almost a third of the world's population have been transformed or touched in some way by the Revolution in Economic Abundance.**

The Anatomy of Abundance

Given the world-wide and sweeping changes the Revolution produced, one would expect it to be a complex of many revolutions: Industrial, Commercial, Financial, Managerial and the like, all of which scholars have identified and analyzed. The interest here is not so much in tracing the history of these transformations as in defining the ingredients of the change. The development of these elements, however, does possess a certain logic, one being preliminary to and necessary for another in a loose historic order but not rigidly chronological. Rather the different phases of the Revolution overlap and interact so that, while distinct, they blend into and reinforce each other.

This blending and interaction among the components of the Revolution makes distinguishing among and listing them somewhat arbitrary. Six will be identified and considered. 1) First of all, the Revolution began with a fundamental change in the economic motivation of a dynamic segment of the population.

2) Their dynamism, by finding new forms of energy and new sources of raw materials, channelled a larger part of the population into industrial production. 3) The harnessing of the gain-motive to the scientific spirit produced an increasingly sophisticated technology. 4) These changes, in turn, transformed industrial production and socialized work. 5) Mass production, consequently, required new methods of managing, financing and marketing the increased out-put. 6) Finally, this complex transformation, industrial, social and financial, required a larger economic role for government.

The most fundamental, and therefore the least understood, change was the motivational. The change consisted first of all in perceiving the economy as a nation-wide network of people producing foods, manufacturing goods, and selling them at home and abroad. Formulated initially by a few savants, this concept of the macroeconomy was grasped by more and more in the business, commercial and financial communities and finally became commonplace with the general public. This contrasts sharply with the ignorance of the peasant in the field, the housewife at her loom or the sailor in the forecastle two centuries ago for whom such data was impossible and, if available, would mean nothing. Related to this conception but pertaining more to economic motivation was the understanding that economic self-interest in driving the economy was socially beneficial. This did not mean that entrepreneurs, managers and bankers of the last two centuries were more socially minded, moral and just than their Medieval and Roman predecessors: they may have been worse. But they saw their actions, not as just fulfilling their own ambitions, but as contributing to the growth of the national economy and, thereby, somehow helping even the workers and customers they exploited. There are several factors which contributed to this mutation.

Sir Josiah Child expressed the consensus among both popular writers and serious scholars of divine approval of economic growth. Given England's superiority in agricultural production and commercial technology, he predicted that she "is wonderfully fitted by the bounty of God Almighty for a great progression in wealth and power."[1] Christianity, especially that influenced by Calvinism, took a more tolerant view of business, accepting diligence, frugality and thrift, all prescriptions for creating wealth, as virtues in the layman's vocation. The role of the entrepreneur as sparking the economy was touted by both French and British economists.[2] But the most influential work was that of the Scots philosopher, Adam Smith, whose *An Inquiry into the Nature and Causes of the Wealth of Nations*[3] convinced his and subsequent generations of the social beneficence of economic self-interest. Smith argued forcefully that self-interest need not be tempered by concerns for the common good since most such simply covered up selfish intentions. Furthermore, a true self-interest was inherently social since a person in his or her economic dealings had to consider the other party's good in order to achieve one's own.

These ideas will come up and be discussed and criticized in later chapters. Enough here to see how economic ambitions received a shot in the arm from the increased social acceptability of economic self-interest.

While the generation and controlled use of steam power can mark the beginning of the Abundance Revolution, self-interested gain- and profit-seeking have unleashed a continuing search for new sources of energy—electrical, geothermal, biological, atomic, solar—and new and more efficient fuels—wood, charcoal, coal, oil, gases, nuclear fission and fusion. Matching these is the development of new techniques to find new minerals and metals, producing new kinds of raw materials and improving the productivity of fields, herds, fisheries and forests.

What may be called the Technology Revolution embraces all of the above and goes beyond into research into the human psyche, the constituents of matter and the universe itself. Before the 19th Century scientific research was pursued here and there by amateurs, that is, individual scientists driven by curiosity and the desire to know, for most, profiting from their discoveries of minor consideration. Today, scientific research is tied for the most part to economic gain, scientists forming an elite of well-paid professionals. Scientists, writes Teilhard, are no longer, "a type sporadically distributed throughout the human mass," but are "functionally linked together in a vast organic system that will remain in future indispensable to the life of the community."[4] **Linked to economic gain-seeking, The Technological Revolution is not petering out. It is just beginning.**

These vast and continuing changes in productive know-how had and have produced a revolution in production. Abundant sources of non-human energy centralize manufacturing in a factory where men and women tend machines and thus work to their rhythm. Now too people come to work instead of working at home and, before mass transit, clustered their hovels and cottages near the factory district. Mass production, furthermore, has radically changed industrial craftsmanship. Now few workers produce for personal sale; most are integrated into a productive process set to the rhythm of machines, each worker completing a small part of the final product. **Mass production, therefore, is socialized production, which necessarily is standardized production, appealing to common-denominator wants and marketed nation- and often world-wide.**

Paradoxically, even as the worker's contribution to the whole has been fractionalized, the worker bears a greater burden of responsibility because a moment's inattention or a small mistake could botch thousands of items, shut-down an assembly line or maim or kill one's self or another. Above and around the basic worker-producer is a host of support personnel and a hierarchy of managers. Thus the basic distinction between employees is not based on working conditions—blue vs. white collar—but between those who oversee the whole of production and thus make decisions affecting the whole and those who see only part of the process and thus do what others bid.

Mass production has also revolutionized how businesses are managed, financed and their products and services marketed. Business has now become a profession for which students can prepare right up to the doctoral level. The science of gathering and analyzing data is now requisite for decision-making and management has become a learned technology which is transferable from private business to public agency and from steel-making to agribusiness with hardly a change in stride. Out of these revolutions emerged the distinctive institution of industrialized countries, the transworld corporate aggregate, employing thousands of people from janitors to research scientists and marketing billions of product throughout the world. While the vast majority of firms employ less than 100 workers, these aggregates set the business skyline. Their ownership is collective with thousands of stockholders, including huge financial trusts. Management consists of a team of professionals who accede to power most often by an internal process of co-option. Managers seldom are majority owners; nevertheless, they make the operating decisions.

Corporations in turn are set in their own economic environments. Most are faced with large professional and industrial collectives which, national in scope, represent the craft or class interests of groups of employees. All are enmeshed in a network of other businesses: with some they compete, from others they obtain supplies and to others they sell product or service. All these relations are in constant flux as markets change, new products and production methods are introduced and managements shape up or go slack. To fail to respond to this discipline spells stagnation or demise because huge sums of money are on the prowl to buy into or to buy out faltering managements.

These sweeping changes in how people live and are organized in making their living have greatly increased the economic role of governments. Industrial urbanization requires more government services: police and fire protection, waste removal and water, roads and traffic control, schools and social and welfare assistance. National governments' spending and taxing have become the largest single items affecting the pace of the economy. They maintain extensive networks of agencies to preserve industrial competition and peace, to oversee working conditions, to regulate commerce and communication, and to stabilize securities and money markets. The U.S. is the largest employer, buyer, insurer and debtor in the world. **In sum, while big government is spawned by big business, all have**

become recipients of government largesse but the biggest still are large corporations.

These then are the ingredients of the Abundance Revolution which in 250 years has transformed life and living in affluent economies: a self-interest which both impels and implements the expectation of continuing economic growth; a constant stream of technological innovations; a progressive penetration into and control of nature's powers; an enduring socialization of production and urbanization; an economic scene dominated by complex and transworld institutions; and government influence and action pervading the economy. How these abundant economies will change has unleashed reams of speculation. What is important here is understanding how the experience of economic abundance has modified people's thinking and behavior.

THE AFFLUENT CONTEXT

People who have lived all their lives in the kind of economy described above may require some historical imagination or experience living in a more backward part of a Third World country or that of the urban homeless to appreciate how affluent living differs from life for most people today and in human history. This is not a condemnation of affluent living. **All things being equal affluence is preferable to and more befitting human nature than destitution. At the same time it poses its own set of moral problems.** How this might be is worth closer examination.

Abundant Living

First the text will sketch four features of abundance which importantly fashion how affluent people live. 1) Abundance is abundant, providing an enormous variety and quantity of goods and services far beyond survival needs for most and even adequate living for the least advantaged. 2) Abundance is widely shared through all socio-economic classes. 3) Abundance offers opportunities for most to climb the economic ladder and daily displays examples of the disadvantaged breaking out of poverty.

4) The economy has the stuff to recover from natural or man-made disasters and to rebound from cyclical down-turns.

A leisurely stroll through a super-market, department store or all-purpose hardware store provides evidence enough of the immense variety of goods from which modern consumers can choose. Flip the yellow pages of a city telephone directory and contrast it with what would be a similar business catalogue of London in 1800. Look at homes, their furnishings, automobiles, travel ads, schools, investments, charities: everywhere goods and services for sale proliferate. The problem is not dearth but choosing from an enormous array of commodities of which only the smallest fraction at any moment is of immediate use to an individual. 'Superfluity' is the word such abundance evokes.

In the U.S. abundance is both increasing and widely shared. The real evidence is what people have today they did not have 50 years ago. The real reality of economic well-being is the use and service people get from the things they possess. Real economic growth is indicated by the increased material well-being of men and women. While true criteria, such increases can only be estimated not quantified. Hence, the more mathematical but less realistic monetary measures, family income and *per capita* national income, must be used. Both will be briefly considered, but how people use their income to implement their life-styles must be kept in mind as the real gauge of well-being.

Increasing national income determines, of course, changes in family income. Since *per capita* national income has doubled in real terms every quarter century or so for the last century, the increases, as one would expect, have been spread throughout the economy. Despite the fact that the top 20% of families enjoy 45% and the bottom 20% only 5% of the nation's income, there exists a high degree of income mobility. 60% of families in the two lowest quintiles will in the course of a decade move upward, the families in the lowest 20% increasing their income by an average of 75% and the second by 40%. Meanwhile the top 20% of family incomes will increase by only 5% since 50% of them will drop to lower quintiles. Most of this mobility is the natural result of younger wage earners gaining experience and acquiring better-paying jobs,[5] while retirement and illness are cutting employment and earnings of older workers, each by 50%.[6] Thus 60% of all families can realistically expect their income will increase and at any one time 60% of families will enjoy an income in current dollars of over $50,000.

Another aspect of these increases is that they have been realized in exchange for a much smaller percentage of one's life committed to earning them. Whereas parents and grandparents entered the work-force at sixteen or earlier and worked as long as they were able (no less in the home than on a job), today people most often begin full-time work 5 or 6 years later and anticipate 10 or 15 years of retirement. Their work year is liberally laced with holidays and vacations and their workweek reduced from 60 to 40 hours or less. That for many families today both husband and wife are employed does not suggest that wives and mothers of past generations put in any less hours of work than their daughters and granddaughters today. Complaints of no time today for relaxation should be balanced against the enormous increase in attendance at cultural and especially athletic events.

Overall, therefore, affluent economies still beckon as lands of opportunity. The U.S. economy, for example, has created over a million net new jobs every year since WW II, employing almost 20% more of the civilian population than in 1950. Surprisingly the opportunities here are often seen more clearly by refugees from the Third World than Americans who enjoy and have enjoyed a high level of material well-being for years. Good luck, of course, plays an important part in anyone's career: being at the right place at the right time. But the best luck is taking advantage of the opportunities which are at hand: education, early jobs, acquiring saleable skills and experience, impressing employers with one's willingness to learn and to work. Some early job movement and even false starts in a vocation are to be expected. But career changes often provide a taste of success which becomes a stimulus for more. **Opportunity, like a life preserver, must not only be grabbed but held onto to do any good.**

Abundance provides the means and affluence the will to rebuild after natural disasters and to recover after business downturns. The affluent can view even the worst catastrophe as a set-back not the end. They are not completely at the mercy of nature nor victims of past human folly. Indeed technocrats, in the hope for profits, are constantly seeking new sources of raw materials and energy, new ways to improve the soil's fertility and new methods of production. Similarly, modern economies can and do recover from recessions and depressions without needing outside stimuli. Business can always rely on consumers' buying commodities already produced and on being tempted by anything new. Governments can be sure that their citizens will pressure for more services and assistance. This ferment for more income and more goods is the most important reason why over the last half-century the years of economic growth outnumber the years of stagnation or decline by three to one.

This then is the state of the affluent. They are immersed in material goods and lavished with services, from medicating their arthritis to grooming their poodles. Their desires for what is necessary to survive goes way beyond simply *hoping* for them and even beyond *wanting* them to *expecting* that what they need will be available to them. They have their money problems but by and large they have no trouble satisfying their ordinary needs and the amenities customary in their society. In general they are confident that the economy can overcome disasters and with a little tinkering rebound from downturns. Finally, they feel no discomfiture about their well-being, taking it for granted, because they are largely isolated from the heart-rending poverty of the hard core disadvantaged and those without economic hope.

In short, therefore, this affluent attitude is entirely normal and to be expected, given the experience of wide-spread economic abundance. Indeed there is nothing immoral about the accoutrements of affluence: cars, TVs, nice homes, and so forth. Nor is it immoral to seek them. They can, of course, like every human good, be misused. Still people should be grateful to the technology, business and government which make them possible. On the other hand, stressing the positive features of economic abundance should not prevent seeing its flip-side of negatives.

The Flip-side of Abundance

There is poverty in the U.S. Besides the homeless, most of whom pose social and health problems not entirely amenable to economic solutions, some 15% or over 35 millions of the total population are classified as poor. That is, their incomes, noncash benefits excluded, fall below the poverty line, which for a family of four is about $13,000. While this income level is higher than that of 90% of families in the world, such poverty here is very real since it contrasts glaringly with what most enjoy. The economic hopelessness of the hard-core poor deepens as a more complex technology eliminates lower-skilled jobs and widens the compensation gap, especially the increasingly expensive fringe benefits, between them and more skilled employment.[7]

The poverty of the homeless and hard-core indigent is often confused with a kind of pseudo-poverty that many, perhaps most, people in affluent economies feel. This is the condition of scarcity, more easily recognized as the problem of making ends meet, which was presented earlier as the fundamental problem addressed by economic science. Since scarcity is present wherever goods are priced, it must be pervasive in a modern, affluent economy. What perhaps needs explaining is that, while one would expect higher incomes and greater wealth to alleviate scarcity, the reverse is often the case: the U.S. with its trillions of debt has a more serious problem than Uganda; a family with a 'yuppie' income of $125,000 experiences greater scarcity than Puerto Rico immigrants with $25,000.

The answer, as also the problem, has both an economic and a philosophic dimension, which are more easily seen in the large by looking at the macroeconomy. First, at any moment a national economy, using current capital goods, labor force, technology entrepreneurial skills can only produce a certain amount of goods and services, however they may be produced in a billion different combinations in response to people's wants.

This is called the economy's **production possibility frontier.** Second, producing this output generates the incomes of the economy's workers, managers and investors and the taxes governments collect from them, which incomes, in turn, buy the economy's product. The economy, therefore, is a vast, complex but essentially circular process of producing, generating incomes and spending. Throughout everything is priced because, however prospering and abundant, the economy's output is limited, hence, scarce. So much for the economic dimension of scarcity; now for the philosophic.

Since persons are not limited in their desires to what their incomes can afford and indeed are free in thought and will to want anything they can imagine, scarcity and the need for prices as rationing devices makes for philosophic common sense. Even more so it explains why increased incomes often accentuate rather than alleviate scarcity. Since a person's spiritual as well as material wants need material goods to fulfill them, he or she in a very real sense is an appetite which can never be sated. Moreover, just as a person climbing a small hill sees the horizon expand many times the height climbed, so a household, business or government on experiencing increased income will more often than not **aspire to buy** much more than its increased **ability to buy**. Scarcity in affluent economies tends to be generated more by extravagant wanting than by niggardly production.

Even more so the expectation that incomes will constantly increase creates a buoyancy in the economy which will tend to keep it humming along. Because increased production and spending feed each other, greater output permits greater spending which in turn stimulates more production. This is why indices of consumer and business confidence are closely watched by the high priests of business, finance and economics in predicting the volatile course of the economy.

Such volatility is heightened because growing abundance expands the range of economic opportunities. Schools, remedial and special education, technical training, colleges and universities are available to all who can and would make use of them. Governments spend billions in ferreting out physical and learning disabilities and in improving the employability of the blind, amputees, and other handicapped persons. Some, of course, are excluded from these opportunities because of mental deficiencies or damage. More fail to take advantage of them out of indifference or willfulness and tend to drift into petty crime or to sink into economic despair. That so many, on the other hand, have overcome physical and family disadvantages and achieved phenomenal success in athletics, in the arts and in business testifies to the power of affluence to multiply economic opportunities.

It has also increased the paths to economic success. The professional athlete, even second and third stringers, for instance, have become millionaires. The myriad components of affluent society mean that the ambitious, the imaginative and the bold can build fortunes in ways previously inconceivable. False starts into a vocation can be corrected without disaster. The complexity of modern living also provides a multiplicity of niches into which individuals can suitably fit their abilities and aspirations. Even though the monetary predominates as criterion of success, most people can achieve a comfortable living from doing what they do best and income possibilities can subsidize just about any life style.

The liquidity of wealth, the prices one's property commands, adds its own dimensions to the volatility of modern living. The pervasiveness of prices has in two centuries radically changed the property people hold as wealth. While real estate, homes and rental properties, farms and factories are still the basis for a large part of private wealth, they are a diminishing portion relative to financial wealth: savings accounts, insurance, securities, pensions and social security entitlements. If one's heart is where one's treasure is, then in the old days a person had to stay on the farm in Kankakee. Now when moving to Kokomo people take their pensions with them or with a signature transfer their wealth across the world or change it from one form of investment to another. **Thus the fluidity of wealth adds another measure to the mutability of affluent living.**

The volatility inherent in abundance is reflected in sudden swings in popular moods from euphoria to pessimism at any shift in the economic winds. The media which, as seen before, has to highlight and dramatize every change in the economy under the rubric of "news", will propagate and accentuate people's jitters about the state of the stock market, employment, the deficit, government spending and taxing and all the rest. While subconsciously expecting their incomes to continue supporting their normal plane of living, people in affluent economies are in a constant state of worry how changes, even those remote from their own lives, may affect their jobs and incomes.

Finally, both scarcity and the volatility of living are both heightened and accentuated in a money economy. Since money like water will filter into every crack and cranny of the economy, the inevitable effect of the increased use of money an affluent economy requires is the intrusion of the **cash nexus** into many human relations previously considered sacrosanct. (Cash nexus here simply refers to those transactions which entail the exchange of money for commodities or services.) Money is often suspected of tainting a relationship or activity, as the phrase "filthy lucre" implies. The services a mother performs, works of charity, spiritual counselling, sports and games, politics to a large extent, scholarship and research, all at one time considered too sacred, too pure or too exalted to be contaminated by money, now involve monetary considerations.

Illustrative of this is the change in the words, "amateur" and "professional". "Amateur" formerly denoted people who engaged in an activity for the pure love of doing so. It suggested a disinterested love which would not be sold out for money. When the activity absorbed most of one's life, the advocate had to be independently wealthy, have a patron, or hold a sinecure. Art, music, religion, scholarship, science, sports, even politics were in this sense amateur activities. But "amateur" now connotes one who is a dabbler, hardly proficient, not particularly serious and obviously unable to make a living in pursuit of his or her interests.

"Professional", on the other hand, which was almost a word of opprobrium as suggesting someone who engages in a noble pursuit for the sake of monetary rewards and, hence, is likely to sell out to the highest bidder. While some of this still clings to the word today, "professional" now more usually refers to people who have trained seriously in their vocations and seek to achieve a level of competence which will yield a good living. Granted amateurs have made significant contributions in every field, professionals make the small, even humdrum, but daily advances which carry on a craft, skill, science or vocation and pass it on as an ordered practice. Because they are paid, professionals must act professionally. **Moral squeamishness aside, there is a cash nexus in practically every, even the most exalted, activity.**

In sum, the Abundance Revolution has radically changed the way the affluent people in the world live. It has showered them with a superfluity of goods and services, shared in by the great majority in the world's wealthy countries. This plenty is realize by people who experience many more years of economic growth than decline and with less physical labor and more years of leisure. On the other hand, affluence surprisingly has accentuated the problem of making ends meet and, in the process of increasing opportunities and paths to success, has made the lives of the affluent more volatile and subject to change. With the increased interest in and emphasis on the economic side of life and the more extensive monetization of human relations, people generally are prone to wilder and more frequent swings in mood from confidence to despair with every new economic report. Both the positives and negatives have become part of affluent peoples' moral context.

THE MORAL CONTEXT OF THE AFFLUENT

The Jesuit theologian, Karl Rahner, fingers how the great technical achievements, effecting the economic abundance just discussed, radically transformed the setting within which this world's wealthy must live and develop as human beings. Rahner is worth quoting extensively:

> Our times have been described as the end of the modern age . . . as the age of existential anguish, disillusion and loss of belief in progress; the age of the denaturing of nature, the eclipse of the numinous in the world, the absence of God; of the substitution of the planned product for the natural growth, of addiction and anxiety, of the replacement of the given by the manufactured, of the loss of the center; an age in which, for the first time, the release of the mind from its bondage to nature is being accomplished . . . . Man used to be protected by what is imposed and inescapable, which is nature . . . . He has been largely successful in protecting himself against nature, which he sees as cruel and heartless towards man; he has reared ramparts against her, against her climate and her bacteria, her animals and her power of death. **And behold, in protecting himself against nature he has lost the protection she afforded him against himself, and man is delivered defenseless into his own hands, to all the errant possibilities of his freedom [and] to his own hubris . . . .Man, escaped from nature—protective, nurturing, limiting, formative nature—is handed over to himself, to his destructive intemperance and lack of intellectual bounds.**[8]

Consumerism and Control

A more fabricated, less natural style of living, which abundance promotes, has obvious consequences for living. People who are removed from nature, from dependence on climate, water and wind power, must consciously seek and plan to experience it. Of greater import, many, if not most, people can not run on natural time cycles or their own inner rhythm but must follow the rhythm of machines, clocks, calendars, deadlines, budgets and targets. But the problem in a complex technology is not so much that men and women are governed by machines and clocks but by the people who set the machines and time the clocks. **The question is whether the people who control the machines exploit those who run them: it is a question of power not of productivity, a matter of justice.**

Consumerism, spending run rampant, is always a possible consequence of economic growth and prosperity. When business is booming and incomes rising, households, businesses, governments and non-profit organizations in enjoying more income, seek more and spend more. Governments raise more taxes; firms scratch for more sales; unions fight for higher wages and more generous fringe benefits; schools, hospitals, churches and the arts solicit more contributions; welfare recipients seek larger assistance. The rich no less than the poor, for-profit corporations no less than charities, governments no less than families scramble for more. All of this is a normal effect of growth. Common sense accepts that increased national income has to go somewhere and to someone. If efforts are not made by all sectors of the economy to participate in the cornucopia, then the lion's share will go to the few who control production or, what is worse, to government.

Equally to be expected is that increased income will be spent: this simply reflects the common sense that the fruits of labor and investment are for the purposes of satisfying wants and needs. This is a given in national income analysis. Governments can always be expected to spend all their income—and often more—hopefully on behalf of the public from whom it was derived. Household consumption spending will absorb most of current income and like government frequently require borrowing. Business incomes will go largely to operating expenses and capital investment, with the smaller part to dividends and bonuses. In other words, it is axiomatic that income will be spent, now or later, by one's self or by one's heirs, by governments who tax and spend, by business or personal investment or by charitable beneficiaries of people's generosity.

The question relevant to consumerism is not whether but how income is spent. Will it go for trivialities, for show, for the immoral and debasing, by careless cost overruns or high living disguised as business expenses or necessary 'perks' of office. The point here is that there are two related but distinct criteria applicable to spending, the economic and the moral. The stepped-up pace of abundance and affluence will mean more production generating more income which must be spent in some way or other lest the economy slow down. That still leaves the no less important question: for what purposes the spending is done. **This is the problem of consumerism.**

Related to this is the danger arising from the proliferation of the cash nexus into practically every human relation and the evaluation in economic terms of even the most sacred things. But there is no contradiction in measuring relations and things by both moral and economic gauges. **That children are costly does not deny that they are priceless; that freedom requires paying taxes does not deny that it cannot be bought.** Hopefully all these seeming paradoxes will be resolved as the implications of economic morality are explored further.

Change and Uncertainty

Affluence like a modern metropolis gives the appearance of solidity and permanence. Yet it is teeming with change. Cities with their office buildings, apartments, shopping centers, expressways and bridges; their array of public and private services; the flow of commerce and production, all seems to promise a culture here to stay. But this promise of permanence is predicated on constant change: buying/selling goods, hiring/retiring workers; refitting plants and office space; births, schooling, graduations; collecting taxes and spending the same. The millions and billions of such decisions ultimately decide whether a city will flourish or languish. Written large, the same applies to the economy as a whole. All the features of affluence, the heightened scarcity, wider range of opportunities and more encompassing money economy, makes living more mutable and mobile and life more uncertain.

More varied opportunities increase social and personal mobility. Change, not just increased travel and visiting but uprooting families socially and geographically, is built into affluent living. Some change may be as simple as taking a new job; some may require moving a family. Some is compelled because the job market, like college teaching, is national in scope. Some is self-determined like a mother returning to her profession or conversely an executive wanting to start a family. Family break-ups produce drastic changes. Much change is involuntary: the recall of an executive to the home office, a division closed down, jobs phased out, a worker laid off or fired. More people spend some time in prison today. More are institutionalized because increasingly mobile families cannot care for the mentally ill, the aged or long-term sick.

Change breeds uncertainty, just as affluence breeds scarcity. The affluent, unlike their grandparents, cannot predict their lives. No one has assurance that she will live out her life in the town of her birth or that he will retire from his first job. The village carpenter, as long as he stuck to his trade, was assured a living until he died. People today have no assurance that their job will not change, that the field for which they trained will continue to hire. They cannot be sure that their business will not be sold, that their neighborhood will not decay or their city lose its major industry and employer. The largest corporations are not immune from change. Loss of market, recession, management gone lax, merger, sale or take-over could totally change the employment picture. The young, the unskilled and the discriminated against are especially vulnerable, but even top executives could be swept out in a general corporate housecleaning.

Increased vocational possibilities also magnify uncertainty. With a wider range of opportunities, the young especially find settling on one difficult. Other fields allure, particularly so when an acquaintance grasps success seemingly without effort or trial, while years of patient attention to detail and sacrifice in mastering a craft or profession yield only a modest return. Success, as measured in power or money, is always elusive in a complex society and may seem to be more a matter of luck, privilege or favor than of hard and intelligent work. Changing one's vocational direction is always possible but, even when the means are available, the uncertainties of a new field or a fresh start will still test one's courage.

The freeing of opportunity also means breaking loose from traditional economic moorings of family, neighborhood or town, and socio-economic class. While restraining, they were also supportive, anchorages of security. The son, who followed his father and grandfather into the mines, narrowed his possibilities but assured his livelihood (as long as the mine stayed open). Now children from the same family and education will vary greatly in earning capacity and style of living.

Small towns and neighborhoods presented a sameness in homes, style of living, schooling and recreation which usually stemmed from the fact of a dominant employer or line of production. If business was good, all worked; if bad, all suffered. When misfortune struck, a family could expect the sympathy and support of neighbors. The rebel against this sameness had to leave; the friendliest stranger was barely accepted. Today, there are few neighborhoods in this sense. While families in the same area may generally be of the same economic class, they may work in entirely different vocations and have widely different interests. Even where the old neighborhoods persist, education, jobs and travel have so exposed children to the wider world that their leaving is no longer traumatic. Those who remain, return or newly arrive do so because they have chosen to and not be cause they have to.

Finally, the same socio-economic class does not guarantee the same living standard. In early generations there was less mobility between classes: the children in blue-collar families tended to become laborers; children of upper classes entered the professions, government or business. Only the very ambitious child struggled to rise above his or her class. Now a person may aspire to any vocation and choose to live wherever he can afford to live. Hence, professional, business or work colleagues may come from any socio-economic background. On the other hand, children from the same family and schooling may go off into any vocational direction. People from the same social level may earn greatly different incomes and experience quite different planes of living, for example, between people practicing law or medicine and those in the ministry and education. Like boats freed from their anchorages people mix and mingle as fortune and their inclinations lead them. Socio-economic class still has meaning but the economic part is more important. In concluding from the above, one can acknowledge what many critics of contemporary living assert, that in achieving abundance people have not gained contentment. To the contrary, while glutted with goods, millions are anxious for more. The concern for wealth seems to make them more envious of others' better fortune and more indifferent to others' needs. **Many have demanded of affluence what it cannot give: peace in possessions, fulfillment of one's innermost wants and, in a word, happiness.** Just the opposite, abundance seems to yield frustration, discontent and a cloying surfeit. It has made some people crabbed in their outlook, tenacious of their properties, and paranoid that they might decrease. **In short, affluence seems to have diminished many men and women as persons.**

On the other hand, one cannot conclude that the affluent have lost all moorings and drift on a sea of wants. They can anchor in a community and in a vocation. But this occurs only with conscious choice and after some moving about. That is, the stability of modern life, when achieved, depends less upon physical and social environment, familiar scenes and familiar faces, and more on a person's inner resources and convictions. **It suggests that economic ambitions must be directed toward fulfilling one's moral aspirations.**

Preliminary to this task, the next chapter must identify and explain those principles of action which enter the moral context as providing the specifically economic element of **economic morality**.

ENDNOTES

1. Child, Sir Josiah, *A New Discourse of Trade*, Printed at John Everingham: London, 1693, Preface.
2. A good short presentation of the primitive concept of the entrepreneur can be found in Schumpeter, *A History of Economic Analysis*, Oxford University Press, New York, 1954, pp. 235-7 and pp. 554-7.

3. Smith, Adam, *An Enquiry into the Nature and Causes of the Wealth of Nations,* Encyclopaedia Britannica, Inc., Chicago, 1952.
4. Teilhard de Chardin, Pierre, Tr. Rene Hague, *Man's Place in Nature*, New York: Harper & Row, Publishers, 1966, p. 106.
5. Sawhill, Isabel and Condon, Mark, "Is the U.S. Income Inequality Really Growing? Sorting out the Fairness Question," *Policy Bites,* The Urban Institute, June, 1992, pp. 2-3.
6. ibid.
7. ibid., pp. 3-4.
8. Rahner, Karl, S.J., *Christian in the Market Place*, Tr. C. Hastings, New York: Sheed & Ward, 1966, p. 21.

GLOSSARY

abundance—An economy's ability to produce enough to satisfy everyone's basic needs of food, clothing, shelter, medical care etc. as well as ordinary amenities. This does not preclude the possibility that a minority may for various reasons lack some part of these.

affluence—The secure possession of economic abundance by a large majority of a given population.

affluent scarcity—Economic scarcity, that is, the general tendency of wants to outpace income, accentuated by the aggressive wanting of affluence.

consumerism—A habit of mind, easily aroused to desiring more goods and especially new products because others have them or simply because they are new, without having a real need for them.

entrepreneur—The persons or institutions which assume the risk of initiating and/or financing an economic enterprise.

green revolution—The sharp increase in agricultural productivity in developing countries, especially India, resulting from using modern agricultural technology.

numinous—Pertaining to the Divinity or divine matters.

poverty line—The level of household income, relative to the number of members and usually exclusive of welfare benefits, which categorizes a household as poor. The line is typically set at 50% of the national median family income.

production possibility frontier—That theoretical limit of output, which an economy with its given resources of labor, capital goods and technology, can generate, irrespective of the combination of capital or consumer goods or services it produces.

socio-economic—The cultural pattern of a family or neighborhood, given its economic resources, educational level and social propensities.

technological—Relates to the application of science and theoretical knowledge to industry, manufacturing, commerce or the arts.

QUESTIONS FOR FURTHER DISCUSSION OR RESEARCH

1. Trace the growth of your home town from its earliest days to the present. What were the critical factors initiating and causing its first settlement? What economic factors stimulated its early growth? What is its economic complexion today?

2. What would the poor (not the homeless and destitute, but the family below the "poverty line") have today which even the very rich would not have enjoyed 200 years ago in England?

3. How do you square the chapter's emphasis on affluence with the contemporary facts of increased homelessness, meal programs, high minority unemployment, a large percentage of children living in poverty and other facts of poverty?

ADDITIONAL SUGGESTED READING

1. Asa Briggs, *A Social History of England, New* York: The Viking Press, 1984, chs. 7, 8, 12, and 13.
2. John K. Galbraith, *The Affluent Society*, 4th ed., Boston: Houghton Mifflin, 1984, esp. chs. I-IX and XXII-XXV.
3. Robert Heilbronner, *The Making of Economic Society*, 4th ed., Englewood Cliffs: Prentice-Hall Inc., 1972, chs. 4-7.
4. Karl Rahner, S.J., *Christian in the Market Place*, tr. by Cecily Hastings, New York: Sheed & Ward, 1966, esp. "Railway Missions" and "Parish and Place of Work."

CHAPTER THREE

ECONOMICS AND THE MORAL CONTEXT

That economics has become increasingly important in the moral context of people who enjoy economic abundance can hardly be disputed. Although economics starts from the problem of scarcity, it is preeminently the science of wealth. This is not a contradiction since, as shown earlier, burgeoning abundance accentuates scarcity. Because the wealth of nations and the world have increased beyond what anyone could imagine 200 years ago and abundance spread from England and Europe to every continent, **the problems of scarcity, of making ends meet, have multiplied, become more complex and insistent, and now pervade every facet of life and society.** If, therefore, scarcity is the special province of economists, it should be no surprise to recollect that the sons of Adam Smith, who, if gathered in 1800 from across the world, would have fitted into a small room, now are numbered in the millions, practical and theoretical scholars studying price, production, investment, spending and monetary trends and that economic, fiscal and business news has become the daily fare of the general public.

Two consequences of importance to this study resulted: some understanding of the *common sense of economics* is essential for everyone and no more so than for social and moral critics and, second, some appreciation of how the ubiquity of prices and gain-seeking in a changing and growing economy affect the moral context of contemporary living by tending to divorce price from use, to fragment moral experience and to unsettle normal social relations. This chapter will address both consequences.

"Some understanding" of how the economy works, obviously, disclaims the need for the theoretical knowledge of a professor, the command of economic technology of the practical scientist, or even the pragmatic understanding of the business leader or financier. But it does imply a need to understand how economic considerations are part of daily life and actions and how they are necessary and normal, but not solely determining, factors in the morality of much of modern living. **As such it means a practical acceptance of *scarcity* as a condition of human life, a realistic comprehension of *price, economic value, gain, wealth and the like* as the subject matter of economic science and *self-interested gain-seeking* as the motive force of economic action.** They are, therefore, the first items on this chapter's agenda.

Little more need be said about scarcity than was said earlier: it is every one's problem, no matter how large one's income or ascetic one's wanting and, in fact, abundance accentuates rather than alleviates scarcity. If a reader is wavering about this, he or she need simply recall that prices are proof of scarcity as rain is of clouds and note that abundance produces more, not fewer, prices. That reaffirmed, the chapter takes up the subject matters of economics, examining first prices and economic values and then gain and wealth.

ECONOMIC SUBJECT MATTER

Limiting the discussion to these four subjects is somewhat arbitrary in that many other topics could be considered: wage, interest, cost, profit, capital, money, credit and so on. But all of these are either categories of the four or, like money and credit, are means by which the four function. Besides, the four subjects chosen illustrate sufficiently, without going into the more complex parts of economic science, how economic factors enter daily life and action.

Price and Economic Value

Prices, of course, are met at every turn in life. As evidence of scarcity, they function as rationing devices, measuring out commodities and services to buyers according to the amounts of money they are willing to spend and measuring out money to sellers according to the amounts of goods they are willing to sell. Prices, therefore, assess the sacrifice scarcity requires of both buyers and sellers to effect exchange. At the same time, prices indicate the value of the money and particularly of the commodities or services being exchanged. Prices are, therefore, the goods' value in exchange, exchange value or economic value.

Price and economic value are synonyms. Everything priced has an economic value; everything economically valuable can be priced. Prices are simply the economic value of vendibles expressed in terms of money, the universal means of exchange. As such every exchange and every thing exchanged is linked in a vast, complex and ever-changing web of exchange. In the sale of a pair of shoes, not only is money surrendered but in a very real sense everything else the money could buy is surrendered. Price and economic value, therefore, as synonyms can be substituted for each other without a change of meaning.

As a matter of practice, however, they have different connotations and are put to different uses. Price is precise, mathematical, simple and objective. It is indispensable for empirical research, accounting and mathematical formulations in analytic work. The ordinary business of life could not be carried on without prices. They are as old as civilization itself.

Economic value, by contrast, is less precise, harder to explain, unworkable as a business or research tool, and impossible in mathematical formulations. On the other hand, it is a richer concept, extending to economic relations which are not easily expressed by prices and is better adapted to explaining economic behavior and relating it to the larger purposes of life. Value in exchange gets to the heart of exchange, the trade-offs in costs and benefits involved in producing, selling, buying and using goods.

For all price's universality and simplicity—every child knows about prices—they (and economic values) are peculiar kinds of realities and beings. When Stone Age traders realized that exchanging goods with neighboring tribes was more efficient and less hazardous than fighting and taking, they very naturally came to the concept of an exchange ratio, so many stone hatchets for so many caribou pelts. While they were well aware that the real, *substantive things* were the pelts and hatchets they desired, they realized that their respective scarcity of these items could not be alleviated without the more nebulous *relative reality,* the ratio or rate of exchange. No less, a contemporary shopper as she wanders down the fairyland aisles of a supermarket knows, if she stops to consider it, that none of these thousands of desirable goods would be hers to purchase without a whole chain of prices which brought them from across the world and by people who had no inkling of her existence.

This deceptively simple concept of price has led economists on a merry chase of analysis for 2500 years we know of and probably for other millennia of pre-history. As a review of the tremendous human effort to unearth the many factors which contribute to the formation of economic value and to understand the many roles this most basic cultural construct plays in the economy, this little exercise should help explain the many elements and characteristics of this fundamental, pragmatic, multifaceted and volatile conceptual tool.

A History of Economic Value

The first approach to economic value was ethical: what would be a just rate of exchange. Here Aristotle (384-22 BC) first noted the basic difficulty that justice required that equals be exchanged, while trade required transferring differing amounts of dissimilar things. His solution based a just exchange ratio on the social value of goods, a doctor's services, for example, exchanging for 3 times that of a carpenter. This measure he called 'demand', essentially the dignity and desirability of a good according to community standards and needs.[1]

Christian thinkers readily accepted Aristotle's resolution. Augustine (354-430) conceded[2] that people's desires and not things' intrinsic worth were the appropriate bases for exchange. Aquinas (1225-74) refined this to include the common estimate of producers and consumers and, when the common good required, public price fixing. He conceded that such consensus was never precise and indeed varied from time to time and city to city.[3] Building on these ideas, later scholastic moralists like Scotus, Antoninus, Biehl and the Jesuits, Molina, Lessius and de Lugo, developed a comprehensive theory of economic value which integrated people's desires, the cost of labor and living, the price level and entrepreneurial profit.[4]

Why this elaborate analysis was ignored has been variously explained: differing religious attitudes to business, middle class migrations due to religious persecutions, the movement of trade from the Mediterranean to the Atlantic. But all these reasons yield to the most basic, a shift away from the ethics of exchange to the secular concern for the growth of national wealth. Here the notion of "surplus value" dominated economic thinking, the crude mercantilistic idea, that an economy became wealthy by exporting more than it imported, giving way to the more advanced understanding that surplus value and thus wealth was generated by an internal process of production and exchange.

The century preceding the *Wealth of Nations* in 1776 was dominated by two interests: to comprehend the national economy as a value producing process and to explain how surplus value was distributed. Sir William Petty (1623-97) first outlined the Irish economy, showing that the generation of the stuff from which useful goods were produced could be measured either in terms of resources or man-power. Richard Cantillon (1680-1734), an Irish expatriate living in France systematized Petty's outline, set it in a sociological frame and incorporated the circulation of money and international trade. Quesnay (1694-1774) then completed this first macroeconomic schema with his famous, *Tableau Economique*, as countering flows of product and money which, driven by the entrepreneurial spirit, simultaneously generated surplus value and distributed it throughout the economy.[5]

This French model, while losing some clarity, gained in

practicality when imported into England. David Hume (1711-76) sketched a free-market model, set in motion by the gain motive and correlating in a rhythmic dynamics international trade, changing price levels, money circulation, production and profits, wages and consumption.[6] His close friend, Adam Smith, then fleshed out this skeleton by infusing human aspirations and interrelationships. First, Smith assimilated surplus value into his key concept of exchangeable value, the enduring materiality of useful products making them vendible. Exchangeable value, while mainly generated by labor, results from a complex process, initiated and sustained by people's desires to better their lots in life and increased by capital investment, the division of labor and market expansion, all effecting a wider sharing in benefits. Exchangeable value, therefore, is suffused with Smith's optimism that private interests can be harmonized with the public good, workers' welfare with capitalists' ambitions, industrial growth with rural prosperity. While giving command over labor, exchangeable value is not only the bond uniting but the very *raison d'etre* of economic activity.[7]

When scholars returned to peace-time activities after the Napoleonic Wars, David Ricardo (1772-1823), a retired stockbroker, spotted the fact that surplus value worked contrariwise for distribution and economic growth. Starting with the obvious fact that increasing output tended to lower prices, he fingered the inherent conflict among entrepreneurial profits, labor wages and resource costs, each seeking its share of a declining amount. Ricardo, therefore, concluded that the effect of increasing population and wants to drive resource prices up but wages down to the subsistence level, and of increased output to lower product prices, would so squeeze profits that production would eventually stabilize or decline. Thus economic growth generated its own demise and industrial conflict not harmony.[8]

Both critics and followers of Ricardo rallied against this pessimistic conclusion, insisting that the way labor, resources and capital goods were combined could produce an output whose value must at least cover costs but could generate even a larger profit. John Stuart Mill (1806-73), summarizing economics since Smith, could square declining values with increasing output both because he was philosophically attuned to a no-growth economy and because his latent socialism accepted a role for government in the distribution of economic benefits.[9]

Karl Marx (1818-85), to the contrary, took Ricardo down the way to social revolution. Discarding Smith's vendibility, he asserted that value is generated in production not in exchange, labor skill being the product's use value and labor energy its exchange value. Production techniques and organization, therefore, determine the stages of human development, capitalism being but one moment in an historical, materialistic dialectic. Since surplus value, according to Marx, is but the labor energy the capitalist exploits from the worker, capitalism itself is set on a course of alienating the worker and centralizing, in periodic crises, all capital into one hand. Thus capitalism will beget its own demise when the last exploiter is himself exploited, ushering in the final age of communist abundance.[10] While most of Marx' labor theory of value has been discredited by history, he did leave a lasting legacy in insisting that the economy is all people servicing each other and that economic production should unite not divide people.

Even as Marx and his followers were chasing down the deadend of a labor theory of value, other economists, like Say, Cournot, Gossens and von Thünen, were rethinking the neglected ideas of utility and wanting as value determinants. Almost simultaneously Jevons, Walras and Menger, English, French and Austrian respectively, demonstrated that value was basically determined by the people's desires and the rate of exchange by their willingness to surrender other goods for this. Hence, the value of labor, machinery, materials and other inputs were imputed from the exchange value of the final product and the alternative to which they could be put. All values, therefore, are related horizontally and vertically in an interdependent and mutually adjusting web of exchange ratios, or prices.[11]

This revolution was completed when the synthesizing genius, Alfred Marshall (1842-1924) integrated classical into the new marginal utility analysis. For the first time economists could consistently explain the related phenomena of value, price, wealth, income, wages, costs and gain, and they began to perceive that scarcity was the root economic problem. Further, the Marshallian synthesis easily translated into price theory which, with its elegant mathematical formulas, graphs and schedules, allowed for unlimited empirical and statistical analysis.[12]

This flood of information, in turn, revealed to economists a new menagerie of influences on prices and economic values: changing consumer preferences and fads, advertising, market power, international trade and exchange rates, monetary and credit controls, banking practices and policy, fiscal policy, anti-monopoly, safety and environmental legislation. The list of influences on and functions of prices and economic values is as extensive as the aspects of modern living—innumerable!

In sum, economists in response to the changing complexity of the economy have found the many indispensable roles prices play in contemporary life. Entailing always a material base they are quantitative, measurable and amenable to mathematical manipulation. They express the vendibility of goods and services, their worth in exchange, by embodying both the utility people perceive in the things they consider buying and suppliers' costs of production. Thereby, they reflect community estimates and all manner of social influences. They also motivate entrepreneurship, work, supplying resources, technology and research with profits, wages, and interests. Thus prices and economic values guide planning and action, measure economic success, constitute wealth and bestow power. Finally, they come into being within a constantly changing, multi-dimensional net of other prices and values, all interrelated, interdependent and interacting.

Perceiving prices and economic values as cultural and scientific constructs, which function to help carry on economic business, is integral to a sound economic morality. In seeing them as necessary, ubiquitous, objective, impersonal and volatile tools for exchange, a person can see beyond them to the real things, the services and commodities the exchangers desire. At the same time, it prepares one for the hard reality that paying and getting prices constrains choices and tempers critical judgments but must still be taken into account to achieve ambitions, realize hopes and pursue dreams.

Wealth and Gain

All of these goals, in their economic dimensions, involve realizing gain and acquiring wealth. Both are derivatives of economic value: gain is the difference in economic value some act or process produces; wealth is simply the economic value of one's property and possessions. Their implications for motivating hopes, plans and efforts require some further analysis.

Wealth and economic well-being are often equated as etymology suggests: wealth being the state of weal or prosperity. But there are enough anomalies about wealth which economic morality requires clarifying. For example, while people have and do what could not be imagined 250 years ago, abundance has also changed the content of people's wealth so that the modestly circumstanced may enjoy a material well-being beyond some who are quite wealthy. Also, while the well-to-do may often be called "filthy rich", an air of respect trails the very rich, even when their fortunes are known to be tainted. Again, the pressure for more, even and especially by the already affluent, generates the greatest crime against property and ranks with sex and power in perpetrating wrongs against persons. Finally, though most people prefer to be rich rather than poor, few admit being rich, citing others who "really are rich." All of these ambiguities are reflected in people's attitude to wealth. They suggest the need to look further at wealth as it is in contemporary life and how a true understanding fits into a correct attitude of economic morality.

Indeed, economic abundance has changed the content and role of wealth from what they were several generations ago. Then most wealth consisted of landed estates, factories and other capital goods, and the source of wealth was control of the labor who worked the land and toiled in the factories. Such wealth manifested itself in palatial homes, fine furnishings, jewelry, carriages and the like. Today, while the wealthy may possess an array of comforts and luxuries not available to the general run, most of their wealth is in the form of stocks, bonds, options, rents, savings accounts, pensions and the like, rights to property and income, whose market values largely determine their owners' wealth but add little to their material well-being.

Two facts should be noted about such wealth. First, most of it is **working wealth**, investments in productive properties which must be worked to generate income and, therefore, is a source of wealth for the entire economy, really a form of social wealth. Not to differentiate this from the personal wealth which provides its owner a good living is to misrepresent the effective distribution of the nation's wealth in terms of people's well-being. Second, that this 'paper wealth' can drop drastically or rise dramatically in market value in a day's trading points up what was explained earlier **that wealth is not the goods and rights to income a person possesses but what these things can sell for, their economic value.** Both cases demonstrate that wealth and economic well-being are not one-to-one proportional. This caution suggests the need to examine wealth more closely.

While the content of wealth has been steadily dematerialized, wealth objects must be material in the minimum sense that they are quantifiable, countable and scarce. Spiritual goods, therefore, cannot become wealth-objects: skills, knowledge and moral qualities cannot be weighed, measured or ladled out like soup. Skills, which work up raw materials and are incorporated into a product, even though measured as earning capacity, cannot be called wealth since they cannot be alienated and sold. Even less so are more spiritual goods like virtue, wisdom, knowledge and artistic vision. Not counting them toward wealth is not to demean but to exalt them as pertaining to a higher level of human well-being which wealth can neither express nor attain.

Wealth does imply some permanence. Hence, material goods like food stocks, every day clothing and ordinary home furnishings, whose values disappear with regular use, are not counted as wealth. Similarly, the 'wealth-ness' of property which is subject to inflation and market vicissitudes is not fixed once and forever either. Wealth and a good's utility are related, its economic value or wealthness ranging between the owner's reservation price, below which he or she will not part with it, and would-be buyers' estimation of its utility. However, while the usefulness, service and pleasure goods and services provide are basic ingredients of their wealthness, they pertain more to people's material well-being than does their wealth. Indeed a good's utility is likely to be more constant than its economic value, since it is more individual and personal, while the economic value is social and dependent upon others' tastes and wants, the utility they perceive in it. All this points up the real difference between the wealth a person may claim and the life style he or she may enjoy. **This distinction is critical for a balanced view of wealth, its use and distribution.**

Summing up, an understanding of wealth proper to economic morality will realize that accumulations of personal, family or national wealth are like reservoirs of economic values which past efforts have filled, to which present and future incomes do and will add and which now water current consumption and irrigate future production. But such understanding will also keep in mind that wealth, being subject to social factors and economic influences, can erode and change. Further, a realistic insight into the nature of wealth will perceive that, however wealth may give power, the quality of life depends more on the benefits one's possessions bestow and even more so on the state of one's spiritual well-being. **In short, to gain wealth is a justifiable effort but not as a Good in and for itself.**

Economic gain also suffers from semantic difficulties. In sports to gain on an opponent is considered a virtue but in business and economics gain smacks of taking advantage of another. Thus "gain," whose Latin is *lucrum,* often is seen as "filthy lucre." But no one disputes the rationality of being pleased that a commodity's price is less than expected, of being happy that one's present employment is better than the previous, of rejoicing that the bottom line of the annual report is black not red. Conversely, no one exults that the new car is a lemon, that the new job pays less than the old and that the company is bankrupt. **No matter what problems gain may pose, an economic morality must hold on to this basic common sense that gain is a valid object of personal endeavor.**

Economic gain, put simply, is the difference in economic value of a good or service as the result of a transaction or production. Economists have identified three general categories of gain which correspond to the three fundamental moments of the economy: the sale of capital, human services, and supplies to the firm; the production and sale of the product or service by the business in its market; and the purchase of goods and services by the consumer. The gains realized in each of these actions are respectively economic rent, profit and consumer surplus. Of these profit is most familiar to the general public and will be discussed first.

Profit, to be sure, is an idea which is deemed unsavory by some people and raises the hackles of others. But profit, it must be affirmed, is a perfectly respectable form of gain and, indeed, the only rationale for doing business. This is obvious from considering the opposite: to generate a loss makes no sense whatever from both the social and personal point of view, because a loss means that the business product is valued less by consumers than the materials and human effort used to produce it. **Losses mean for the business, the individuals involved and for society as a whole a worse economic state after the endeavor than before.**

If losses make no sense, are an unmitigated evil and, when inevitable, should be minimized, then the opposite should hold that profits are good and should be maximized. Here ethicians, moralists and good Marxists will start to squirm. Indeed they should because some cautions and distinctions must be made about the profit concept itself. First it should be noted that tax collectors, accountants and economists define profits differently and vary among themselves. Next, profits will be interpreted differently depending upon the state of the business and the laws, social customs and moral principles which the profit-seekers consider relevant to their enterprise.

However interpreted, profits mean the business is doing well, in a general sense, measuring the difference between total income and total costs, both actual and imputed. As such they constitute the reward of investors and managers and arise from three general kinds of activities, 1) from innovating and getting the jump on competitors, 2) from producing more efficiently and 3) from acquiring market power. These will be discussed after a brief look at the two other forms of economic gain.

Economic rent is the difference between what a seller of labor or of productive goods can command and the next best opportunity. This is best illustrated in professional sports where a player may command a salary of a million a year, while, if not employed there, would get considerably less at an alternative job. The difference is called economic rent. A little reflection will reveal how widespread it is. A craft union or professional society, which requires licensing and certification and thus raises labor costs by restricting employment, obtains economic rent. The employee who moves from one firm to another doing essentially the same work but for higher compensation is gaining economic rent. The rocky meadow, good for little but grazing, now sold for a new subdivision earned a handsome economic rent. Indeed, the long range pressure to raise wages and capital, energy and resource prices to match the growth of the economy is the most fundamental form of economic rent which has distributed widely, if not perfectly, the benefits of abundance.

Consumer surplus, while less acknowledged and more difficult to measure, is the most prevalent form of economic gain. Every household purchase is intended to yield consumer surplus at least in the sense that the commodity is preferred to the money to buy it. Consumer surplus, however, is more apparent in the elation experienced in obtaining a bargain, in paying a lower price than the prevailing one or in obtaining more use and service from a good than anticipated. That consumer surplus, even though difficult to measure, does motivate buying is well known to retailers who periodically slash prices or sell generic goods at lower prices. Advertisers also regularly play the theme of 'more value at a lower price'. Professional purchasing agents survive or perish on their ability to realize consumer surplus. Indeed bargain hunting can become a disease, spurring buying whether the thing is needed or not. **All this demonstrates that consumer surplus is a universal object of gain and importantly affects people's material welfare.**

That completes this short treatment of wealth, gain, price and exchange value, those cultural constructs which, while generated in economic acts, direct and guide them. It now entails showing how **self-interested gain-seeking**, the desire for these constructs motivates economic behavior and drives the economy.

Self-interest and Gain-seeking

Self-interest, as shown earlier, is an essential element in all human action. Persons, as agents responsible for their own conduct, have a basic interest to seek their good, as they perceive it, in all they do. **Self-interest is essential to all responsible behavior.** In the inevitable and universal context of scarcity, therefore, where rising and falling prices monitor action, economic self-interest must take the form of gain seeking. (Gain-seeking is preferred to wealth-seeking because the former includes the latter as well as gain which will be used for current consumption.) A brief review of the respective impact of the three kinds of gain, consumer surplus, economic rent and profit, will show how together they generate a dynamic tension which increases and distributes the economy's output.

Gain-seeking will, depending upon the goal of the gain-seeker, variously lower or raise prices. Buyers, seeking consumer surplus, will in general seek lower prices and/or better product. The shop-lifter carries this to extremes in a petty way; the large buyer can in a more serious way by forcing unjust price and quality concessions. Rent-seekers, on the other hand, as sellers of labor move to the higher paying job, and as providers of raw materials, supplies, energy and capital seek markets which command higher prices. They are tempted not only to surpass competition but to eliminate it, thus creating an artificial scarcity and raising prices. The key people, however, are the profit-seekers, entrepreneurs who seek economic gain by assuming risk in committing expenditures in order to produce commodities and services for future sale.

Profit-seekers' interests are bi-valent, seeking lower prices for the labor and resources used in production and higher prices for the product sold. They thus like the base of a triangle hold the two sides together, seeking more efficient work and better quality inputs and trying to increase final sales by selling more and/or charging a higher price. Three courses are open to them: **innovate, become more efficient or acquire market power.** Some businesses are noted for one or other path to profitability; most combine the three in various mixes as circumstances warrant.

Innovators try to get the jump on competitors by coming out with a product which is markedly improved or changed from what is currently available. A lesser variation of this is called **product differentiation**, a minor or cosmetic change appealing to a particular segment of the market. Obviously, the innovator can charge a higher price until other firms begin to match the change with their own versions and thus erode the innovator's competitive advantage. **Productive efficiency** is a form of innovation, since improving output from the same factory or work force will require some innovative improvements in technology, marketing or management. More frequently such changes result from new techniques, better labor skills and improved capital goods. All tend to increase production or to lower costs or both, thus allowing lower product prices and higher sales, both tending to increase profits and eventually wages.

The last form of profit-seeking is gaining market power. Of course, innovation, product differentiation and improved productivity will give a firm a market advantage, but one from which the general public benefits and is eroded by competition. Other forms are not so socially beneficial. Price discrimination is defended in that the different segments of a market are charged different prices equal to their demand. But it does absorb the consumer surplus some customers would realize if all paid a uniform price. Price discrimination is universally practiced at theatre or sport events: those wanting seats close to the action pay premium prices while students seats behind the goal posts are much less. This practice is widely accepted, the public's advantages and disadvantages probably evening out. A less accepted form of market advantage is the crude exercise of economic power: eliminating competitors to raise prices; squeezing workers' wages; monopolizing raw materials; colluding with competitors; rigging bids for government work; or seeking privilege under guise of fair-trading, safety or health rules. The tricks are infinite to the fertile mind maximizing profits by unjust means. In short, profit-seeking is protean, limber and fluid in taking whatever shape and emphasis situations present.

Gain-seeking also drives other economic activities which do not fit neatly under the three discussed. Tax-collectors are pressured to reap larger tax revenues. Businesses, institutions and advocacy groups lobby for larger government favors. Investors revise their portfolios to get better returns. Philanthropies scrutinize possible recipients for those offering the largest benefits for their giving. **Gain-seeking, therefore, drives all economic action and is, indeed, the rational response to scarcity, the condition of never having enough to make ends meet, which infuses every economic activity and relation.**

While gain-seeking in its many forms creates a dynamic tension, keeping a free-market economy both generally growing and in fair balance, two other factors, inherent in a free economy, play important roles in this dynamic. They are *competition and cooperation.* Economic competition, of course, is essentially social in that for people to get what they want they must pay someone else's price. Competition means outbidding others for what one wants: to get more, give more. In the context of scarcity this is a force, which when present and effective counteracts and controls gain-seeking, driving some prices up and others down, thereby further shaping the distribution of gain among consumers, laborers, investors and entrepreneurs.

At the same time, cooperation is also inherent especially in the productive processes of the economy. Such cooperation is more than the social network mentioned above: it implies that people work together for a common end. B.W. Dempsey expresses it well. "Cooperation in the economic process is both implicit and explicit. Factors of production working together on a job are obviously cooperating. Less obviously, but equally importantly, factors working upon different jobs, but with the object of exchanging the surpluses arising from the specialization, are also cooperating toward a common objective, namely, the provision of an improved standard of living for both."[13] Competition and cooperation will be encountered again later on. **Now they should be kept in mind as the tie-rods and struts which counter the stresses on the economy gain-seeking produces.**

An economic morality which would be relevant to contemporary life must accept the universality as well as the necessity of gain-seeking in a free-market economy. It must acknowledge the deep cultural roots in Western Civilization of a gain-seeking which destroyed the status and privilege of feudal society, steered economic ambitions away from land ownership to commercial and industrial enterprise, and carried European culture along with its products throughout the world. While gain-seeking is responsible for untold plunder, exploitation and misery it has also shifted the burden of hauling and heaving from men to machines, expanded people's horizons and increased their mobility, and lifted from untold millions of the world's underclass the cold hand of debt and economic stagnation. To be convinced one need only contrast Western-style with those developing economies where the feeble spark of gain-seeking has not been fanned into self-reliant, self-fueling economic growth.

As to a free-market economy it should be apparent that it compensates those who consult their own interests. Those who supply the goods and services most wanted are most liberally rewarded. Those who anticipate consumer trends get the jump on competitors. Those who are most truly innovative can become fantastically rich. Those who seek better paying jobs have more income. Those who shop intelligently enjoy a better living. Considered from every angle, gain-seeking is both a powerful energizer of economic growth and that valid principle of action which directs the free market in distributing its abundance.

But like any strong human drive, self-interested gain-seeking will get out of hand and destroy as well as improve. That, of course, establishes the need to blend moral convictions into that attitude and temper of mind called economic morality. To appreciate better that necessity it would be helpful to look at some of the moral dangers and pitfalls gain-seeking presents.

PERILS AND PITFALLS

Anyone who has zipped along expressways and been in an accident or seen a near miss can appreciate that the headlong course of self-interest and economic abundance would be strewn with perils. New kinds of wants and products are created which because of their novelty will present problems. Prices may play an excessive role in daily life and the superficiality of economic transactions may come to characterize much of social intercourse. A fuller discussion appeared in an earlier work as *The Anguish of Affluence.*[14] Here just the three moral reefs listed above will be explored.

The Perils

Increasing one's material possessions is inevitable—except for the heroically ascetic—in an economy generating more and more abundance. Someone has to get the increased income if the lion's share is not to go to the already super-rich or, worse, to government. Increased income increases one's wants, combines them in more complex bundles of satisfaction and seeks from them more psychic satisfaction. All pose the danger of materializing one's values.

As income increases wants accumulate. Children take for granted and as given wants their parents struggled to fulfill and now hanker for satisfactions their parents had never imagined. In this way, generation after generation, increasing income and scarcity spawn more and more wants. Furthermore, these increased wants are combined in more complex bundles of satisfactions. Compare, for example, contemporary automobiles, those marvels of speed, efficiency, comfort and styling, with those of 30 or 40 years ago.

The dimension of wanting most often overlooked, however, is what can be called *want symbolization*. Ignoring it misses an the important dynamic of wanting things and ministrations more for the spirit than the body: to love and be loved, to know and be known, to have power, to be respected and held in awe, to possess beauty and be admired. Too frequently people consider only its baser manifestations, emulation, envy, dilettantism and tyranny,[15] ignoring the kinder impulses of the heart, gratitude, social concern, generosity and commiseration. **All in all, increasing abundance generates in every way more insistent material wants, which can distract from life's higher goals.**

Responding to this proliferation of wanting, suppliers have, as one would expect, created commodities and services which satisfy wants more swiftly, more conveniently, in larger doses and more complicated patterns. Moreover, scientists, driven by intellectual curiosity as well as profit-seeking, generally outpace popular imagination in finding new uses for known materials like oil or aluminum and in discovering new applications of medical, chemical, biological, electrical and physical principles.

More remarkable, in a sense, are the services abundance has generated. Supplying information, for example, by mail, advertising and catalogues has made international and transcontinental buying almost foolproof and transmitting it by computer has revolutionized finance, marketing and management. Insurance also, while as old as trading itself, is peculiarly modern in its pervasiveness. People can be insured against all the most likely risks, fire, illness, death, retirement, unemployment, home and traffic accidents. What private business cannot cover, governments of affluent countries do.

Less understood and more castigated is the financial activity called speculation, which is really a form of insurance. In very volatile markets, like spot and future trading in moneys, stocks, bonds, stock options and basic raw materials, rapid and cumulative price changes can endanger the buying and selling of those who must be in these markets. Speculators assume much of this risk by betting against market swings, often realizing fantastic profits or disastrous losses. In summary, these and a wide range of personal, family, household, health, environmental and educational services can make things easier in today's faster paced life. As a result, however, people are more dependent on others and more exposed to manipulation.

More income and greater scarcity obviously generate more prices and changes in prices. Price changes, in turn, because of any of a host of influences, sets off a chain of changes in other prices, some markedly, some minutely. Since every price (economic value) is set in a multi-dimensional web of prices, wages, salaries, bonuses, royalties, taxes, rents, dividends, all prices mutually affect and are affected by each other. Hence, every decision to buy or sell begins a line of consequences for incomes, jobs, growth and survival. As a forest is continuously dying and renewing itself, so too this kaleidoscope of prices is constantly reshaping the economy, some gaining and some losing.

Many people, however, are needlessly tyrannized by prices and price changes: buy or sell now or do without! But just the conviction, that there are substitutes for every job, every product and every item on the supermarket shelf, frees one from the power of price. Being aware of all the factors which effect prices helps people to respond more intelligently to prices which adversely affect them and helps them wait out the change or to seek alternatives. In neither case do they become passive victims of prices but use them to their own advantage. Another benefit of a modest understanding of prices is acquiring the habit of distinguishing between what a commodity or service sells for and what it is good for. Too many people take for granted that a high price denotes high quality because they lack confidence in their ability to judge quality on their own. But confusing exchange value with use value is both bad practice and bad economics. It reverses the causal relations: utility, as shown earlier, is a determinant of price, not price of utility.

These cautions have universal applicability. While price, gain, wealth and the other economic relational constructs are necessary to guide and monitor economic activity, they arise out of and change with the flux of production, exchange, investment, saving and the rest. The substantial reality behind this fluctuating net of prices is the enjoyment things give and the use to which they can be put. **The benefit goods and services provide, their utility, is the real and relatively constant source of material well-being. Losing sight of this truth is one of the more serious perils of the pervasiveness of prices.**

But to caution against the tyranny of prices is not to denigrate them. As pointed out earlier, the vast system of national and world prices is a way in which total strangers, even enemies, can exchange commodities, jobs and capital to their mutual benefit. Paradoxically, this is possible because the economic act, while social, can be and usually is superficial: trade only requires that people relate to each other in the narrow way of one person surrendering what another wants in exchange for what he or she wants. No deep personal commitment, as in marriage or other forms of community, is needed: a person can stay with an unlikable boss if the job is good and the wages fair.

The superficiality of exchange relations can, however, imperil the more personal kinds of relations if the economic aspects begin to dominate: a marriage, for example, reduced to an economic *quid pro quo*, a cold mutual self-interest replacing its initiating intimate love. Most acts in which the economic predominates are transient and ephemeral: the transaction done, the relation terminates. Such acts are individual and complete, so much for so much, reflecting no obligation prior to nor promising commitment beyond this exchange, this deal. Given the volatility of prices, gain-seeking, unalloyed by any sense of permanence, tends to flit from one deal to another, regardless of consequences to others. Impatient with slow organic growth, which might unite others for a common goal, it lives for the moment, the next bargain, the next killing, the next quarterly report, oblivious of long run consequences. **Such** gain-seeking is close to becoming an ingrained selfishness.

The Pitfalls

That self-interested gain-seeking needs to be controlled in no way denies that it is essential to make the economy go. But more so perhaps than other kinds, economic self-interest is inclined to a selfishness, tending to greediness and injustice. People must, therefore, be as open and objective in scrutinizing it as they can be. First, all self-interest is egocentric in this basic sense that people are responsible for their own lives. But a self-interest, which is exclusively concerned with self and ignores the network of personal and economic relations which is the matrix of all human action, changes the dictum from "I am responsible *for* myself," to "I am responsible *to* myself." Such self-interest in the economic sphere, given disparities in talent, energy and fortune, will generate huge inequalities. For the self-interest of the single-mindedly ambitious will be concerned about others only as means to their own ends, mindful of others only to advance their ambitions.

Such gain-seeking is not a factor just in the lives of captains of finance and industry. It does describe more modest lives: the consumer who can never pass up a bargain whether needing the good or not; the worker never satisfied with any job but flits to every new one offered; the executive whose appetite for more income and power destroys the business which provided them. Such self-interest has generated spectacular successes and tragic failures, very frequently in that order. However it may be, such self-interest produces moral entropy, the dissipation of moral energy and dissolution of moral ties. It also violates economic rationality by quenching the cooperation essential to business processes and by setting individuals one against the other. All the above indicates quite clearly that gain-seeking is a form of self-seeking and, as such, seems fixed on three anchors of self-centered individualism. As a maximizing principle under conditions of scarcity it seems to pit all constituencies of a business against one another: workers, managers, and stockholders, each against the other, and suppliers and consumers against all, each competing for the biggest slice of the business' pie. Second, gain-seeking seems to compound this struggle by excluding from consideration any other's well-being except one's own. Last, being its own rationale, it would seem to preclude any values beyond itself.

As to the first, the term "maximizing" needs explanation. In economics it can never mean "unlimited", which would deny scarcity and thus economics itself. Gain-seeking, therefore, as a maximizing principle can only mean the largest possible amount in a given set of circumstances. This, as we saw, means at the national level being limited to the economy's production frontier and at the company level to the firm's productive capacity. Both, of course, can be increased but at any one moment these capacities are finite. Furthermore, a person's gain-expectations are limited by the gain rationale itself. If a business would grow, all or most involved with it must intend to gain. Thus to preempt all gain to one's self deprives others of their hopes for gain and destroys the very expectations which energized the company's growth. Maximizing gain, therefore, can only mean realizing the best possible gain, given the physical limitations and the need to share gain with all who contributed to it. **Moderating gain-seeking within the limits imposed by the possible is simply economic common sense.**

Secondly, while gain-seeking is self-seeking, it is not asocial or anti-social. Gain like economic value depends upon the worth other people put on one's property. Gain-seeking, therefore, requires offering what others want, and competition for gain means out-bidding others in offering more of what buyers want. All of this was discussed earlier. But gain-seeking is structurally social in that, in a free economy, it is premised on others also gaining. Production, for example, is not just a collective effort but a truly social process in that it not only combines in a mechanistic way the skills, talents and wealth of its many participants but in a more profound sense blends the gain-motives of all its contributors. Indeed every transaction, intended to lead to further business, requires both buyer and seller to consult each other's interests. Exploiting one's comparative advantage, remember, creates an advantage for someone else. The strong to take advantage of their strength need the weak, the clever the stolid, the skilled the unskilled, the boss the worker. **Gain-seeking is not only social but at heart it requires complementarity, mutuality and cooperation.**

Indeed unrestrained gain-seeking (greed really) defeats itself by ravaging the market or situation where it gorged. Besides turning off people who resent being used, economic greed destroys the continuity of business relations and, become short-sighted in pursuit of the immediate deal, loses sight of the long-run. Finally and most disastrously, it demoralizes and embitters the associates and employees, who in seeking their own interests, contributed to the organization's success. Gain-seekers, who would squeeze every drop of gain out of every transaction, inevitably desiccate all their human relations and reduce everything to its economic value.

Gain-seeking's supposed third anchor in radical individualism, that gain and gain-seeking are their own rationale and need no validity beyond themselves, presents more difficulty than the previous two. Indeed, gain-seeking is justified for the same reason economics is justified: since scarcity is inherent in the human condition and only scarce goods have economic value, seeking to increase the economic value of one's work and possessions is simply common sense, needing no other justification. Being, therefore, secular, utilitarian and concerned with material goods, economic self-interest seems closed to any values or purposes which transcends gain-seeking's goal of increasing income and wealth. Gain-seeking from this perspective would seem to exclude all the values stressed earlier, respect for persons and their social nature, community and sharing and values which transcend this life. **In fact, the problem is so fundamental to the very thesis of this book as to require the rest of it to answer it.**

With this, having examined the moral perils and pitfalls economic principles presents, the book can turn to the nitty-gritty of blending moral convictions into economic common sense. This will be done in five stages, each covered in a chapter.

1) It will examine the differences between moral and economic values and how the latter can be fitted into a value hierarchy. 2) The discussion of economic justice will center on the preeminent rights of the individual and social rights of persons. 3) Chapter 6 will demonstrate how gain-seeking is best controlled by directing it toward achieving higher moral values. 4) Chapter 7 will go further in showing how concern for the ultimate meaning of life requires both a certain indifference to income and wealth and a willingness to share them with others. 5) The final chapter will bring all this together by showing how the moral and economic enterprises work together for an integrated life.

Such an agenda well advises to get right to it.

ENDNOTES

1. Aristotle. *Nichomachean Ethics.* Tr. W.D. Ross, Oxford, 1905 bk. V, chs. 4-5.
2. Augustine. *The City of God*, Tr. M. Dodds, Chicago, 1952, bk. 11, ch. 16.
3. Aquinas, Thomas. *Summa Theologica*, Tr. Fathers of the English Dominican Providence, New York, 1911-20, II-II, p.77.
4. Spiegel, Henry W. *The Growth of Economic Thought*, Englewood Cliffs, NJ, 1971, pp. 202-5.
5. Schumpeter, Joseph. *A History of Economic Analysis*, New York, 1943, pp. 209-43.
6. Hume, David. *Writings on Economics*, Ed. E. Rotwein, Madison, WI, 1930, passim.
7. Smith, Adam. *Wealth of Nations*, Ed. Edward Cannon, New York, 1937, bks. 1 and 2.
8. Ricardo, David. *The Principles of Political Economy and Taxation*, Homewood, 1963, chs. 1-8.
9. Mill, J.S. *Principles of Political Economy*, Boston, 1848, bk. 2, ch. 1 and bk. 4.
10. Marx, Karl. *Capital*, Ed. F. Engels, Tr. S. Moore and E. Aveling, Chicago, 1952, chs. 1-12, 16, 24-25.
11. Schumpeter, pp. 825-9.
12. Marshall, Alfred. *Principles of Economics*, New York, 1980, passim.
13. Dempsey, Bernard W., S.J. *The Functional Economy*, Englewood Cliffs, NJ, 1958, p. 21.
14. Danner, Peter L., *An Ethics for the Affluent*, Lanham, MD, 1980, pp. 35-8, 98-100 and 130-6.
15. For a more pessimistic look at baser want symbolization see: Smith, Adam. *The Theory of Moral Sentiments*, New York, 1822, p. 46 and p. 153, and especially Veblen, Thorstein. *The Theory of the Leisure Class*, New York, 1912.

GLOSSARY

complementarity—The properties of things such that each supplements the others' functions, e.g. work and tools.

consumer surplus—The gain realized in purchasing a commodity at a price less than anticipated or in getting more than ordinary service from a good. When noteworthy, it is called a bargain.

cultural construct—A standard, custom, guide or measure, developed from cultural relations or social practice. While not substances, they are real measures of objects and behavior.

economic rent—Strictly defined, economic rent is the increase in the value of a product, resource or skill whose amount is fixed but demand is increasing. More loosely defined, it is the increase in value when demand increases much more than supply.

economic value—Economic or exchange value is the estimated market price of something or its equivalent if available for sale.

exchangeable value—The materiality of a saleable object, allowing it to be alienated, to become another's property. By contrast, services, according to Adam Smith, while they can be bought and sold, cannot be alienated.

moral context—The total implication, including intentions and circumstances, of an act or course of action for one's final end and purpose.

moral entropy—A pattern of behavior tending to dissipate one's moral convictions and principles.

political economy—A comprehensive view of the economy from the perspective of the national political state.Today called the **macroeconomy.**

price discrimination—The practice of charging different prices to different segments of a market, e.g. according to seating at a concert.

product differentiation—Slight changes made in an otherwise standard product to appeal to different consumer preferences.

profit—That form of economic gain which rewards the risks taken by entrepreneurs and investors in a business venture.

spot and future prices—The spot price is the current price of a commodity being sold today; the future price is the current price of a commodity to be sold at some specified future date.

surplus value—The net increase in the value of goods and services an economy produces. Economists have variously ascribed it to a net balance of trade, business profits, labor productivity, economic rent etc. Now they attribute it to the complex of factors causing growth.

utility—Utility is the anticipated use or benefit an economic good is expected to provide. **Marginal utility** is the increase in benefit an additional unit is expected to provide.

value formation—The market process, including all the determinants of supply and demand, by which prices of economic goods and services are generated.

want symbolization—The psychic satisfaction, beyond the good's usefulness, which it is expected to provide.

TOPICS FOR FURTHER DISCUSSION OR RESEARCH

1. Demonstrate how each of the synonymous terms, price and ex change value, illustrates well some but not other aspects of these things: a pound of butter; the annual tuition you pay; household tasks various family members perform; income tax payments; one's weekly pay check.

2. Critique Veblen's chapter 17, "The Higher Learning as an Expression of the Pecuniary Culture," from *The Theory of the Leisure Class.* From your perception of higher education in the U.S. today, how relevant is his view? has higher education become more utilitarian? remote from practical living?

3. Trace the growth and spread of one of the many consumer or productive innovations since World War II, like television, international communication, fast-food restaurants, robotization, computers and the like. Show in a general way, but with some defensible data, the effect of the innovation both in creating new wants and new industries servicing the wants and in eliminating other wants and other industries or jobs.

ADDITIONAL SUGGESTED READING

1. Robert Heilbroner, *The Worldly Philosophers,* New York: Simon and Schuster, 1953.
2. Bernard W. Dempsey, *The Functional Economy,* Englewood Cliffs: Prentice-Hall, Inc., 1958.
3. Thorstein Veblen, *The Theory of the Leisure Class,* chs. 1-4 and 14, Boston: Houghton Mifflin, 1973.

CHAPTER FOUR

MORAL AND ECONOMIC VALUES

This chapter shifts from the economic goal of orchestrating material well-being to the more encompassing moral purpose of personal fulfillment. As very complex beings, humans have many dimensions by which they can excel (or fail) as persons: by attaining superior health, physical strength and bodily agility; by acquiring the material goods which bestow easeful living; by achieving respect and honor from and power over others; by knowing more about and understanding better one's nature and world; by a more refined appreciation of art and nature; by developing a more sensitive attitude to and respectful conduct toward intimates, associates or just anybody; and, for believers in life after this, by a closer union with God. All—and everyone could add others—are ingredients of a good life and contribute to personal growth.

No one, of course, can realize all these goals to the same degree in a life time nor are they equally desirable toward achieving the fullness of human personality. Arranging them in a hierarchy according to a person's ultimate end and purpose is the work of ethics and the moral sciences which, therefore, deal with **Values**, those features of people (including self) things and relations, perceived as Goods worth pursuing. (Note the capitalization of "Values" and "Goods". For clarity sake from now on these words will be capitalized when having a moral meaning and lower case with an economic sense.) Espoused and ordered hierarchically, governing Values become guides of conduct and determine a person's character. Since such Values are personal, qualitative and freely chosen, they are essentially different from economic values, which are set by the market, quantitative, and given. Nevertheless, the use of the same word for different realities suggest some connection. Exploring this will be the task of this chapter, first looking at moral Values as they relate to moral growth.

MORAL VALUES

Values are learned by experiencing them, a daily occurrence for most people, though often unheeded. Value espousal happens more rarely and often unconsciously. When espoused, Values become guides of conduct and determinants of character.[1]

The Value Experience

However tuned in or tuned out, people encounter Values at every twist and turn of life. The pleasure from an ice-cream cone is a Value experience no less than the lightning perception that a certain person is the most wonderful woman in the world. While worlds apart in their impact on a person's life, they share common features as Value experiences.

First, the experience of Values like all human knowing comes through the senses: tasting, touching, seeing and the rest. But the Value experience goes beyond sensation to an immediate perception, that is, without conceptualizing or reasoning, of the object as Good. Thus the will comes into play, simultaneously desiring, preferring, loving. This action of the will is not inevitable. A person may have eaten many ice-cream cones before the will jogs the intellect to perceive the cone as Good. Even more startling is realizing that someone known for years is really special as a role model, friend or beloved. In intuiting immediately the object's Goodness and worth, a person knows and loves, perceives and prefers simultaneously, knowing more clearly by loving and loving better by perceiving. **Willing illuminates knowing and knowing intensifies willing.**

Knowing how Values are experienced suggest what they are. As products of intellect and will together they are things and persons, their natures, features and qualities which are known as

Good, that is, they are loved and preferred when known. In a strict sense a Value may not tell one more about an object. Rather the object is now seen in a new light. For example, I may well have known and heard for many years of the things Aunt El did for others but it only dawned on me recently that she really is a kind person, indeed, kindness personified. In the parlance used here, she bears the Value, kindness. It may be that for the first I have come to understand kindness and may begin to see it in others. **My experiencing this Value, therefore, tells me more about my perceptiveness and the quality of my likes and dislikes than about the bearer of the Value.**

Once sensitive to Values, people begin to realize how prevalent Values are. Individuals, groups or classes of people bear Values, as do the qualities they possess and the things they do, whether conscious spiritual, vital or sensual acts, unconscious responses, or instinctive reactions. Individual acts or feelings differ as Values from one's moral character and intentions. Relations may be evaluated according to the persons related, the kind of relation or the quality of the relationship. Things may also bear sacred, spiritual, cultural, pleasing or useful Values. Also, persons must and some things may be preferred as Values in and for themselves while other things, tools, instruments, techniques, plans, symbols or anything useful, are means to other Values: they are means-Values. Last, Values are categorized according to whom they are valuable, in the way they are valuable and for what end they are valuable.[2]

Values, the above makes plain, are both objective and subjective. As the qualities people, things, relations and so forth bear, Values relate to objective realities: Values are objective. As the perception/preference that these qualities are Good, Values are the product of a subjective experience. **They arise in my experience; they are my Values.** The Value experience is, therefore, subjective and very personal. Just as the born-blind could never fully appreciate the Sistine Chapel, so too the self-centered could live with saints and still steel themselves against concern and compassion for others. Values, to repeat, are founded on the nature, features and relations of objective reality but come into being when someone perceives and prefers them as Good. All the above suggests that Values encounter people at every turn in life and whisper to them at every level of their beings and personalities. While most acts of preferring are probably instinctive, reflexive and habitual, people are, either consciously or unconsciously, evaluating persons, things, acts and relations, judging them pleasant or unpleasant, beautiful or ugly, good or bad. **All life, viewed horizontally or vertically, is Value-laden. When a Value becomes habitual it acquires tremendous, even if subconscious, power in one's life and conduct.**

The Value Espousal

Values indeed can be more than preferences. Scruton stresses their importance in practical reason. Unlike preferences, he insists, we defend our Values because, "we learn to see and understand the world in terms of them . . . . A Value is characterized not by its strength but by its depth, by the extent it brings order to experience."[3] For Rescher Values not only serve as norms for judging the goodness or badness of objects but also as purposes or goals for overt action.[4] Allport locates Values deep in the personality "as a belief upon which a man acts by preference." This "deeply propriate disposition... reveals a person's intentionality or the central theme of his striving."[5] Finally, Angell emphasizes the social significance of Values, seeing them as "continuous qualities of life we desire to see realized."[6] **The sum of these remarks leads to the conclusion that Values can be internalized as principles and criteria of conduct and, when so espoused, make a profound difference in a person's moral life and development.**

Value espousal, therefore, is more than a passing experience and, like a bethrothal, suggests a more permanent commitment to a Good, one powerful and comprehensive enough to be a dominant force in one's life. (While eliminating trivial or ephemeral Values, this does not rule out some lower Values like the pleasures of liquor or sex from being a dominant force in one's life.) Some Value espousals may be as dramatics as Saul's on the road to Damascus; others may be recognized only after years of influencing conduct; others again may lie in the unconscious and never be acknowledged.

However perceived, dominant Values are dynamic, coalescing about them lesser Values, wants and habits, every act or choosing to act confirming or eroding these central Values. They are like search lights on a dark night, pointing out and facilitating certain courses of action and predisposing one to certain kinds of responses, choices and actions, whether immoral, moral or indifferent. Although powerfully predisposing, such dominant Values are not set in concrete: they can be eroded by conscious contrary action. Thus higher Values, espoused with some conviction can displace lower Values, and unfortunately, lower Values can erode higher Values.

The notion of higher and lower Values implies, of course, that Values are not equally important for right conduct but can and should be ranked according to their authority for moral action. Indeed, everyone, consciously or not, develops a Value hierarchy. Although each person's rankings, being imperfectly done, will differ from everyone else's, there are certain disposition in human thought by which Values can be organized into a theoretically correct Value hierarchy. These disposition include the **ways of preferring Values and the principles of preferring, which in turn determine the Value modalities or categories.**

The Value Hierarchy

Ranking a Value means putting it ahead of some Values and behind others. Preferring, therefore, is expressed either as a 'placing before' or a 'placing after'. The former stresses the positive preferability of the Value over others, the latter the subordination of this Value to others. The former expects to overwhelm vice with virtue by looking toward higher moral expectations; the latter by the more ascetic way of achieving virtue by eradicating vice. Both ways are necessary; neither can be pursued exclusively. A Value espousal is both an achievement (placing before) and an incentive for the better (placing after).

The rules of preference can be reduced to the one principle, **that an absolute Value is to be preferred to a relative Value.** According to Scheler, the more absolute Value leaves the conviction that preferring another Value to it constitutes a falling away from a higher state of Value-existence.[7] Since there can be only one absolutely absolute Good and Value, an existing infinite Being, all other Goods and Values share in absoluteness to the extent that they possess the features of absoluteness. These, as experience demonstrates, are four: **duration, unity, depth, and fulfillment.**

1) The **longer-lasting good** is preferred to the transient, just the reverse, of course, for evils. An **eternal** being simply endures: there is no past or future but only an eternal present. Thus the more enduring a Value, the more absolute it is: love is for a lifetime; lust for a night of pleasure. 2) The more **integrated, indivisible or simple** a thing the more absolute its Goodness: erasing the smile ruins the *Mona Lisa*, removing the carburetor impairs but does not ruin an automobile. Art bears a higher Values than a machine; loving than hearing. 3) The more **basic** the Good the more to be preferred. Health, presupposes life, which presupposes being. Hence, being is the more fundamental, more basic and deeper Value, just as an infinite and eternal Being must be *the* absolute Value. 4) Values which are more **fulfilling**, which yield a deeper **contentment**, are preferred to shallow pleasures. (Studying economics *is* more satisfying than an evening of rock!!!)

Applying these four rules of preferring establishes what Scheler calls **Value-modalities**, categories of Values in order of their absoluteness.[8] At the lowest level are **sensual Values**, given in sensation and perceived as yielding pleasure and pain. True Values, they are ranked across a spectrum of agreeable to disagreeable. Pleasure/pain are transient, partial, and peripheral states of feeling. They are real and important indicators but not the substance of well-being. At a higher level **vital Values**, relating to life and well-being are ranked from lively to lifeless, **those relating to plants and animals** are ranked from noble to base; and **those relating to tools, machines and symbols** from useful to useless. Such Values evoke the feeling-states of gladness or sadness, of feeling healthy or ill, of succeeding or failing. Although material Values, thus terminal, they do last for some time. While means, they require some integrity: a wounded dog cannot hunt. Though enhancing living, they are not of the essence of human life.

Spiritual Values surpass the previous two in their degree of absoluteness. They are classed as **aesthetic Values**, beautiful to ugly, as **ethical Values**, right to wrong, and as **intellectual Values**, true to false. While requiring material expression, these Values supply humans' enduring and existential appetite for the Beautiful, the True and the Good, all essential for personal fulfillments. They rank just below **sacred Values**, the highest modality, ranking from holy to unholy. The sacred, in a sense, encompasses all Values because every category, pleasure/pain, lively/lifeless, useful/useless, beautiful/ugly, true/false, and right/wrong can be referred to absolute being. Every person, animal or thing can be perceived in the light of absolute existence and Goodness, correlating with the religious concept of the sacramentality of all things. But above all the modality of the holy/unholy applies to the Value of the human person and preeminently of an infinite person. Granted a supreme being, he/she would exist eternally, absolutely unique and simple, perfect in all respects and the source of all being. Human persons, to the extent they share this absoluteness, should also be perceived as sacred and holy.

[A word is needed about the Values, efficient/inefficient and useful/useless, which are of particular concern for economists. These Values, of course, belong to the second Schelerian modality. About them two points must be made: 1) both these Values are means-Values and imply, therefore, another Value which pertains to the substance or qualities of the object under consideration and 2) this more fundamental Value could belong to any of the categories from the sensual to sacred described above.]

Having presented what Values are, their variety, experience, espousal and formation into Value hierarchies, this section is completed by seeing how the objective, not the subjective, aspect of Values serves as both criteria and purposes of conduct. Distinctions here are subtle but decisive, the basic principle being that an act should be pursued not because its object is valued but because it is Good. Values are important motivators of action but not the ultimate criterion: they only mirror, not establish, the object's Goodness, which is, therefore, the ultimate criterion of the act's morality. Also because the end sought is Good and not just because it is valued, the object's Goodness becomes the ultimate purpose for acting. Even less should an object be valued because it is wanted, but wanted because it is valued. That is, while valuation logically precedes purpose, the valuation itself arises from the intellect seeing and the will choosing the Good of the object. Once the Value is espoused, the will then further steels purpose. **Thus Values by illuminating others', as well as one's own Goodness, become both guides and goals of conduct and thereby contribute to moral growth and check moral decline.**

MORAL PROGRESS AND PATHOLOGY

The connection between the many dimensions of human excellence (and failure), listed earlier, and the Value modalities just described is not accidental. One's moral growth governs the Values he or she espouses, espoused Values reflecting one's moral maturity. That is, a person's Values and moral conviction mutually determine and corroborate each other. **Value perceptions of external Goodness are internalized and then externalized in moral conduct. Values perceiving and preferring only self will be externalized as selfish and anti-social behavior.**

Values and Moral Growth

Despite the complexity of the human person and human civilization, purpose is evident in the lives of individuals and more apparently in the ascent of the human species. From the prehominoid tool-maker to the hunter and gatherer of food and from that to the crop cultivator and animal herder, people through the millennia learn to live together as tribal cave-dwellers, then communal farmers and lastly urban artisans and traders. From belief that life has some ultimate meaning, *homo sapiens* tries to plumb the meaning of all things, wresting from them power to exploit the forces of nature and to enhance living. This sweep through human history may be conceived, as does Teilhard du Chardin, as an evolutionary cosmogenesis, a world coming into being. As Teilhard sees it, all things, material, living and human converge in Omega, human purpose blending into the Divine, Supreme Act of Love.[9] **However far one is disposed to go with this vision (or myth), it is a captivating expression of the human species' purposeful ascent from the cave.**

Everyone can, in a sense, replicate this ascent in his or her life. While a person's physical growth is for the most part dictated by one's biological clock and the general pattern of native endowments and circumstances, the important decisions and ultimate direction of life is within one's purpose and intention. Many people, of course, are vague and inconstant in their moral aspirations. But those whose intentions are clear and in focus exercise that most precious power of personality, its transcendental drive, which is nothing other than moral growth.

The Swedish psychologist, Eduard Spranger, pioneered the conception of personality growth as an organic process,[10] from which many scholars have drawn inspiration. Spranger's analogy was that just as the tree grows from seed, transcending yet contained within it, conditioned by its environment but transforming it, so the human person grows in a complex, yet systemic and interdependent way. Spranger conceives the ego as a congery of many drives: an organism struggling to survive; an appetite to satisfy wants and to achieve fulfillment; a desire to know and to create beauty; a seeker for the meaning of everything and an aspirer after ultimate reality. While thus striving for self-fulfillment, the ego also reaches out to other human beings, either to impose its will on them or to identify lovingly their Good as its own. **Growth in personality, therefore, is a spiraling movement, thrusting upward and expanding outward**

yet rooted in a person's most elemental needs and wants.

The self, therefore, at any moment is a specific fusion and interfusion of these elements. The particular blend at any point in time determines the tone and texture of character and sets the general tenor of behavior. At the same time it conditions how a person conceives and treats things and people from simply using them as means to one's own end to perceiving the sublime in everything and everyone. Hence, personality and moral growth translates in practice to what a person judges to be the Goodness of other people and other things and what is to be considered worth striving for. Thus, moral growth is linked to **Value espousal** as one side of a coin to the other.

People's Value hierarchies, however, do not have the logical tidiness of the earlier analysis but display the messiness of living. In the swirl and bustle of life the Value experiences of most people may reflect their physical environment, economic circumstances and social circles rather than purposeful preferences. Certainly, a person's Values tend to mirror others' Values and especially one's class and societal Values. A person may even hold Values which are almost contradictory, which could eventually precipitate moral crisis unless the conflict is spotted and the Values adjusted. But, however slip-shod Value systems may seem to be and to have grown haphazardly, they do not just happen but display some real effort. The Values which dominate people's lives are the result of deliberate espousal, of a searing experience, or habitual repetition. Some degree of purposefulness can be detected wherever a strongly held Value is evident. The lengthy catalogue of words describing moral states demonstrates the need to identify how ruling Values specify one's general moral condition.

The **aesthete**, for example, suggests a refined sensuality which may be further specified by the **gourmet** in dining, the **paramour** in sexual affairs and the **connoisseur** in imbibing. A grosser sensuality is practiced by the **hedonist, glutton, rake or harlot**, and **drunkard**. The **austere** person, discomfited by sensual Values is at the other extreme, as also the **abstemious, prude** and **teetotaler.** Vital Values are a dominating mark of the

champion in sports, the **powerful** in politics, the **successful** in business, the **hero** in feats of daring, and the **star** in entertainment, their opposites being the **failure, powerless, coward and so forth. Talented** usually denotes the person whose ruling Values are spiritual (not necessarily holy) to an exceptional degree. In aesthetics it is the **savant**, possibly a creator of art and literature but especially a person most sensitive to artistic and natural beauty. The **scholar** is distinguished by his or her devotion to knowing about people, their history and world, and worlds beyond this one. The **benevolent** are those who seek the Good in all people and things. The **saint** raises this love to another dimension, seeking the reality and love of a Supreme Being and seeing all reality in the light of that Good.

While few people, with the rare exception like a Thomas More perhaps, would find it possible to encompass the suavity of the bon vivant, the self-confidence of the successful, the sensitivity of the artist, and the nobility of mind and heart of the scholar and lover in total dedication to and love for God, most acknowledge that the complete person must incarnate in some fashion all the Value modalities, sensual, vital, useful, spiritual and sacred. Some people realize a semblance of this ideal after a lifetime of effort. Most achieve a patchwork of Values, a system not entirely consistent and in some state of flux dependent upon the person's moral complacency or uneasiness. Almost all have to struggle against an innate tendency toward corrupting all Values, the most sacred, into ugly caricatures.

Values and Moral Decline

Early Christian and Medieval moralists called this tendency the *fomes peccati*, which transliterates into English as "tinder of sin," meaning the disposition of the human person's flawed nature to act contrary to moral convictions and principles. Frequently, they took as text the Apostle John's warning against the **sensual body, the lustful eye and the pride of life.**[11] Even without ascribing to this theological explanation, people can acknowledge, what most ethical systems accept, that actions seldom match aspirations and intentions, that material rewards in this life rarely equate the intrinsic worth of contributions, and that, efforts to the contrary, people's lower Values tend to crowd out higher Values and debased Values to evict true ones. This warp in human nature toward the perverted Values of sensuality, superficiality and arrogance—how the Johannine text might be understood today—can be considered *the* moral problem just as scarcity is the economic problem. Being both ego-centered and other-related in workable and working tension, humans must balance the two proclivities, personality disintegrating, when either overpowers the other. **Most people, however, are biased more toward self-absorption than prodigal benevolence to others. Abundance, it will become abundantly clear shortly, tends to heighten this bias.**

Self-indulgence, as St. John suggests, progresses through distinct but related stages. The **sensual body** refers to people's natural attraction to pleasure and avoidance of pain, including anything which disturbs a person's ease. Pleasure is, of course, Good and pain evil, and are so perceived/preferred in valuing. They are particularly important as signals of what to seek and what to shun for those Values which relate to preserving life and perpetuating humankind. Though not needed, they heighten spiritual and even sacred Values. Pleasure-pain corrupts, however, when they are sought or avoided for themselves, divorced from any higher Value. Gross sensualists are barred from experiencing not only spiritual and sacred Values but often the vital and useful when pleasure is pursued to the person's physical harm or even destruction.

The love of ease is similar to the love of pleasure in that the ease-loving want above all to avoid pain and not have their pleasures disturbed. Ease and rest are, of course, necessary for the human animal. But a love of ease, which procrastinates doing what should be done or avoids duty altogether, precludes, like the passion for pleasure, aspiring to higher Values. At advanced stages of sensuality the person becomes mired in pleasures and is wearied of them and everything else.

The **lustful eye** refers to a person's attraction to the superficial. It especially warps those Values which relate us to others, the useful, the vital and the spiritual. While the lustful eye looks beyond the pleasure an object bears to its attractiveness, it stops short at surface seduction and beauty. Beauty, of course, naturally attracts: the object's charm luring the beholder to its inner reality. But the shallow, sentimental and superficial Values of the lustful eye gravitate to glitter and glitz, preferring styling to substance, *kitsch* to art, wit to truth, information to understanding, manners to morality. In everything their intention is to be adorned, enhanced and noticed. Restless, faddy and eager for the new, such people are basically rootless, not resting long enough to savor the Goodness of others, seeking rather to be admired than to admire.

Pride of life, the highest stage of ego-absorption, paradoxically almost transcends it. As self-glorification which wealth and public acclaim can nourish, this arrogance is not incompatible with a Spartan disdain of riches and indifference to others' regard, displaying a negative conspicuous consumption and crude manners. What the proud prize is power over others; parading wealth or courting public good-will are subordinate to their dominant Value, power.

Pride in one's worth and acknowledging the good wealth and power can do are defensible. Authority is justified when used to help others develop as human beings. Heroes challenge others to emulate their achievements. But the pride which glorifies one's strength, wealth, power or whatever to others' harm may often cultivate lower at the expense of higher values. But it wreaks greater havoc by perverting some of the noblest Values: artistic sensitivity into snobbishness, patriotism into nationalistic chauvinism, erudition into intellectual despotism, moral conviction into religious tyranny and maternal concern into smother love. **There is no Value pride of life cannot pervert, because like sensuality and superficiality it has the ego as its ultimate and only referent. In effect, it denies that anything or anyone, except one's self, bears an absolute Value.**

Thus the same spiraling movement is seen in moral decline as in moral growth: the lowest to the highest Values can be perverted and the movement downward wrongs a larger and larger circle of people. As with moral growth, character corruption does not occur according to the logic of Value perversions, lowest to highest, but like any disease it can infect any segment of the moral spiral and from there spread forward or back. The dynamics of moral progress and moral pathology are the same as the dynamics of the Value hierarchy, whether whole, perverted or, as is true of most people, some brew of both.

However the effort people make, the link is clear: **Value espousal and personality growth and Value perversion and personality decline are organically and creatively interdependent and interacting.** Even more so, the development of a Value system becomes almost the embodiment of a Personalist credo: in seeing beyond the materiality of one's self and others to an even deeper Goodness, a person opens to and becomes committed to others. Thus a person's inwardness is turned outward to the Good of others. **Above all, with each movement up the Value ladder the individual is progressively freed to seek higher Values and to fulfill his or her transcendental destiny.**

Having related Values to moral growth and decline, the chapter can now examine how Values apply to economic living today.

THE ECONOMIC DIMENSION

The first task here is to see how economic values and moral Values fit together. Though the words suggest relationship, linking them goes against the grain of contemporary economic thinking. At best, most economists today will concede only that exchange ratios (market values) adjust a given supply of economic goods to a given pattern of wants which more or less reflect personal and social Values. Many, if not most, economists prefer to explain the economic process as free of Value judgments.

The Utility Link

Such enfranchisement does make sense because economic values are not Values. This becomes more obvious if price is substituted for economic value. Values are **subjective, qualitative and free**. Though derived from objective Goods, they are intensely personal. Even social Values, like love of Shakespeare or patriotism which belong to the patrimony of a people's culture and are shared by many, are unique to each person in the manner and intensity of their espousal. Values, while ranked, cannot be quantified, weighed, measured or numbered. They are, therefore, free both in that a person can freely espouse them and in espousing one Value a person need not surrender another.

By contrast, price is **objective**, generated by the market or at minimum by bargaining between buyer and seller. Price is **quantitative**, however fluctuating and ephemeral, the exchange ratio between an amount of money needed to buy an amount of product or services. Price, therefore, always **constrains**. The sacrifice required in every purchase is itself coercive. To bargain at all, even when advantage seems almost completely on one side, is itself constraining. To pay any price acknowledges some lack of freedom, the power the market has to ration what one wants or desires.

These distinctions between moral Values and market values inspired economists to fashion a neat science of prices, quantitative and antiseptically free of moral Values. But just as physicists, biologists and other scientists have, economists find it necessary to address problems today which are Value-laden and have returned to the tradition of the early economists that social issues and social Values are also the stuff of economic thinking. Indeed, they are finding that the most controversial economic issues, like economic growth, full employment, deregulation, social planning, income distribution, environment and so on, all have Value dimensions, which must be considered if one is to address them at all. Thus how Values influence economic values and, more so, how price formation, the generation of economic values, conditions the espousal of personal or social Values become matters of importance.

The key unlocking this problem is understanding two Values, **efficiency and utility** which economists must consider, however Value-free they hold their science to be. Efficiency is the ability of a person or instrument to produce a desired effect. Its measure is the ratio of work outcome to energy, fuel, time or money input. Its virtue is economizing, the habit of using time, effort and resources in the most effective way. Hence, it is a form of prudence dictated by scarcity. Efficiency, therefore, is a Value with universal applicability: not only money, but words, gestures, sounds, labor, energy, time and resources of every kind must be economized. Frequently, efficiency is contrasted to caring and concern for others. Indeed, the overly efficient can be cold, unfeeling, and even cruel, but the slip-shod and slovenly will often defeat their good intentions by using money, energy and time carelessly. Efficiency, therefore, must be tailored to the goal proposed: where the goal is persuasion efficiency may be warm, gentle and consoling.

Essential to efficiency is utility, the use to which a thing can be put. Useful things or people possess utility, are seen as fit to produce a desired purpose: they are means to an end. They relate, therefore, to a specific exercise of efficiency. Utility and efficiency are desirable qualities of objects which are perceived/preferred, that is, are experienced as Values. As such, they belong to the vital modality, Values which pertain to the material quality of life. Since the Value, utility or useful, is determined by the Value, efficient, which, in turn, is specified by the purpose, end or goal desired, both are **means Values**, not Values-in-themselves but Values-for-another. Their Good is a means to another Value, be that pleasing/painful through all the Value modalities to the holy/unholy. Utility, therefore, becomes the focus of this analysis since it is a major determinant in the generation of market values.

Unfortunately, economists, concerned more to explain prices and economic values and not being particularly sensitive to philosophical niceties, have relied on two quite different meanings of utility, neither of which is completely explanatory of the phenomena. Economists, inclined to a labor theory of value, like Smith, Ricardo, Marx, Mill and the Classical economists generally, explain prices in terms of the human effort embodied in the product. They tend to follow Locke in locating utility in the commodity: "The natureal worth of anything consists in its fitness to supply the necessities, or serve the conveniences of human life."[12] Economists in the marginal utility tradition like Jevons, Menger, Walras and most economists since 1870 stress the psychic effect of utility, the satisfaction the consumer derives from the product. Marshall, as so frequently, formulated the contemporary usage: "Utility is the correlative of Want or Desire," and "the total utility of anything to anyone . . . is the total satisfaction or benefit it yields him."[13]

The very difficulty economists had in pinning utility down as either useful qualities or psychic satisfactions hints what common sense experience underscores that utility is really neither. Utility is not the useful properties which the manufacturer hopes the product has, because what the consumer perceives as useful and the producer intended may differ widely. Nor can utility be the psychic satisfaction the customer experiences. First, satisfaction is an effect, not a cause, of the purchase. Second, satisfaction differs widely from customer to customer and even the same customer's wants change over time.

Thus both the ambiguity of analysis and the evidence from experience force the conclusion that utility, while it must encompass both the useful qualities of the commodity and the psychic satisfaction derived from them is really neither. In fact, utility is the **perception** of those desirable properties of the commodity, and, being desired, the good is preferred to the extent of sacrificing money and/or other goods to get it. **Utility is the Value, useful or beneficial, the object's perceived and ranked usefulness or benefit toward realizing another Good, be it material, vital, spiritual or holy.**

Actually other economic concepts confirm this conclusion. **Marginal utility** analysis, for example, says that the subjective evaluation of a good depends upon the amount of the good the potential buyer already has. Satiety in this sense is simply the realization that one has enough of a good thing and more would be simply superfluous if not harmful. Further, when more of a good is available more usage is found for it. Advertising is especially fecund in suggesting how products can service more of people's wants and needs. On the other side of the coin, the concept of **opportunity cost** argues in the same sense. In expressing what a buyer must forego to obtain a good, opportunity cost measures the demander's **estimation** of the hoped-for gain. What one is willing to sacrifice weighs the intensity of desire for the preferred commodity.

All arguments, therefore, persuade to locate utility among the vital Values in the Schelerian hierarchy. All things, objects, services, persons, groups, and relations, therefore, can in a thousand different ways bear the Value, useful and, being a means-Value, it takes on the coloration of whatever end, purpose, goal or Good proposed, be it secular or sacred, material or spiritual. Buyers can use the same product to express love or to satisfy lust. Sellers can regard their product as a source of profit or as fulfilling others' wants, as feeding their greed or expressing their personalities. Thus utility bridges the gap between economics and ethics. "To adopt a value," writes Rescher, " is to espouse principles of policy in the expenditure of resources."[14] If I really espouse a Value, I should be willing to put my money where my mouth is.

This definition of utility will have little effect on economic analysis. It does, however, make a significant difference in locating moral responsibility in economic actions. Here Bohm-Bawerk's principle of a century ago is appropriate: while scarcity determines how high prices **will** rise, utility determines how high they **may** rise[15]. From this one could argue that wanting and preferring are more cogent market forces than producers' costs, profit intentions and market power. While this point is moot, especially in particular circumstances, what is clear from Bohm-Bawerk's principle is that Values, others' and one's own, determine the prices of commodities needed to achieve those Values more so than the commodity prices determine Values. **In short and as a general rule, people get what they are willing to pay for.**

While no one really denies this rule, fudging it allows rationalizing much misdirected tampering with the market, while extenuating people's responsibility for their economic choices. It does not say, on the other hand, that the intensity of a Value experience is proportional to the price paid for the means, nor (what is sadder) that the person with an intensely held Value can always afford the means to it. It does mean that widely and fervently held Values increase the prices of the means, testing people's Value espousal by their willingness to pay the price.

Moral Values in the Market Place

In this way Values enter the market place. While they themselves are qualitative, free and collaborative, the products and services needed to realize them compete in the market place. Consequently, what sells will be supplied. The demands of a mass market will be catered to over the wants of the discriminating few. The opportunity costs, therefore, of art, virtue and integrity may rise not because they are less valued than before but because alternatives are wanted more. That base, warped and materialistic Values are indulged, while higher, true and spiritual Values are ignored, is the fault not of the market but of people's Value priorities. **People are not prurient because pornography sells. Pornography sells because people are prurient and suppliers cater to their pruriency.**

Economic abundance has certainly abetted the national decline in Values. By raising the ante it has tempted more people to gamble on a course of crime and violence. But disgraceful as America's crime record is, it only involves a minority. Abundance has affected the Values of the great majority in a less dramatic but more universal way. Because mass markets are profitable, the lowest common denominator Values will be serviced ahead of quality preferences. Popular entertainers, for example, will earn more than serious artists. At the same time, shrewd marketers may discern profits by selling differentiated products to segments of the market, often at varying price levels so that, if one cannot afford the best, good alternatives are available.

All things considered, therefore, abundant economies do enrich existence, pouring out goods and services to sustain life better and to make it more pleasant. The world's poor, having glimpsed affluent living, hanker after it. But while life for the affluent may be richer, it seems to be less fulfilling. With more income people seem to enjoy life less. This is attested by people every day: their wanting and having more of the already plentiful seems only to satiate without satisfying.

This certainly applies to gross, and often tragic, sensuality, which like addictions to drink, drugs, sex, food and the like not only cost much money, time and energy but yield diminishing pleasure. Milder addictions afflict many more. Almost everyone, for example, accumulates things beyond their usefulness, a fact which rummage and garage sales testify to every weekend. Abundance indeed permits one to become hooked on any kind of pleasure from sports to tavern hopping. Most such habits are relatively innocuous and generally pleasurable. But they go far toward explaining the profitability of bars and restaurants, the incomes of athletes and entertainers, and the profits from tobacco and liquor.

The lure of superficial glamor is for many people no less nourished by economic abundance. For the wealthy and especially the new-rich, to be in fashion, to have showplace homes, to attend the best schools and to travel in style is requisite to circulate with the 'best' people. People of modest incomes are more likely beset by the allure of the trivial and vicarious glamor. The lure of the trivial is no trivial matter when it triggers impulse buying. For families, however well-heeled, who consistently expect the next paycheck to recoup today's overspending, the allure of the trivial can be very compelling and, in cases, disastrous. But the pursuit of vicarious glamor can be the most insidiously trivial. Good grooming and dressing attractively, of course, can show respect for others and one's self. But certainly the flood of novels, magazines and advertisements touting vicarious glamor is big business and widely patronized in abundant economies.

Abundance, finally, nourishes arrogance, the pride of power, and the desire to lord it over others. Most frequently those who bear authority in government, business and public affairs, while they need more help, easy travel and quick communication, will hanker for perquisites become pre-requisites. Consequently, the courtly elegance of their accommodations and their insulation from physical discomfort significantly differentiates their life-styles from the commonality. Carried to excess this desire becomes a costly drag on government or business. Even in moderation it saps their authority by making calls for sacrifice and restraint sound hollow and hypocritical.

While the 'perks' of office symbolize power, the reality consists in disposing millions and billions of private or public funds, thereby affecting hundreds of thousands of lives. Of course, top corporate and government officers hold such power, but it may be shared by people down the bureaucratic ladder by dominating a key committee, by getting one's ideas ingrained into company policy or agency regulations or by chess-like moves through and up the power structure. More open power is played out in dispensing funds to implement programs, in making grants and signing contracts, in hiring and firing, and, most dramatic of all, in buying out or into another business. All of this is as old as business. What differs today are the financial techniques, the size of the transactions and the danger of playing with other people's money, all factors which makes for ego-glorification. **Economic abundance both provides the means and makes the possible pay-off worth the risk.**

Sketchy though the preceding is, it suffices to show how affluence can feed the *fomes peccati*. It enables not only a gross sensuality, crass superficiality and blatant pride of power, but permits a climate in which the majority can pamper their desire for pleasure and comfort, abet their preference for the specious and glamorous, and feed their appetite for ego-glorification. It, however, must also be conceded that such tendencies by absorbing enormous amount of money, income and goods stimulate economic activity. Thus Mandeville's paradox that private vices are public virtues is resurrected in modern form. Undoubtedly, underneath the current concern for business ethics and economic morality there lingers the unarticulated fear that reining in people's materialistic tendencies, their *fomes peccati*, will impair economic growth. **This is but one step from arguing that abundance not only makes people follow base and/or warped Values but requires it.**

That jarring statement should make one pause to consider the malaise which affects modern living. To the daily toll of moral and social tragedies, broken marriages, abandoned and abused children, promiscuous sex, drug and alcohol addiction, crime and social rancor, economic abundance makes its special contribution to popular distress in combining people's congenital gravitation toward base and perverted Values with the heady dynamics of economic self-interest and competition.

The Econo-moral Malaise

Three constituents of this moral unease can be identified as the *poverty, self-centeredness* and *futility syndromes.* The first, of course, recalls that abundance by heightening people's wanting faster than their increasing income can satisfy them generates a more intense scarcity. Whatever amenities a person does enjoy, he or she can always see more they would like which others have, in all this the siren calls of pleasure and glamor aggravating their frustrations. The poor here, while far from destitute, suffer poverty more acutely because others have so much more. For the moderately situated the poverty syndrome may take the form of seeming to run faster and working harder yet advancing little. All these add to a psychic tension: a touchiness at any slowing in the growth of real income and positive alarm at any signs of recession.

The **self-centeredness** syndrome is the hydra-headed self-interest which does energize the economy but, as egocentric self-seeking can produce moral and social entropy, reducing personal and cultural ties to cash nexuses and as profit-mongering treating people as means and abusing their rights as person; as competition pitting people against people and class against class; and as exclusively this-worldly lacking ultimate end and purpose. In its milder form the me-first attitude is still quite nasty, touchy about rights, property, pleasures and social approval, tending to wrap a person in a cocoon of selfishness, an emptiness care and concern for others would fill. The more virulent form certainly eases men and women toward the pride of power, manifested in a greed which lusts to control people and in an egoism which distorts and debases the most sacred Values in craving to dominate others.

In a sense the worst form of the econo-moral malaise is the **futility syndrome**, the feeling that the rat-race of survival and the pursuit of wealth have no ultimate meaning, that all the good things abundance provides do not add up to satisfaction. Unmoored from the traditional restraints of nature, affluent men and women have flimsy defences—recall Rahner[16]—against their own perverse tendencies. The incoherence of their lives is further aggravated by the corrosive effect of affluence on social institutions and by the difficulty produced by modern mobility of sinking roots in community, social groups and vocation. Further, the impersonality of the market, the fleeting character of business relations, the fickleness of wealth and the instability of prices, and the intrusion of the money motive into the most sacred ties seem, for many people, to bleach out all the colors of human potentiality and to leave only the dull gray of meaninglessness. Written large, this frustration feeling takes an almost masochistic delight in national self criticism and has become cynical at government chicanery, business fraud, class disharmony and personal disloyalty. All these frustrations are accentuated by the chaos of much of urban living, the pollution, noise, competitive rat-race, dysfunctional institutions, and the often gross and always disproportionate gain by the cunning and greedy.

All of this speaks of a worsening social climate and a decline in national character and of a fostering of a matrix singularly stifling of true growth in personality. Responses to this social malaise are as varied as the social scientists and moral philosophers who have struggled with it. Most can be grouped under three broad headings: rugged individualism, social paternalism and social estrangement. Each view is myopic in one way or another. While they tend to modify each other, taken together they would form an incohesive patchwork. Nevertheless, each reflects important insights into the spirit of contemporary society and affirms Values which could and should be incorporated into a more consistent vision of the ideal.

The rugged individualism of someone like Ayn Rand,[17] with its deep roots in Social Darwinism and laissez-faire liberalism comes closest to embodying the American practical wisdom, that one makes it on one's own. The absolute freedom it touts is not universally enjoyed but only by those strong enough to wrest it for themselves. It is also opposed to government welfarism, unless one can bend the state to benefit one's self, one's class, or one's group. These contradictions reveal its radical weakness against the socializing forces in American society.

As it fades, social paternalism, of which B.F. Skinner is representative[18] gains in acceptability, especially among academics, social planners and social engineers. It rests on the twin pillars of absolute individual liberty and government welfarism. It assumes the radical equality of all individuals for those characteristics which can be defined and classified by law and thus conditioned: population, education, income, social deviance and the like. Absolute egalitarianism will prevail except, of course, for the social planners. As Orwell predicted, all animals are equal but the pigs more equal than the rest.

The most radical solution is that of Herbert Marcuse.[19] For him the "warfare and welfare state" is a "thoroughly static system of life, self-propelling in its oppressive productivity and in its beneficial coordination." The affluent, therefore, no matter how comfortable and provided with labor-saving gadgets, and however the fiction of liberty, are really slaves: their thoughts one-dimensional and their souls contained in material possessions. While preaching a thorough hedonism, Marcuse could suggest nothing better than dropping out of society.

Thus the Marcusan Great Refusal stands squarely against a personalist philosophy. Espousing Values which transcend the goods abundance provides and freely choosing among them deny Marcuse's assertion, that people are contained within a materialistic status quo. Industrial society is not bound to "inherently necessary goals" and ceases to be an essentially static dynamic. Unlike squirrels racing in a revolving cage, people possess purpose beyond just producing and consuming.

On the other hand, a personalist philosophy agrees with rugged individualism that the human person is ultimately responsible for his or her own life and actions. It also agrees with social paternalism that the individual is essentially social. It, however, does not combine the two synthetically, but blends them organically. Personalist individualism is not aggressive like laissez-faire individualism nor defeatist like Marcusan individualism, but perceives the person as interacting with others, drawing sustenance from communion with them and supported by society's institutions. Personalism, while espousing the whole panoply of Social Values necessary for public order, economic prosperity and national defense, accepts them as belonging to one's Value system and not imposed *a priori*. **Personalism, therefore, preserves the ancient concept of the common Good as a personal Good of each citizen and not as a collective Good imposed by the state.**

Thus personalism maintains the delicate balance between personal self-determination and social conditioning and bonding. While defending the right and necessity of all to formulate and espouse the Values and personal goals they perceive as right for themselves, a personalist philosophy promotes the Values which foster the Good of others, of society and of all humanity. Since Value espousals are sign and substance of moral growth, personalism goes beyond what Allport calls the "clamorous immediacy of the body and ego-centeredness,"[20] to concern for others, for the general welfare and transcendent purposes.

More specific to this study, it is abundantly clear that economic abundance can have deleterious personal consequences, can poison the moral climate, can corrode the cohesiveness of society and even destroy the moral fabric and social bonds which hold the economy together. At the same time, there is little chance that people who have experienced economic abundance will surrender it without social upheaval. Indeed, even the most vocal critics of industrial economies never suggest turning history back to a pre-abundance age and are forced to accept the principles, self-interest, competition, cost cutting, profit maximizing and the rest, by which market economies operate.

Thus the issue is joined. However incompatible they may seem to be, moral principles and economic principles are both necessary for people to develop to full humanity in abundant economies and even more so to maintain the dynamism of abundance while preserving the integrity and cohesiveness of society. Personalism suggests how their integration may be realized.

ENDNOTES

1. This and the following section relies heavily on Max Scheler, *Formalism in Ethics and Non-Formal Ethics of Value*, trans. by M. Frings and R. Funk, Evanston: Northwestern U. Press, 1973.
2. Rescher, Nicholas. *Introduction to Value Theory*, Englewood Cliffs, NJ, 1960, ch. 2.
3. Scruton, Roger. *The Aesthetics of Architecture*, Princeton, 1979, p. 32.
4. Rescher, pp. 2-3.
5. Allport, Gordon W. *Pattern and Growth in Personality*, New York: Holt, Rinehart and Winston, 1965, p. 454 and pp. 126-7.
6. Angell, Robert C. *Free Society and Moral Crisis*, Ann Arbor: Universty of Michigan Press, 1965, p. 18.
7. Scheler p. 99.
8. *ibid.* pp. 105-10.
9. Teilhard du Chardin, Pierre, *The Phenomenon of Man*, New York: Harper & Row, 1965 and *The Divine Milieu*, New York: Harper, 1960.
10. Spranger, Eduard, *Types of Men,* trans. P. Pijors, Hulle: Niemeyer Verlag, 1928, pp. 88-106.
11. 1 John, 2:16.
12. Locke, John. *Some Consideration on the Consequences of the Lowering of Interest,* 1691, in *Works, London*: 1777, v. II, p. 28.
13. Marshall, Alfred. *Economics of Industry*, London: Macmillan, 1958, pp. 61-2.
14. Rescher, p. 134.
15. Bohm-Bawerk, Eugene. *Positive Theory of Capital,* New York: Speckert & Co., 1930, p. 159.
16. Rahner, *op.cit.*
17. Rand, Ayn, *For the New Intellectual,* New York: Random House, 1961, and *The Virtue of Selfishness,* New York: New American Library, 1961.
18. Skinner, B.F., *Beyond Freedom and Dignity*, New York: Knopf, 1971.
19. Marcuse, Herbert, *One-Dimensional Man*, Boston: Beacon Press, 1964.
20. Allport, pp. 126-7.

GLOSSARY

absolute—Anything free from restrictions, hence, unlimited, independent and unconditional. **The Absolute** is the ultimate basis of all thought, evaluation, reasoning and existence.

cosmogenesis—The formation of the universe as an ordered system, here assumed as an evolutionary process but not necessarily without an initiating cause.

egalitarianism—The doctrine that all persons possess equal rights. Its extreme form holds the theoretical right of everyone to an equal share in material well-being and political power.

hedonism—A philosophy which makes pleasure people's highest good. Also a tendency to excessive pleasure-seeking and self-indulgence.

hierarchy—The arrangement of a set of people, groups, classes of things or qualities ranked systematically from highest to lowest.

homo sapiens—A family of the primate order of vertebrates who are distinguished by possessing reason.

intentionality—The power of acting by design and for a purpose.

kitsch—An excessive sentimentality in art and floridity in decoration.

laissez-faire liberalism—An extreme form of economic liberalism, which maintains that government intrusion into the economy should be held to the minimum.

opportunity cost—Any alternative good or action which must be given up in obtaining what one does choose. The opportunity cost of a new job is surrendering one's current job.

organic—Pertaining to the constitution or organization of any complex, living thing and by analogy any association of people organized for a common goal or purpose.

paternalism—A way of governing a business, organization, or society, tending to deprive subordinates of freedom and responsibility.

perquisites—Any benefit or privilege, beyond compensation, which is attached to performing a job or service.

propriate dispositon—A predominant temper of one's mind and bent of one's actions, often so intimate and personal as not to be recognized by one's self.

sacramentality—The perception of a person or thing as a sign or symbol of something sacred.

Social Darwinism—A social philosophy of the late 19th Century which applied Darwin's theories of natural selection, survival of the fittest and evolutionary change to the economy and argued, for complete economic freedom as essential for economic progress. Herbert Spencer in England (1820-1903) and William Sumner in the U.S. (1840-1910) were its leading proponents.

systemic—A quality or condition which affects the entire organism and, by analogy, any social institution.

TOPICS FOR FURTHER DISCUSSION OR RESEARCH

1. Review Scheler's Value-modalities: holiness, moral goodness, truth, beauty, well-being and pleasure. What are your pre dominant Values, if any, in each modality? Rank them from least (one) to highest (ten) effect on you and your conduct.

State, if you can, a person or persons whom you admire and after whom, perhaps, you pattern your behavior in each modality. (There is, of course, no right or wrong answer here, but only more or less truthful results of self-analysis of what Values are dominant in your life.)

2. How would you rank the *fomes peccati*—pleasure-seeking and love of ease, the appeal of the glamorous and self-embellishment, and finally self-glorification and dominating others—as influences on your behavior? (The last sentence above, of course, applies here as well.)

ADDITIONAL SUGGESTED READING

1. Kenneth W. Stikkers, "Max Scheler's Contributions to Social Economics," *Review of Social Economy*, (December, 1987) v, XLV, no. 3, pp.223-242.
2. Nicholas Rescher, *Introduction to Value Theory*, Englewood Cliffs: Prentice-Hall, Inc., 1969, chs.1-3.
3. Herbert Marcuse, *One-Dimensional Man: Studies in the Ideology of Advanced Industrial Society*, Boston: Beacon Press, 1968. Intro. and chs. 1-4.

CHAPTER FIVE

SELF-INTEREST AND SOCIAL JUSTICE

The first four chapters of *Getting and Spending* have set the stage for the real work of integrating economic common sense into those moral virtues which pertain most especially to economic and business activity. The first is **justice** which mandates respecting others' rights to gain in the common pursuit of income and wealth (Getting). This is balanced by **moderation** which directs people's material well-being (Spending) toward fulfilling higher Value aspirations, including sharing one's well-being with others less fortunate. Next the **spirit of poverty** guides a person's total economic effort (Getting and Spending) beyond the vicissitudes of a volatile economy toward an ultimate meaning by emulating the generosity of a bountiful Providence. Given the social nature of the economy these virtues do not fray but reinforce economic relations. Consequently, the moral and the economic, though distinct but life-long enterprises which must be pursued simultaneously, are complementary and can be meshed into an integrated pattern of life.

The subject of this chapter, therefore, is **justice** which, according to Aristotle, consists in obedience to law and fair-dealing.[1] Put another way, it is the consistent moral habit of respecting the rights of others, individually and collectively, and of one's self. In regard to economic matters, it especially applies to controlling economic self-interest wherever this involves others' rights.

ECONOMIC SELF-INTEREST

Self-interest, of course, is concern for those things which a person conceives as conducive to his or her ultimate Good. In this sense, as was stated earlier, all must be self-interested: all are **rightly** concerned about their own Good. Self-interest, however, can become so concerned about self that it violates the Good and rights of others. Economic self-interest is particularly prone to selfishness, in pursuing one's own Good hindering others from seeking theirs. Justice, therefore, is needed not to suppress self-interest but to monitor and guide it.

The Dilemma of Self-Interest

This suggests the dilemma of self-interest for economists. While the freeing of self-interest since the 16th Century by the progressive elimination of government regulations on industry and commerce was enormously successful in stimulating economic growth, it unleashed a monstrous greediness causing untold human suffering. In downplaying the latter, many economists opposed self-interest to benevolence and altruism and often identified it with selfishness.

With this, of course, they flew in the face of human experience that self-love and self-interest does not exclude involvement with and care for others. No less than Adam Smith affirms: "How selfish soever man may be supposed, there are evidently some principles in his nature, which interest him in the fortunes of others, and render their happiness necessary to him, though he derives nothing from it except the pleasure of seeing it."[2] Despite this, many economists forced their analysis to explain every economic act and decision as motivated *solely* by a self-benefiting gain-seeking. Concern for the public Good is even more of a problem for scholars who stress the egocentricity of economic self-interest, since even the freest market economy needs at minimum a public order for the economy to work at all. Responses to this dilemma are as varied as the economists who wrestled with it, but they can be grouped under two broad conceptions which still differentiate political philosophies regarding government influence on the economy: the minimalist

Conservative and the more interventionist Liberal approach.

The latter may be traced back to Thomas Hobbes' (1588-1679) basic tenet, that people in their struggle for wealth, power and glory, need an all-powerful state to control and arbitrate their strife.[3] Conservative thinking, on the other hand, tends to follow Adam Smith's insistence that individuals are best able to define their own Good and, in pursuing it, achieve unintentionally the general Good more effectively than if required by public policy.[4] Economists, struggling with the issue over the last 200 years, drew from both, each with a unique answer. J. S. Mill, the most influential economist of the third quarter of the 19th century, epitomized the Victorian compromise in defending laissez-faire capitalism and the freedom to work and employ capital as one chooses as essential for economic growth, while predicting economic stagnation and the need to subject income distribution to social customs and law.[5] Karl Marx was both more logical and unreal, predicting that the absolute economic freedom capitalism required would in the process of generating economic growth concentrate more and more capital in fewer and fewer hands and by exploiting surplus value drive the working class into the proletariat until the last exploiter was himself exploited ushering in the communist era. Then self-interest would be replaced by communist altruism and freedom, and the state would wither away.[6] (How ironic Marx's idealism in view of the history of human repression by geriatric bureaucrats clinging to power!)

More contemporary scholars, Robert Nozick and John Rawls, have their own versions of self-interest and the general welfare. Nozick recalls the Lockian/Hobbesian state of nature in which autonomous individuals possess inviolable rights to life, health, liberty and property.[7] While holding that egocentric utility determines action and that a minimal state is sufficient to protect rights, Nozick, nevertheless, requires a more interventionist state to protect current entitlements and rectify past injustices. John Rawls, while reasoning within a neoclassical economic framework, holds firmly Kant's principle that a person is an end and never a means. At the same time he admits large inequalities of talent, fortune and power which he justifies if they compensate by benefiting others, especially the least advantaged in society. Hence, Rawls justifies the overall beneficence of the free-market economy if two conditions prevail: 1) the market system itself is justly structured and 2) its very inequalities produce efficiency, that the more valued replaces the less valued, that waste is constantly being eliminated and that the more productive use of labor and capital supplants the less productive use.[8]

Personalist Self-interest

In contrast to the preceding efforts a personalist approach accommodates self-interest as easily and cleanly as an Olympic diver knifes the water from ten meters. In so doing it includes all the Values previous philosophers and economists sought: freedom and responsibility; efficiency and public direction; concern for others and for the general welfare. Personalism, as described earlier, is essentially social and society is a person's natural habitat. Personal self-interest, therefore, includes sharing in the common Good as well as others' Good, thus imposing the obligation to contribute to both.

Since the Good is right for persons, a personalist self-love requires respecting others' rights as persons, their physical needs but above all their **freedom, sociality and transcendence**. This obligation, of course, implies a duty which further implies a debt, something due to another, for example, for past help, loan, kindness or whatever. What is owing another in repaying a debt, of course, is right for that person. This is obvious in the case of a wrong done another or in repaying one's debt to parents, friends, teachers and the like. But what is owing in the opposite direction: parents to children, teachers to pupils, mentor to tyro and the like? Here personalism, as was shown earlier, evokes the mystery of personality: that every person, no matter how inconsequential, obnoxious or even vicious, says something important about what it means to be a person and, therefore, is owing this ultimate respect.

Respecting one's own and others' rights, therefore, in all their dimensions, physical, economic, political, aesthetic, moral and religious, as a way of acting, does not come easily or spontaneously but requires insight, effort, and determination. Its exercise needs sensitivity to others, objectivity about self and self-control. Only with practice is the habit gradually formed. **Given what it is called upon to do, justice, the virtue about to be explored, is neither simple nor simplistic.**

THE VIRTUE OF JUSTICE

While most people today, when talking about justice, think of court judgments or legal decisions mainly about economic rights, they miss the richness of the many levels of benevolence this virtue urges.[9] The following will only discuss four of its dimensions, all of which are intertwined because justice as a moral attitude is whole and not bits and pieces. The four are: an internal harmony, ordering and balancing one's knowing and wanting; a general virtue, the habit of respecting others' rights; a social virtue, governing a person's relations to other persons, to a group or to society as a whole, and the relation of the group/society to the individual; and last as the basis for public policy. Justice thus covers the field of human action, and a personalist approach comes closest to developing a unified field theory of justice. But in no sense is the theory complete or set in concrete. Indeed, such a conception of justice would immediately entail injustices by failing to respond to changing circumstances and human needs.

Justice as Internal Harmony

Fundamental to being right with others is being right with one's self. This is the internal harmony in which the unruly passions of sensuality, greed and anger are subject to a firm will enlightened by understanding of what is important in life. Socrates was the first to develop this moral hierarchy as told by Plato in his *Republic*.[10] There Socrates compares personal harmony with public order in which all classes stick to their respective duties without meddling with that of others, the philosopher-kings ruling wisely, the guardians maintaining internal order and external defense and the general citizenry, moderating their own demands, provide the material needs for living.

Thus Socratic justice was primarily an internal peace and harmony, a good beyond all other goods, one worth dying for as he demonstrated in the peace and equanimity he met an unjust sentence to death. Christian scholars incorporated this noble statement almost as such into Christian spirituality. Augustine added that "reason must be subject to God if it is to govern as it ought the passions and other vices."[11] Aquinas goes further, identifying Socratic justice with Adam's rectitude before the fall, "his reason being subject to God, the lower powers to reason, and the body to the soul."[12] **In short, people find it impossible to be right with others if not right with themselves.**

Justice as General Virtue

Aristotle carried this internal rightness forward, insisting that justice "is the actual exercise of complete virtue."[13] Put negatively, arrogance, envy, anger, licentiousness, avarice etc. impose on and abuse others. On the other hand, justice by obeying laws and rendering to each what is due relate people positively, safeguarding their rights to share in the economic, political and cultural common Good and in private dealings rendering equal for equal.[14] **Put positively or negatively, this principle says that a just person, as a general rule and practice, holds it as a matter of obligation to respect the rights of others.**

"(It) is in the United States," writes Allan Bloom, "that the idea of rights has penetrated most deeply into the blood stream of its citizens and accounts for their unusual lack of servility."[15] The real revolution of 1776 was not just breaking away from England but establishing a state specifically to protect its citizens' rights. That in itself explains the reverence Americans have for the Constitution and what they demand first and foremost from government, to guarantee and defend their rights. "From our knowledge of our rights," continues Bloom, "flows our acceptance of the duties to the community that protects them."[16] Even though Americans' conceptions of rights resonate with legal and juristic overtones, **personal rights are not bestowed by the Constitution but are derived from one's being, nature, sociality and individuality as a human person.**

"Right," while derived from the Anglo-Saxon *riht,* can be traced to the Indo-European root of the Latin *rego* and *rectus.* Its etymology, therefore, suggests to rule (to regulate), to make proper (to correct) and to straighten (to rectify). All in the final analysis relate to the power to achieve one's purpose or Good. Perhaps the slang "Right on" says it all: a person is exactly on target for what he or she wants. Rights, therefore, are appropriate for and proper to a person, since they are necessary to fulfill one's destiny as person. Because rights are due to others, they impose the obligation to respect them and thereby set the rules for dealing with others. **As a general virtue, justice is sensitive to the whole gamut of rights to which any person, one's self included, can lay claim.**

Rights are both common to all people as due to a person and particular as due to an individual. Rights possessed by all may be physical and biological, like the right to space, food, shelter, clothing and other possessions, the right to health care, sexual integrity and the like. Spiritual and religious rights include freedom to learn, to express thoughts and feelings, to associate with others, to love and be loved, to worship as one chooses and to pursue one's personal destiny. Altogether they stem from the essential features of personality: freedom/responsibility, individuality/sociality, and transcendence. Related to all of these, as means to personal ends, are economic rights, to gain and to have the opportunity to gain, to cooperate in an economic enterprise and to compete for scarce goods.

All rights, of course, are specific and particular since they belong to individuals. Here is the real test of a just person's sensitivity because rights do change, not essentially, but as the individual changes in age, size, sexual power, health and bodily integrity; in mental acuity, emotional stability and state of stress; in education, training, experience, cultural and social development. Past events can change one's rights: the convicted criminal loses some; the compensated accident victim regains some. Thus a person's rights and the respect due them are grounded not only in his or her common humanity but in every changing nuance of individuality and circumstances. Justice, therefore, can never be a state achieved once and for all, but rather is an attitude which, while flowing from an internal harmony and a deep and imperturbable conviction of the dignity of the human person, is ever sensitive to new conditions and different needs of people. **In this sense it is a general, or as Aristotle called it, a complete virtue.**

Justice as Social Virtue

As complete virtue justice is necessarily social. As an internal harmony and righteous action to others, justice not only establishes right relations and corrects wrong ones but widely practiced fosters the common Good and general welfare. Thus justice is *the social virtue*, the glue holding society together.

Society, of course, has its origin in people's social nature, that inescapable fact of human existence and basic human condition, that each person is conceived, born, lives and develops related to other people. But human sociality goes beyond mere relatedness to more radical qualities and needs of their material/spiritual natures. As human, each person develops by drawing on the common pool of humanity. As unique, each is obligated to contribute to it. As limited, a person needs others to fulfill his or her biological and material needs. As transcendent, a person needs inspiration from others to aspire beyond one's present state of being.

Persons are truly the proper subject of knowing and loving: their materiality attracts others; the mystery of their transcendence echoes to the mystery of one's own. In knowing others people know themselves; in loving others they love themselves. Each glimpse into another human heart reveals more of one's own. Beyond self-knowledge people expand their experience many times by drawing from the common reservoir of human love and knowledge. Only through such sharing can persons slake their thirst to know and love all things human. **Such sharing is the root of human sociality and in turn requires and creates society.** It is this concept and reality which can bear some elucidation.

"Society" has acquired many meanings, for example, as a social pecking order, as simply an organization of people with a common purpose or as other people generally. As used here "society" will include features of each, a relationship among people, a common Good, and a bond of welfare (or illfare) tying all to each. In particular, society must be distinguished from the state since people belong to both simultaneously. While both are natural, they are distinctly different. Society arises spontaneously, is loosely structured and is all inclusive; it may leap national boundaries or several may be defined within the same state. The state, on the other hand, is formally constituted, highly structured and excludes or limits non-citizens, even those living within its boundaries and part of society.

Thus they differ basically in the factors entitling membership. Society, being all inclusive, not only tolerates diversity but flourishes by integrating ethnic, cultural and intellectual differences. The state, on the other hand, while also needing citizens of varying talents and interests, requires a certain *homogeneity*, at least in the sense of a general knowledge and habitual observance of its laws and constitution. While these differences create tension between society's Good and the state's, that tension need not be destructive. **Each needs the other: society without civic discipline tends to anarchy; the state without tolerance to tyranny.**

That this distinction is not trivial is witnessed by this century's deplorable history of violations of society's principles of universality and diversity. Country after country, the most powerful as well as most paltry, have liquidated—mass murdered!—or forcibly "re-educated" millions of their own citizens in the name of ethnic or ideological purity. Even nations, constitutionally pluralistic, will tolerate for decades systemic injustice to religious, racial, sexual or disability minorities and only with much prodding try to right the wrong.

Paradoxically people most insistent of their rights may cause their erosion. Those who demand that government act against the most trivial infringement of their rights will eventually weave a web of legal restrictions about everyone's freedom. On the other hand, those who flaunt their rights by lawbreaking, upsetting public order and violating others's rights destroy the very conditions which preserve personal liberty. Common sense, as usual, lies in the middle: the state must tolerate personal and cultural differences; society needs law and order so that integrating those differences may proceed peacefully. How personal and common rights interrelate and must be respected simultaneously needs further development.

To begin, society is that all-embracing and many dimensioned network of human relations in which every person is set from the moment of conception and can neither flee nor destroy. Most relations result from others' decisions, like family, school, neighborhood and business; others arise simply by chance; and again others from a person's own choices. However the web is woven, society is like the air people breath, a Value permeating every phase of life. Variously viewed as an **association of persons**, as a **cultural climate** and as a **commonwealth of goods**, society's facets are so intertwined that the relations binding people are simultaneously personal, cultural and economic. Analyzing each separately will help to esteem this complex Value as it deserves.

Society as an *association of persons* bears the marks of diversity and complementarity. People need each other and are attracted to each other because they are different. The most obvious paradigm is human sexuality: men's need for and attraction to women and women to men and parents' love and need for children and children for parents are the very sources and perpetuation of human society. Civilization itself builds on differences. The variety of personal talent, training, interests, opportunities and ambitions is essential for survival. Psychologically people need others' scrutiny and evaluation of their Values, ideas and actions. Society itself develops from cultural cross-fertilization and the challenge arising from differing customs and life styles. **Hence, any form of bigotry—ethnic, gender, religious, economic or whatever—not only violates personal rights but cuts at the very roots of society and civilization.**

In an association of *persons* differences require complementarity because persons can be subordinated functionally to achieve a common purpose only by respecting their natures as persons. The distinction is subtle but decisively important. People can be used, and most are in one way or another, as means to achieve another's purpose, for example, workers hired to increase profits, the same as one would buy a machine or feed an animal. With tools or animals their purposes are subsumed into that of the owner and their use as well as their care is subordinated to that end. But with persons there is an all-important difference: workers have aims, purposes, goals and destinies which must be respected. Indeed in most such relations complementarity goes both ways: in using each other, both must respect the unique Good of each.

Complementarity, therefore, produces not only individual Goods but a common Good. Given fundamental equality as persons, when individuals complement each other in an activity by pooling their different talents and skills, each seeks his or her Good in the common result, which, therefore, is a Good for each individually and a **common Good**. Regardless of who directs the activity, provides the financing, or assumes the risk, all titles to a share in the benefits, everyone involved must realize a good. The paradigm of this is again gender complementarity. While men and women can use each other as means, instrumentally, as in prostitution, in a truly personal and loving relationship each achieves his or her own Good, moral, biological, emotional and intellectual, by providing and being a Good to the other.

Such mutual use and benefit characterizes, each in a different way, the relations between parent and child, governor and governed, teacher and student, artist and audience, employer and employee, buyer and seller, lender and borrower. Certainly one party can take advantage of the other, using the person as instrument. But if each is able to find some fulfillment of those qualities of personality, self-knowledge and self-awareness, freedom and responsibility, sociality and individuality, materiality and transcendence, then the relationship partakes of complementarity. **Obviously, if the sharing is more equitable and evenly beneficial, the more just and more truly social the complementarity will have been. Conversely, the more one party uses another as means, the more that person's personality is abused and the nature of society violated.**

Such cooperation for a shared benefit is, of course, a form of communication, which more strictly defined, is the mark of society as a *cultural climate.* By that is meant all those institutions and individual actions by which people transmit their intentions, thoughts and feelings in words, signs, symbols, gestures and artifacts. Culture is especially manifested in a nation's language and mathematics, those two products of a people's collective intellectual experience. But it includes their literature, painting, sculpture and architecture; their religious, educational, civic and political institutions; the very manner and dress of the people.

The vehicles of culture are a country's churches, schools, monuments, public buildings, civic festivals, concerts, plays and movies, its commercial and industrial establishments. By all these ways people communicate their religious and moral sentiments; their respect for government, the political process, laws and legal procedure; what they learn, how they feel and how entertained. This is the social environment which encompasses everybody. **Willy-nilly, loving it or not, people must share in and contribute to society as their cultural climate.**

As suggested above the cultural climate requires a *commonwealth of goods*, public buildings and gathering places whether publicly or privately owned. But society, that vast network of human relations, requires much more. Most basically the commonwealth of goods refers to the public patrimony of land, climate, natural resources, rivers, lakes and harbors. It includes the infrastructure of highways, railroads, airports and air lanes, telephone lines and communication satellites, factories, office buildings and shopping malls, homes and the utilities which service them. All of these things are public in the sense of being necessary for the daily business of life, that complex and ever changing mesh of human actions we call the economy.

More important than things are the skills of people, their coordination, knowledge, research and risk-taking. These most intimate and personal abilities make the economy go, but they are social and socially productive only in cooperation with others. (Most people are so specialized that they could not survive on their own.) **As a commonwealth, therefore, the economy generates commodities and services which are produced socially, priced socially, marketed socially and enjoyed socially. Private wealth, therefore, is individual only in the sense that laws protect the private ownership and use of what are really social goods.**

Just as with rights, society is a many-faceted reality, and the Value, society, contains depths of Goodness which cannot be captured even in this, perhaps, too extensive treatment. But having done so, the text returns to the virtue of justice with a clearer understanding of its social dimension. Respecting the rights of others, difficult as that proves to be, is not enough. **Rights must be seen in their relationship to and effect on that all-permeating and indispensable Good and Value we call society.**

This emphasis on others' rights and on the social Good is distinctive of medieval moralists' conception of justice as pre-eminently a social virtue. Thomas Aquinas, the foremost among many, fashioned from Classical philosophy and Patristic theology a comprehensive moral system which placed social unity and order as paramount human Goods and affirmed the duty to respect personal rights as essential to the public Good. When abuse of others' rights also disrupts public order, Aquinas calls the obligation to rectify not only the abused rights but also the public order **legal or general justice.**[17] The obligations on individuals to advance the general welfare he calls **contributive justice. Particular justice**, on the other hand, he sees as respecting rights in interpersonal relations **(commutative jus-**

tice) and safeguarding individuals' rights to share in the general welfare **(distributive justice).** Justice for Aquinas, therefore, is not a state of righteousness achieved once and for all but a constant effort, habit forming, to respect everyone's rights, individual, personal and collective.[18]

Thus the medievalists developed a **unified-field theory of personal justice** which safeguarded the rights of individuals as well as the common Good. It prompted obedience to just laws and induced a general concern for society and the obligation to re pair systemic and social injustices. No less this social virtue was sensitive to and respected the rights of individuals in personal dealings and in participating in the general welfare. **Inherent in, therefore, and prerequisite to any degree of social order, citizens of the state and members of society must be imbued with a lively sense of justice, which simultaneously expresses an inner harmony, a sensitivity to others' rights, and an abiding concern for the general welfare.**

Like much of medieval culture, Scholasticism's inspiration tended to dry up, and in confronting the new currents of self-interest, capitalism, nationalism and religious reformation begot more skepticism than conviction. Rene Descartes (1596-1650) in searching for certitude[19] concluded that all things could be doubted except one's internal states of consciousness, including a sense of self-interest and self-preservation. Thus modern philosophy, starting from this radical egocentricity and individualism, wrestled with both preserving and controlling individual freedom in the context of the sovereign national state. **Hence, moralists were less interested in justice as personal virtue and more as a quality of public life and policy.**

Justice as Public Policy

Thomas Hobbes' radical individualism of universal, unlimited and inalienable rights to life, body and property needed an all powerful state to impose justice and arbitrate private conflicts[20], establishing order through people's "fear of greater injury."[21] Such yoking of anarchy to autarchy urged philosophers to seek a firmer foundation for public policy in a moral sense, social mores or general utility. Rejecting all these as circumstantial, Immanuel Kant (1724-1804) postulated as basis for just public policy the duty to obey the innate, universal maxim, that "everyone can have what is his own secured against the action of every other."[22]

Critics, however, criticized Kantian duty as ambiguous: it could mean undeviating obedience to laws and customs or unique convictions impervious to criticism. Much philosophical effort went toward resolving this antinomy. G.W.F. Hegel (1770-1830) developed his dialectical method to bridge the chasm between self and society. He postulates the person as pure thought, subjective, indeterminate and universal, which in knowing itself becomes determined universality, which as the concrete concept of freedom, knows itself as different from others and possessing abstract rights to body, actions and material goods.[23] These subjective rights, embodied first in the family, are objectivized in laws and protected by private institutions and public force. The individual, therefore, in associations outside the family, realizes freedom in the nation state, which is open to the will of all and is for the good of all. Thus citizens, in doing their duty achieve their rights and are confirmed in freedom and goodness, when they subject their wills to constitutions and laws as immutable principles.[24] **In this way, Hegel through the dialectic preserves rights, freedom and public order, and public justice is not just protected, it is fulfilled.**

J.S. Mill, on the other hand, being pragmatically British, starts from the personal experience of justice as being compelled by law to do or to refrain from doing something.[25] From such compulsion a person can infer the right to so act. Further the state's obligation to punish wrongdoers implies its duty to protect citizens' rights. Hence, Kantian duty, for Mill, is obedience to such rules which rational people adopt for their collective interest. The principle that rights should be protected because they benefit the general welfare leaves, however, the dangerous inference that rights may be violated which seem to harm or are simply indifferent to the public good.

Many more philosophers, Nietzsche, Dewey, Moore, Sedgwich to mention but a few, have participated in this effort to square preserving personal freedom and self-interest with fostering the public good. But de-emphasizing justice as a personal virtue, modern moralists oscillate inconsistently between advocating the widest scope for freedom and investing more power in the state to punish violators of others' rights and to coerce acting for the general welfare. Despite people's inability to find a firm base for personal rights and the justice obligations which flow from them, people generally are convinced that a well-regulated public order preserves personal freedom and rights. Further, most agree with Nozick that public policy should recompense past injustices, whether private or public, and with Rawls that it should benefit especially the least advantaged.

But such an idea of justice falls far short of the work of justice as a personal virtue. At minimum, justice preserves an equanimity which flows from an internal peace and harmony. It oils interpersonal relationships by a mutual sensitivity to rights. Even more effectively than the most enlightened legislation, a keen and broadly shared sense of justice sustains state and society as a healthy habitat for human persons. As a moral Value, justice undergirds one's total personality in all of life's phases, and permeating every quirk of character maintains a serenity in all life's vicissitudes and trials. It especially distinguishes the person of moral integrity in matters of business and economics.

ECONOMIC JUSTICE

Economic justice, of course, is not a particular kind of justice but simply principles of justice applied to activities whose most prominent component is economic. Nor is it suggested that justice is concerned most of all with economic matters. Quite to the contrary, the most frequent and most heinous violation of justice are acts against personal not property rights. But since every economic act is social, involving at least one other person, it is subject to criteria of justice. Moreover, abundance has so accentuated and complicated the economic aspects of contemporary living that the principles of justice as they apply to business and economic dealing needs special treatment. Hence, too, the spate of new courses in business ethics.

But the discussion here will not address the myriad of ethical issues economic justice entails—they need a tome of their own—but will make the one point **that a sensitive sense of justice fits well with and corroborates the basic rationality of economic action.** It will apply this precept to all manner of exchanges (commutative justice), to obligations arising from one's role in society and in subaltern organizations (contributive justice) and to the individual's right to share in a common Good (distributive justice). While a bit old-fashioned, these terms conveniently organize the analysis of justice according to its multi-faceted obligation to respect others's rights.

Commutative Justice

Commutative justice applies to every kind of economic exchange. As the specifically and characteristically economic act necessitated by scarcity, economic exchange not only spans the range of economic activities but is the **essential economic act.** In exchange not only are commodities, services, properties, rights, moneys, options, etc. transferred but money circulates, prices are formed and wealth is created. Unlike with animals, exchange is the universal and inevitable task of the human species. Because of scarcity, exchange is **competitive**: buyers bid against buyers; sellers against sellers. Because it is social, exchange requires **complementarity**: without buyers there can be no sellers; without sellers buyers.

A sense of commutative justice in the course of exchange will keep clearly in mind that scarcity with its consequences of competition and complementarity is inevitable; that the purpose of exchange is to enhance the well-being of the exchangers by surrendering what they desire less for what they desire more; and that the economic constructs, money, prices and wealth are not the purpose of exchange but only the necessary means to effect it. **Thus there are two distinct but related aspects to every act of exchange: the moral, how the respective well-**

being of the exchangers is *affected* and the economic, how efficiently the transaction was *effected*.

Although these aspects cannot be separated, they can be examined individually, thus showing how injustice may violate either economic rationality or morality and how violations of the one violate the other.

To begin then, both buyers and sellers have moral rights to honest treatment in negotiation, to trust that agreements reached be honored, and to an overall civility in dealings. Sellers have the right to be protected in their property, to have access to their markets, to sell to whom they choose and to withdraw their goods from sale. This argues as a general rule against monopoly, closed negotiations, and collusive bidding. Buyers have similar rights: access to the market, not being barred by irrelevant criteria like sex, age, religion, race, or political persuasion; and the right to honest presentation of the goods for sale. All these moral precepts obviously make for good business relations. In sum, therefore, commutative justice requires **respecting others' moral rights by not taking advantage of them.**

Stating this comes to the heart of the econo-moral problem. First the facts: while everyone is faced with scarcity, people differ in the advantages they possess in knowledge, experience, mental acuity, risk willingness, economic resources, and family influence and thus enjoy differing economic advantages, some in one way, others in another. Given these, exploiting one's ad vantages is eminently rational: a person should do that which he or she does best or which pays the most. The common sense of economic competition, therefore, is that people can and should use their advantages to attain their ends. Even more so following one's comparative advantage, as shown earlier, benefits both buyer and seller and their competition. How then can taking advantage of another be unjust?

The distinction to be made may seem minor but it is decisive. Justice allows one to use his advantage *over* another but forbids taking advantage *of* another. This is not semantic quibbling but cuts cleanly to the core of the issue. Exploiting one's advantage is the essence of free-market competition. As a principle of competition, using an advantage over others, far from degrading competitors, respects them as equals in seeking the same goal, while differing in their pursuit of it. Such competition, moreover, does not cross economic orders: suppliers compete with suppliers and demanders with demanders. Following advantage, therefore, is both social and socially beneficial because it urges competitors to their best contribution to the economy and in general rewards proportionately. **While charity may be needed to override justice in particular situations, a just competition is, in general, the most effective way to counter the limitations and restraints imposed by scarcity.**

Taking advantage *of* another, on the other hand, violates both economic and moral principles. Exploiting one's own advantage in such a way as to destroy a competitor's advantage is both unjust and harms the market because it limits the buyers' choices. For example, a large firm may use its advantage in volume to lower prices below costs so as to destroy a smaller producer which has the advantage in more personalized service. Even more obviously unjust and uneconomic is the advantage taking which crosses economic orders: the seller, for example, who takes advantage of buyers' ignorance and credulity, and less frequently buyers of sellers. The list of fraud in exchange is never ending, ranging from deceitful advertising, to every form of "bait and switch" selling, to complex, recondite and ambiguous contracts, to shoddy goods and service, noxious and unsafe products and so forth through every twist and turn of the selling process. More reprehensible is the deception which can foul industrial relations: tricky wage contracts and forcing employees to work under unsafe conditions and in a manner and at a pace injurious to health; and, on the other side, workers' loafing and feather-bedding on the job. **The possibilities are legion today by which human ingenuity can cheat, defraud, hoodwink and endanger others. Whatever the form, fraud destroys the trust which bonds exchange so that a reputation for, or just rumors of, underhanded dealing can be financially disastrous.**

Injustice in the more economic aspects of trade, generating

gain, forming prices and creating wealth, is considerably more elusive. Unlike medieval moralists who pursued the phantom of the just price, in this era of absentee, scientific, and linked pricing, where one seller's price becomes another's cost, the ethician is faced with a range of highly volatile and frequently discounted prices, very few of which buyers are forced to pay. In such a context it is really impossible to talk about *a just price* but, at best, *a range of just prices.* On the other hand, profits and earnings can be enormous, suggesting that prices can be bloated. A seller, trying to be just, or critics, passing judgment on a transaction, must resort to general principles applicable to economic exchange itself.

Essential to free exchange is that each party gains. But since there is neither more commodity nor money than before but merely a transfer of both, the gain must consist in that each prefers his or her present to the previous state. Both have gained. But have they gained equally? equitably? They are not likely to have gained equally, since buyer and seller come to the exchange with different resources, desires and purposes. Even so they could have gained equitably if each is better off than before and reasonably satisfied with it. Equity in exchange is compared to the arithmetic mean. Just as the average is the same for all the numbers in the set, so too the market price is the same for both buyers and sellers, some influencing the market price to raise it and some to lower it. Consequently, the final price is like the average of the hopes and fears of all in the market. As such no one gets all he or she wished nor loses as much as feared. While no one is entirely happy, all are better off.

In today's mass and impersonal marketing (much transcontinental and even transworld) and scientific and impersonal pricing just pricing can be assumed if certain conditions prevail: there is no evidence of collusion; government has not intruded unduly into the market; prices are clear and unambiguous; there is no evidence of fraud and other forms of advantage-taking; the market is open and accessible to many; prices perform their designed functions of allocating goods and rewarding participants; and finally both buyers and sellers are disposed to return to the market. All are marks of a truly free and effective market.

A person's business dealings begin to be colored with justice when he or she combines these principles with a lively respect for other people and their rights, in a manner to inspire trust, treating them with honor, civility and the firm intention not to take advantage of their weaknesses. Respect for the human person is particularly important in dealing with shop, office or sales personnel. Two universal maxims should be kept in mind: the manager-worker relationship is complementary, not instrumental; trust is generated by neither management nor labor trying to take advantage of the other. **These principles, whatever knotty issues the ethics of exchange may present, are basic to a just attitude in all one's economic and business dealings**. Even more so they apply to *contributive justice* and one's role in society and the economy.

Contributive Justice

Contemporary **me-first** individualism probably finds contributive justice and the obligation it imposes to support not only society but lower order private associations most difficult to accept. But this form of justice protects both community as a human Value and the right to participate in whatever form of fellowship one chooses, family, church, team, club, business or professional association. Further in respecting personality, freedom and individual differences, contributive justice matches a person's obligation with his or her capabilities and role in society and other groups.

In general, therefore, contributive justice follows the principle, **to whom more is given, more is owed**, and varies its burden of obligation proportionately to wealth, talent, ambition and charisma. Contributive justice in this sense is like the harmonic mean, the product of two numbers divided by their mean, while both contribute to the final number, the larger contributes more, the smaller less. Thus, contributive justice, although pre-eminently social, imposes a personal duty and only secondarily requires alerting others to their obligations by persuasion or general rules or laws. **In other words, contribu-**

tive justice will develop a personal concern and regard for society as a fellowship of persons, as a cultural milieu and as a generator of wealth, and will accept the obligation of material support, implied with each.

As belonging to a fellowship of persons, everyone has the obvious and overwhelming obligation to respect the rights of other human beings. Abusing others, demeaning them, violating their rights or stealing their property, destroys human relations and in so doing undermines society. It goes without saying that everyone is obliged to obey just laws and, specifically in this context, laws applying to business. Indeed free markets require closer observance lest playing fast and loose with laws invite government legislatures and agencies to weave a more strangling web of regulations. Last, of course, taxes to support all the many services of government, police, courts, schools, parks and so forth, are generally, if painfully, accepted as owing in justice. Non-government agencies have no less claims for support when they perform the same services.

In no sense is this truer than in maintaining economically society's cultural constituent. Money writes, teaches, paints, acts and sings in the sense that art, literature, scholarship and moral thought need material support and will seek whatever market that does so. Art and entertainment, especially, will sink into the vulgar, bizarre and debased if there is not the kind of assistance which subsidizes striving for the more exalted and challenging. Since there are no laws, rules or even guidelines governing obligations to support culture and the arts other than what government wrests by way of taxes, a pragmatic contributive justice is the most effective way to preserve the vitality and variety of education, music, art and entertainment.

The material needs of the personal and cultural constituents of society imply an obligation to contribute to and maintain its economic dimension. Most people subconsciously accept that what they can draw from the economy must be roughly proportional to what they contribute or have contributed to it. For many, if not most, of wealthy Americans a distinguishing feature is their affirmation of the stewardship of wealth, the obligation to use their surplus wealth in a socially beneficial way, to provide opportunities for the dispossessed, to promote civic ventures, and to assist education and cultural programs. The poor and disabled are faced with the same obligation that to take from the economy they must give to it. They can do so by their example of patience under adversity, their zest for life and their efforts to overcome their handicaps. In this way they contribute to the economic commonwealth and can, like everyone else, rightly feel entitled to share in the common fund of economic and social goods.

Distributive Justice

The essence of distributive justice in its economic dimension is respecting everyone's right to share in the benefits of the economy. In the direst circumstances this means a minimum of food, clothing, shelter and health care needed for survival. In more abundant economies this social minimum should be more copious and diversified. For active contributors to the economy's output the share should roughly match their contributions. The basic problem is that, with universal scarcity, an economy can never produce all its participants feel entitled to. In the private sector they will compete for larger shares of the output pie; in the public domain for budget-breaking handouts.

Economic growth, of course, will ameliorate the strife but poses its own difficulty. In free markets, which are designed to reward the more efficient production, investment and buying, growth is achieved by stimulating self-interest, quite the opposite of sharing with the least advantaged in society. Economic rationality, therefore, can see how abundance and poverty could increase hand in hand and conclude that those, who for one reason or another, bad luck, bad habits or poor employability, make no contribution to overall production, are a drag on the economy and exacerbate the problem of sharing.

But a sense of contributive justice, reflecting both a deep concern for the disadvantaged and the rationality of self-interest as the energizer of economic growth, will want to alleviate the direst distress and will join with others in promoting government and private programs to establish more equitable and effective opportunities for the poor. Instead of allowing them to wallow in economic despair and to moulder on welfare, distributive justice will try to jump-start their self-interest by first guaranteeing their basic needs and then making available ways to regain their self-respect, repair their employability, arouse their self-interest and get into the economic mainstream. **Thus self-interest, the very human drive which can make distribution worse, can become a means toward its amelioration.**

This ideal that sharing and growth proceed hand in hand is represented symbolically in the geometric mean, the square root of the product of two numbers. This suggests that distributive justice is realized when the social minimum reflects the productivity of an economy where the self-interest of both capital and labor motivates them to cooperate in generating more and more output. Such an ideal, of course, will not by itself clarify all the complexities and resolve all the ethical conundrums of contemporary industrial relations, welfare policies, tax laws and business regulations. Basic principles can not substitute for empirical knowledge and experience but they are essential to the moral attitude necessary for addressing problems of distributive justice.

In the private sector, the bone of distribution fought over often bitterly and of most consequence to the general welfare is the wage contract. Medieval moralists discussed this as the just wage theory but, like the just price, so many factors are involved in wage determinations that at best one can talk about "a just wage" and not "the just wage." Nevertheless, certain principles of distributive justice must attend negotiations if equity is to be realized. 1. Disadvantages (usually of the worker) cannot be abused, nor irrelevant criteria, such as race, gender, religion and the like determine employment or compensation. 2. Where wages are the main support of the worker and his or her family, a basic living wage is required by commutative justice. 3. The right to seek gain is a universal right, as much that of the employee as the employer.

4. Since a business is an essentially collaborative process,

requiring complementarity and cooperation, growth in earnings should be shared by all in the enterprise to the extent of their contributions. 5. An awareness of the universality of scarcity will warn that the demands on the business will always exceed its resources. Justice will seek parity for the business' constituencies in sharing shortfalls. 6. Above all, amidst the demands on the business, a just person will make every effort to keep the enterprise going, realizing that an ongoing operation has some chance of working out of difficulties to the good of all, a defunct one none.

All of these principles, with appropriate adjustments, apply to government officials at every level and also to citizens in their evaluations of officials and agencies. Some additional ones should be considered. 1. First and foremost, it is incumbent on both officials and the general public that government's limited but lavish largess reaches its intended beneficiaries and is not dissipated by a perverted self-interest in peddling influence, inter-agency squabbling and administrative waste. 2. Concern for the disadvantaged in society should direct more effort and money to encouraging aspirations rather than to rehabbing failures. 3. This applies the general principle that public policy should walk the tight-rope between caring for the poor and sustaining the spirit of economic self-interest, the ideal being that the latter implement the former.

4. The present generation owes to future generations and especially today's children an educational system which will prepare them for high-tech living and an environment and planet both salubrious and bountiful in natural resources. 5. International equity in an increasingly interdependent world insists that wealthy countries help redress the destitution and dearth of capital of poor nations. It goes beyond this in urging a freeing up of trade between nations as the way, despite the difficulties involved, of increasing world well-being and amity.

The list could go on and on of economic issues which justice should address. Enough has been shown to demonstrate that it in every way corroborates economic common sense. Requiring an internal peace and harmony, justice is a firm habit of respecting every person's rights and the personal, cultural and economic ties which bind people in society, in the family and other associations and especially in business. Producing peace, justice is like a gyroscope responding to every change in one's self, in others, in the texture of society and pattern of living, continuously readjusting one's internal equilibrium and relations to others. **Firm but flexible, just persons control their self-interest, are a calming influence in political and business controversy and sources of strength upon which others rely as moral points of reference. The word describing them is "integrity."**

This quality then becomes prerequisite for setting one's sights on Values and goals which transcend economic well-being.

ENDNOTES

1. Aristotle, *op. cit.*, V, 1129.
2. Smith, Adam, *The Theory of Moral Sentiments*, New York: Evert Duyrinck et al., 1822, v. 1, ch. 1, p.1.
3. Hobbes, Thomas, *Leviathan*, New York: E. P. Dutton, 1950, ch. XIII.
4. Smith, Adam, *Wealth, op.cit.,*, pp. 423-4.
5. Mill, John Stuart, *op. cit.*, bk. 2; *On Liberty*, ch. 5 and *Utilitarianism*, chs. 2 and 3, Chicago: Encyclopaedia Britannica, 1952, v. 43.
6. Marx, Karl, *op. cit.*, chs. XXIII to XXXII.
7. Nozick, Robert, *Anarchy, State and Utopia*, New York: Basic Books, Inc., Publishers, 1974.
8. Rawls, John, *A Theory of Justice*, Cambridge, Mass: Harvard University Press, 1971.
9. Josef Pieper's short but comprehensive treatment, *Justice*, (Tr. L.E. Lynch, New York: Pantheon Books, 1955) is highly recommended. There Pieper draws out the radically provocative (at least for moderns) implications of classical and medieval analyses of the rights of persons as individuals, sexual beings, and citizens as well as economic agents.
10. Plato, *Republic*, pp. 357-366 and 587-8.
11. Augustine, *City of God*, ch. 21.
12. Aquinas, I, q. 95 a. 1, ans.
13. Aristotle, bk. 5, ch. 1.
14. *ibid.* chs. 2-4.
15. Bloom, Allan, *The Closing of the American Mind*, New York: Simon & Schuster, 1988, p. 166.
16. *ibid.*
17. Aquinas, II-II, q.58, a.9, res.2.
18. *ibid.* a.1, ans.

19. Descartes, Rene, *Method of Rightly Conducting the Reason*, Tr. E.S.Haldane and G.R.T. Ross, Chicago: Encylopaedia Britannica, 1952, v.31, pp. 41-68.
20. Hobbes, Thomas, p.120.
21. Spinoza, Baruch, *Ethics*, Tr. W.H. White, Cambridge: Oxford Press, part IV, prop.37, schol. 2.
22. Kant, Immanuel, *The Metaphysics of Morals*, Tr. T.K. Abbott, Great Books,Chicago: Encyclopaedia Britanica, 1952, v.42, p. 275.
23. Hegel, G.W.F., *The Philosophy of Right*, Tr. T. Knox, London: Oxford University Press, 1967, intro. par. 31. 24. Hegel, G.W.F., *The Philosophy of History*, Tr. J. Sibree, *op. cit.* pp. 364-5.
26. Mill, J.S., *Utilitarianism*, Great Books, Chicago: Encyclopaedia Britannica, 1952, v. 43, p.468.

GLOSSARY

anarchy—A state of political disorder as opposed to **autarchy**, a state of autocratic rule.

antinomy—A seeming contradiction between two rules or the seeming irreconcilability between two principles or conclusions.

commonwealth—The body of people constituting a state or an organized political community. **Common wealth of goods** by analogy refers to the common aggregate of public and private goods by which a people carry on their daily lives.

dialectic—A branch of logic, teaching the art of disputation, referring here to Hegel's method of drawing a synthesis from a thesis and anti-thesis, which synthesis becomes the thesis of a further antithesis. Marx adopted this method, expressing it in materialistic terms.

geriatric—Referring to old age or to elderly people.

homogeneity—An identity or similarity of kind or nature.

illfare—The state of doing poorly especially in an economic sense.

moral relativism—The philosophic doctrine which denies all objective moral criteria or standards. Moral judgments about right or wrong are entirely relative to the situation and person.

mores—Customs or conventions imbued with an ethical significance or having the force of law.

neo-classical—In Economics this refers particularly to the economic thought of Alfred Marshall who synthesized the Marginal Utility analysis of the 1890s with the earlier Classical Economics of Smith and Ricardo.

unified-field theory—A theory in any science or discipline which purports to explain all the phenomena of the science in a logical and coherent fashion.

TOPICS FOR FURTHER DISCUSSION OR RESEARCH

1. Review the recent troubles of the Texas and California S & L industries, which produced so many examples of costly failures. Demonstrate from them that even legal policies, which reveal poor economic judgment or mismanagement, may also violate both contributive and distributive justice.

ADDITIONAL SUGGESTED READING

1. Josef Pieper, *Justice*, Trans. L.E. Lynch, New York: Pantheon Books, 1955.
2. Bernard W. Dempsey, S.J., *The Functional Economy*, Englewood Cliffs: Prentice-Hall, Inc., 1958, chs. 9, 11 and 19.
3. Edward J. O'Boyle, "On Justice and Charity", *Review of Social Economy,"* v. 49, no. 4, Winter, 1991, pp. 578-595.

CHAPTER SIX

MODERATION AND GAIN-SEEKING

Moderation to many is a namby-pamby kind of word, evoking little heroism and no romance. It sets ill with people used to instant gratification and attuned to quick, often violent, solutions to problems and difficulties. To some it connotes a joyless puritanism, to others a Milquetoast caution. But a true moderation is neither spineless nor insensitive to pleasure and pain. Rather it controls the appetites not by suppressing but by guiding them. Above all, just as justice subserves economic self-interest by maintaining right relations with others, so moderation supplies motive and meaning to self-interested gain-seeking by directing its proceeds toward achieving goals higher than sensual, superficial and egoistic ones. **All told, moderation is a flexible and unassuming but tough virtue.**

This chapter begins with a brief survey of human appetites, preliminary to analyzing gain-seeking as an appetite not only distinguishable from the other vital appetites but fundamental to all economic action. Acknowledging the gain appetite's susceptibility to the downward pull of the *fomes peccati*, the chapter will, nevertheless, then demonstrate that economic agents are not always nor solely the beneficiary of their own acts and that moderation in fact can control, without suppressing, the gain appetite by directing it toward higher human Values, including concern for others.

THE APPETITES

The appetites are matter for this chapter because gain-seeking is really an appetite, the appetite for wealth. Furthermore, since all wants and needs are satisfied by the action of one or several appetites, appetency is an action of concern to economists and some general observations about them is in order. Consequently, while this fascinating subject is best left to philosophers and psychologists, some treatment here is necessary as preliminary to analysis of gain-seeking.

The Appetitive System

Although few people can readily define an appetite, everyone acknowledges them as necessary for survival. A moment's reflection on them will indicate that people have built-in adaptations and acquisitive propensities for objects which gratify their physical or spiritual desires. Some appetites are activated in a single act as a baby takes to suckling, others develop with maturity and again others must be cultivated and practiced. In this regard, of course, people differ greatly according to their natural appetitive endowment and their individual development, experience and aging. In addition to these differences in personal appetitive dispositions, appetites themselves are distinguished by the functions they perform and by the properties of things which actuate them.

In general, appetites can be ranked much like Values. At the lowest level are appetites which function through various physical systems, alimentary, sexual, circulatory, emotive and the like. Their objects are mainly means to other ends: the **vital** appetites for food, drink, air, rest and sex, all necessary for human survival and the **acquisitive** appetites for every kind of material good, necessary, useful or simply desired for living. (Here too is located gain-seeking, the **economic** appetite, to be discussed shortly.) The sense appetites function through the different sense organs, ears, eyes, mouth, nose and touch. Their objects, respectively sound, color, flavor, odor and resistance, can be sought both for their own sake and for an ulterior end, either vital or spiritual. Finally, the spiritual appetites through the faculties of mind, will and aesthetic sense seek respectively knowledge, goodness and beauty just as ends in themselves. Though ranked in this distinctive way, the appetites in action are not sealed off from but filter into each other. Indeed they almost always act conjointly, seeking to capture an object as complex as the human act itself. **But however appetites may blend together in operation, each seeks the properties connatural to it. Thus a uniquely differentiated object will require a distinctly different appetite.**

These remarks, sketchy as they are, are sufficient to give an inkling how marvelous the human appetitive system is as the way of taking hold of the reality of one's self, of others and of the material world. As such too they are great sources of gratification and pleasure. Because they provide pleasure, appetites pose a problem, implied in the frequently held but erroneous opinion that pleasure and pain, the former sought, the latter avoided, are objects of the appetites, if not *the* objects.

The confusion is understandable because pleasure and pain often accompany an appetitive act, but making them the reasons for seeking or avoiding an object is to put the incidental ahead of the essential. Pleasure, as Aristotle pointed out 23 centuries ago, only supervenes on and completes the act.[1] It only signals that the appetite is functioning properly on an appropriate object; just as pain indicates some malfunctioning. One encourages continuing or repeating the act; the other warns against it. Neither, of course, determines whether a particular act should be done: a painful medical procedure may save one's life; the pleasure from drugs may be addictively killing. Even less so does either signify an act's moral goodness or badness.

Nevertheless, pleasure and pain should not be ignored: they do signal that an appetite and its organ is doing well or that some pathology or abuse is impairing the appetite. Indeed the pleasure/pain calculus has important uses. Declining pleasure from repeated gratification of especially the vital and acquisitive appetites may warn that the particular appetite and its organ are over-used; increasing pain clearly signals misuse and abuse. But neither is definitive regarding the moral desirability of continuing or stopping the act.

Indeed pleasure/pain may be the very worst guide of conduct. It most menaces moderation in abetting the lower appetites' tendencies to excess. The slide from eating heartily to gluttony, from social drinking to tippling, from an occasional snort to dependence, from casual sex to lechery, from sufficiency of material goods to glut has occurred too often to need documenting. All testify to the *fomes peccati* at work. The decline is especially accelerated by the propensity to sensuality but it can be helped along by a silly superficiality, the need to be one of the crowd, and by the desire to stroke or inflate one's ego. **In sum, the vital exuberance humans share with other species requires controlling the appetites just as herds need culling, forests thinning, orchards pruning and gardens weeding.**

This review of the human appetites, admittedly sketchy and unscientific, corroborates, however, what personalism, Value theory and justice analysis concur in affirming an ordered hierarchy in the nature of the human person. This the book insists, must necessarily be reflected in the principles and operation of economic morality. That in turn requires locating gain-seeking, **the economic appetite,** in the person's appetitive system and examining its function in human conduct.

The principle used to distinguish the economic from other, especially the vital and acquisitive, appetites is the same given earlier, that each appetite seeks the properties of an object which are appropriate to it and to which it is connatural. Properties uniquely different from those sought by other appetites will, therefore, require a distinct appetite. Since price, gain, profit and wealth, being subsidiary to the physical benefit an object provides, are distinctly different from the object's utility and contribution to well-being, and since the gratification they produce is more intellectual than sensual, **gain- or wealth-seeking, the economic appetite, must be identified as different from all other appetites.**

The Undifferentiated Economic Appetite

Through most of the history of the moral sciences the appetite for gain and the vital and acquisitive appetites have been so intertwined that moralists generally treated them together and made little effort to distinguish between them. This made sense in earlier ages because wealth objects, though presumably commanding good prices if sold, were mainly desired as gratifying a sense of luxury, of vanity and/or of power. However used, wealth was *real*, land, buildings, clothes and the like, as opposed to today's *paper wealth*, claims against property and rights to income, having purchasing power but no sensual appeal.

Of all the ancients Plato insisted most adamantly that gain-seeking and the lower appetites mutually fed and motivated each other. In the *Laws*, therefore, he argues for limiting personal wealth, restricting foreign trade to necessities and isolating the populace from foreign innovations. In effect Plato would suppress gain-seeking, insisting that a stable and moral society required a zero-growth economy.[2] Aristotle agreed that excessive gain-seeking and disordered appetites were linked but, in distinguishing between commodities' proper use, to satisfy human wants and needs, and their secondary use, to exchange and accumulate wealth,[3] he establishes different principles to control each. Moderation achieves the mean between repression and self indulgence and liberality by using surplus wealth to help others achieves it between prodigality and niggardliness.[4] In this way Aristotle was able at least to tolerate trade.

After Plato and Aristotle the most popular ethical systems were Stoicism and Epicureanism which, while derived respectively from reason and refined sensibilities, differed little in practice. A scholar-politician like Cicero (106-43 B.C.) reflected both, comfortably combining high-minded philosophizing with enjoying great wealth obtained by exploiting the provinces. The harsh Stoicism of Epictetus (55-135) was practiced most rigidly by Christian hermits who spurned both profits and pleasure. Augustine, seeing Roman decay and Vandal fury, exhorted his fellow Christians to use but not enjoy this world's pleasures.[5] His warning against profit-taking cast a thousand year suspicion on commercial enterprise. Aquinas, like Aristotle distinguishing between wealth and vital appetites, still links them, since money is the universal means for indulging one's concupiscence.[6] He was, however, more tolerant of profits earned justly and used to benefit others.[6] This grudging concession to profit-taking was enough to nudge later moralists, both Catholics and Protestants, toward accepting slowly and laboriously, the possibility of economic gain being morally justifiable.

The first break in the suspicion clouding commerce came from an unlikely source. John Calvin (1509-1564), despite his doctrine of salvation by divine predestination, taught that while a person could not be saved by good works, he or she could not be saved without them.[8] Whatever one's vocation in life, everyone was called to live industriously, frugally and soberly, using the good things of life but enjoying them in moderation.[9] In a commercial city like Geneva, which he dominated almost like a theocracy, banning both licentiousness and dishonesty, Calvin's doctrine became a blue-print for business success. Montesquieu (1689-1755), although only peripherally touched by Calvinism, disengaged the gain appetite from the vital appetites one more notch. Reversing their influences, he makes the desire for wealth a means for controlling the lower appetites: "When a democracy is founded on commerce, private people may acquire vast riches without corruption of morals. . . because the spirit of commerce is naturally attended with that of frugality, economy, moderation and rule."[10]

Across the Channel this idea formed a comfortable conscience for English scholars, policy-makers and businessmen like Child, Mun, North, Petty, Cantillon and the like, exhilarated by the 17-18th centuries' expansion of Britain's commercial empire.[11] Bernard Mandeville (1670-1733), the "pothouse" philosopher, then took the next radical and upsetting step, asserting in his *Fable of the Bees* that economic avarice and unbridled sensuality were the true causes of economic growth, while frugality and sobriety depressed it.[12] His cynical sophistries, born of Hobbesian individualism, set off the altruism egoism debate, which involved all the great moralists of the 18th century, Bishop Butler, Shaftesbury, Hutcheson, Hume and Smith, and is reflected in the 19th century philosophies of Kant, Reid and Bentham. This debate provoked the final disengagement of the gain from the vital appetites.

The Gain and Vital Appetites Disengaged

This was accomplished by Francois Quesnay, David Hume and Adam Smith, all three political economists, social philosophers and friends. Each conceived the economy as a dynamic system of countering flows of product and of money, both driven by self-interest. Quesnay located this drive primarily in the class of entrepreneur-farmers whose effort produced and whose investment increased the **stuff** of material wealth.[13] Hume universalizes the entrepreneurial spirit as an instinctive urge competing for profits, which he calls "liveliness".[14] Finally, Smith insists that private gain-seeking by requiring mutuality, reciprocity and harmonizing economic purposes achieves, as by an Invisible Hand, the public Good more effectively than by planned public policy.[15] Thus the three and economists following them, while never intending to downplay business morality, nevertheless, **in disengaging gain-seeking from the vital and other appetites, denied in effect its need for moral controls and freed it from moral tutelage.**

Throughout the 19th century economists stripped gain-seeking further of moral implications. In the Neo-classical system it becomes simply an amoral axiom of rational behavior, the premise of a logic of choice under conditions of scarcity. For economists of this mind, economics has lost all normative content and shed every subordination to moral disciplines. They take for granted that economics is a technical, Value-free, positivistic and quantitative science. Despite this, gain-seeking since Smith has not had an easy time of it. Some have defended it as a universal, economic cure-all. Others have ascribed to it at one time or another every ill which besets the modern economy. It is usually treated as the logic of choosing between costs and benefits, as an instinctive reaction to gain and loss possibilities or as the essential function of economic acts. Bundle all these functions together and it looks like a human activity behaving like an appetite. Even a cursory review of the treatment of gain-seeking in some of the principle systems of the last 200 years will suggest the same.

Despite the spectacular increases in productivity of industrial economies, major economists like T.R. Malthus (1766-1834) and J.S. Mill echoed Ricardo's conclusion that gain-seeking produced its own demise. Marx went further. With him the Medieval infinite appetite for riches re-appears as the capitalist's compulsion to accumulate capital wealth by exploiting labor. Such exploitation by producing periodic and worsening crises of over-production, mires the proletariat deeper in poverty and drives craftsmen and smaller capitalists into the proletariat. When inevitably the last exploiter is exploited, Communism is ushered in. Marx could, therefore, castigate the appetite for wealth as capitalistic greediness, while preserving its sociological function in the inevitable transformation of Capitalism into Communism.[16]

At the other extreme Herbert Spencer (1820-1903) and Charles Sumner (1840-1910), the chief protagonists of Social Darwinism, argued that unrestricted private freedom to gain, and untrammeled competition were necessary not only for economic progress but for enlarging human liberty. Where Smith saw expanding economic freedom as revolutionary and salutary, Sumner hardened it into dogma.[17] His almost moral fervor was matched by R.H. Tawney's (1880-1962) countering attack on the profit motive. In his *The Acquisitive Society* Tawney details the evil effects of gain-seeking, undermines its moral sanction and argues for its control.[18] These proclivities, translated into the arena of social legislation, inclined conservatives to heed J.S. Mill's principle of avoiding legislating private morality except to protect the rights of others.[19] The more socialistically leaning argued with the Webbs (1858-1947) for more controls on gain-directed free enterprise, often echoing the thought of G.W.F. Hegel (1770-1831): ". . . Society has the right and duty of acting as trustee . . . substitut[ing] for [private] extravagance the pursuit of the ends of society and the individuals concerned."[20]

Well past the first quarter of this century a moral streak, more or less discernible, ran through most arguments for and against gain-seeking. More recently the debate has purged moral considerations and become strictly technical. In it economists are now joined by physicists, biologists, climatologists, ecologists, demographers and such like in warning of economic catastrophe. Economic growth and, implicitly, the gain motive which fosters it, they predict, will beget its own demise either by destroying investment and innovation incentive or by the more technical way of depleting natural resources, destroying the atmosphere, dissipating energy, garbaging the earth, and by people proliferating beyond earth's ability to feed them. The problem being a-moral, the guilt must be impersonal: Government, Big Business, Society but never people's excessive appetites! This "de-moralization" of the wealth incentive over the last two centuries has been matched by the progressive dematerialization of wealth itself. While the wealthy generally live sumptuously, the largest part of great and even modest fortunes consists of rights to property and claims to income, all of them devoid of sensual appeal. Often homes, jewelry and art are kept more for their market value than their intrinsic appeal. Indeed people commonly equate the quality of purchases with the prices they pay. **All demonstrate that a good's economic value, while related to, is distinctly different from the use and pleasure it gives and, consequently, is the object of a unique appetite.**

THE ECONOMIC APPETITE

Preliminary to this analysis it is necessary to be clear about the point of the question. A comparison might help. Just as eating is both the action of a vital appetite and a function studied by the science of dietetics, so too gain-seeking is the act of a special appetite, thus coming under moral scrutiny, and a function fundamental to the operation of the economy, hence, a subject of economic science. Furthermore, just as the appetite for food involves many other appetites even the most spiritual, so too the economic appetite is closely linked to all, especially the sense and vital, appetites by providing the means to get the scarce, material goods or service the appetites seek. **In short, gain-seeking can be studied as economic principle, as moral act or as both functioning together.**

Consequently, it is again worth emphasizing that scarce material goods and services have two functions: they can satisfy some need or want and they can be exchanged for other scarce things. As distinct functions they are subject to different criteria: the satisfying function to moral and other criteria; the exchange function to the test of economic efficiency. While viewed differently as appetite and economic principle, gain seeking is always both simultaneously, its distinct operations mutually influencing each other. Such would be expected, given the assumption of a fundamental order in human nature. **Indeed that assumption implies that the moral principles applicable to gain-seeking are consistent with and corroborated by its economic principles, and vice versa.** With these clarifications, it is now necessary to examine gain-seeking as a human appetite.

Gain-seeking Distinguished

Gain-seeking, the economic appetite, is a distinct appetite because its object, the properties of things it seeks, differs from all other, especially the vital and possessive, appetites and because its nature and function is unlike any other.

These functions, while distinct, are obviously related: price is paired with a thing's utility; wealth with well-being; gain with increased desirability; gain-generation with improved productivity. Both sets of properties are real but utility, well-being, desirability and production improvement are inherent qualities while prices and the rest are relative to the thing's exchange value. The physically real changes slowly, the economically real, being more abstract and relative, constantly. Economic values, therefore, even though related to physical goods as means to acquiring them and as such subject to constant market changes, are, nevertheless, **true objects, sought in and for themselves,**

of the distinct and unique economic appetite, which is at the same time the principle of economic change.

While the price of a steak may change the next hour, once sold the price is realized once and for all. The money gained from selling can purchase whatever one would, precisely because the price is nothing more than a mathematical ratio, the amount of money gained for the amount of steak surrendered. By contrast the qualities of the steak, once consumed have yielded their specific benefit and are gone. Obviously, of course, one may have survived by eating the steak but starved clutching the money. **All these differences point to the same conclusion that a commodity's economic properties are objects which require an appetite uniquely connatural to them and distinctly different from other, specifically the vital and acquisitive, appetites.**

The facts of exchange suggest the nature of the economic appetite. The universality and volatility of prices mean that people, whether realizing it or not, add to or dissipate wealth in every exchange, implying a real distinction between the utility and exchange value of property and services. Further, the complexity of modern economies requires a money, an economic good wanted for no use except that it is easily calculated, safely stored, readily transferred and universally accepted. All point to an appetite which can now be identified as the **calculating function of the practical intellect**, measuring the ratio of gain to sacrifice in every transaction. As such, the economic appetite, while implementing sensual and acquisitive appetites, is a real propensity and craving for gain. Being rational and sophisticated, it must be cultivated and developed: in some people it almost never is operative; others have honed it to a keenness which almost senses bargains and profitable investments.

The gain-appetite, therefore, although concerned with material things, seems more a function of the mind than the body. This is confirmed in that this appetite, unlike the vital and acquisitive, is not really subject to satiation, the appetites' warning of enough. More may be harmful: indulgence beyond satiation causing physical revulsion, impairment, disease and even death. The desire for wealth, on the contrary, knows no satiation. It may remain keen when other interests fade and the passions are calmed. It can be stimulating to the extent of addiction. For some it promises security, for others the spice of gambling or the challenge of competition. Generally, it gains the respect usually accorded the wealthy, however the source of their wealth. While often contemned by the morally fastidious, it may narrow one's vision but sharpens one's wits and is universally needed in business and in varying degrees in governments, non-profit organizations and households. **All told, the gain appetite is tougher, more resilient, longer-lasting and more universal than the vital or even the sense appetites.**

In sum, gain-seeking, its natural propensity become addiction, poses a greater moral danger. Accumulating wealth does not diminish but increases social respectability and prestige. Addiction receives no warning from the body, nor abates with age, a person never realizing how greed dominates one's life. All helps explain the paradox that objects, having little or no sensual appeal, nevertheless, may evoke irresistible desires. Its moral danger is evidenced in that most of the world's crime is provoked by greed for money and gain and this is confirmed by the common experience that the loftiest aspirations can be eroded and degenerate into a consuming passion for money. These reasons warrant the Classical and Medieval philosophers' naming it **the infinite appetite for riches** and helps explain why the moderns, after divorcing it from moral tutelage, cast about for other, usually political, ways of fettering its drive. Given gain-seeking's economic function, all this suggests a problem.

To put the problem in perspective, it would help first to recall that economic morality consists in applying to every day conduct two distinct sets of criteria, one economic, the other moral. As an economic act, each instance of gain-seeking expands the economy if only by a millimicron. Multiplied a hundred million times, however, in the social interplay of seeking profits, economic rents and consumer surpluses by producing, consuming and financing goods and services, economic growth becomes measurable and significant. As the principal motive driving the economy, gain-seeking is subject to economic judgments. At the same time, it is an appetite subject to moral criteria about its appropriateness as to time, place and other circumstances, of the way and manner of its doing, of the agent's purposes and the act's consequences for others. In assuming, therefore, a basic coherence in life and human nature a person must conclude **that both moral and economic precepts are valid and, blended together, guide a person's gain-seeking.** While such simultaneity makes neat distinctions difficult, it will still help to examine separately gain-seeking's economic and moral functions.

Gain-seeking's Economic Role

The economic role gain-seeking plays can be no better illustrated than by a trip through a large supermarket with its thousands of commodities worth millions of dollars, gathered from every corner of the globe from people who had no idea of the ultimate buyers. Any item traced back through shipper, manufacturer, farmer, farm supplier and so forth reveals a price set and paid at each stage, each party in the process hoping to get a price larger than the costs of labor, raw materials and the rest, in a word, to gain. If disappointed, they may withdraw from this market or even from the industry. If successful, they may expand. **Thus gain, wealth, profits, money and the like, all conventional and cultural constructs which satisfy no want or need themselves but are universally serviceable in producing and bringing goods to market, are objects of a voracious appetite.**

This appetite, expressed especially as the entrepreneurial spirit, distinguishes the industry and commerce of abundant from survival economies. By stimulating research and invention it largely shifts the burden of hauling and heaving from men and animals to machines, spectacularly increases people's mobility and expands their boundaries. It devises ever more ingenious ways of using human skills, raw materials and sophisticated technology to generate an ever larger, more diversified and more desired output of material goods and services. Abundant economies, consequently, are able to support a larger population more generously over a longer life, and to devote a greater part of societal wealth to education, medical research, artistic effort, a wider range of entertainment and moral and religious concerns. For all the evil gain-seeking has perpetrated, it is being emulated in economies, formerly ideologically opposed to it and in cultures alien and foreign to it. Despite the complaints levelled against gain-motivated economies, even their most bitter critics prefer them to government-controlled economies.

Gain-seeking, besides dramatically increasing production, helps distribute that output more effectively. For a free market can operate only on the two bases of what consumers want enough to pay the sellers' prices and what sellers will offer at prices which compensate their efforts. That is, markets reward gain-seeking: those who lower costs gain more profits; those who seek better paying jobs enjoy higher incomes; those who search for bargains live better and more cheaply. **Consequently, also the free market coordinates gain-seeking: widely practiced, it will be widely shared. If not, the lion's part of output will go to the few who control critical pieces of the economy or, worse, to government.** This affirmed, the darker side of free-enterprise gain-seeking can be viewed squarely: the misery visited on the poor, the slavery and exploitation of labor, the spoliation of the land and pollution of the environment, the carnage of wars of conquest, all the terrible injustices wreaked on the poor and weak by the rich and powerful seeking gain and wealth. Against this backdrop, the question is inevitable whether gain-seeking must inevitably produce such effects.

Put another way, the question asks whether self-interested gain-seeking inevitably tends to selfishness or whether it can intend an altruistic end. Self-interest itself, of course, is not selfishness: as shown earlier, the Good for which a person acts consciously may be for self or for others. Economic self-interest differs somewhat in that it usually encompasses the material *benefit* the act produces. Hence, the question really asks whether self-interest always means self-benefit. Many economists in identifying the two try to shoehorn acts done to benefit others into a person's utility preferences. Such mental gymnastics are unnecessary against the obvious fact that people often seek gain not to benefit themselves but others because they see the act as a good thing to do. Some simple empirical observations will demonstrate that self-interest and self-benefit are not identical, that a self-interested act may be done to benefit someone else.

Because of scarcity gain-seeking always involves exchanging property or services usually for money. Wanting what each other has, buyers and sellers seek to improve their conditions, to gain, by mutually surrendering some of their property for some of the others'. Gain, therefore, is the difference between what exchangers obtain and what they surrender. In real life such transfers of property differ endlessly, producing a continuum from purely selfish stealing, in which the thief's benefit is the owner's loss, to altruistic giving, in which the owner's voluntary loss becomes the beneficiary's gain. Between these extremes property transfers mingle self- and other-benefit in as many combinations as human ingenuity can devise. Those closest to outright theft are fraudulent exchanges in which one party (usually the seller) takes advantage of the other, benefiting at another's loss or lesser benefit. At the center of the transfer continuum would be voluntary and equitable exchange, including lending at interest, where each party benefits at or near parity. Lending one's property, charging no fee or interest, bespeaks some real altruism, the borrower benefiting while the lender does not lose. Even more altruistic is a kind of reciprocity in gift giving, in which the recipient is expected to return a like gift, not equal in value but in affection. At the end, the pure gift, no return expected or possible, yields a net gain since the recipient benefits more than the giver loses.

In hiring or selling human services there is the same balancing of work against compensation and a like exchange continuum, mixing variously self- and other-benefit. Employment can range from slavery through different degrees of exploitation to mutually satisfactory labor contracts. From there workers' benefit may, by way of various kinds of make-work, exceed the employer's. Even more so is compensation now for some anticipated future service. Last and most purely altruistic is compensation for no and no expected work done. Conversely, the work arrangement could reverse the range from no work done through various kinds of feather-bedding, to mutually satisfactory contracts, to working for less than the going wage and on to out-right volunteerism. The common thread running through all three real-life patterns of exchange is not self-benefit but gain-seeking. Whoever or however the exchangers benefit, they intend to make things better. Thus, scarcity still ruling, each party to the exchange must be concerned to use limited means efficiently and, thereby, to realize a greater benefit for whomever intended. Gain, therefore, is still the drive of even the most altruistic economic action. As an essential economic principle, gain-seeking, therefore, because it is potentially of benefit to either or both exchanging parties, is subject to moral precepts.

In much the same way gain-seeking is open to ethical implications on two other accounts. As a maximizing principle gain seeking would seem to require extracting as much profit, rent and consumer surplus as possible, suggesting a gain-seeking run rampant and becoming the infinite appetite philosophers condemned. Such is not the case, however, because gain-seeking is confined within the overall production frontier and more specifically by the gain desires of all others involved in the transaction. Justice itself, as good business practice but more so as a moral guide, will impose limits on gain-seeking by mandating honest dealing with workers, suppliers, customers and governments. Thus the distinction between maximizing, in the sense of getting all one can, and optimizing, getting the most possible given all relevant circumstances, opens this aspect of gain-seeking also to moral considerations.

Finally, economic competition, with its social component that third parties are always involved in and generally beneficiaries of competition, also has moral implications. Competition, especially among sellers, both tends to lower prices and diminishes each's market power. Paradoxically, this means less rivalry and more cooperation. Where markets are subject to wild swings in prices, competitors are more willing to accept rules of the game and to abide by them. On the other hand, the fewer the competitors, the more intense is the rivalry and greater the temptations to immoral practices, spying, luring others' employees, infringing on patents and the like. For the same reason, the fewer the competitors and the larger each's market share, the more they are prompted to collude, to rig bids and to set prices. **The evils which moralists commonly rail against are misdirected against competition but should be aimed at unprincipled rivalry.**

These considerations demonstrate that gain-seeking has several possible beneficiaries, is limited in its compass, and varies greatly in its beneficence depending on how extensive the competition and/or bitter the rivalry. The stage is thus set for examining a moderation, crafted for gain-seeking as a necessary and important economic principle and as an avid appetite. The objects of this appetite, although abstract and lacking in sensual appeal, are not only eagerly sought in and for themselves, but also serve as means by which especially the vital and acquisitive appetites obtain the objects they seek.

A MODERATION FOR MODERNS

That kept in mind will make for more precision not only about what moderation here is to moderate but also how a lack thereof affects others, the economy as a whole as well as the agent's well-being. For example, it is hard to conceive of excessive gain-seeking not involving fraud, coercion and other injustices, not having an impact on the economy. Furthermore, by providing the means to obtain what the other appetites seek, they obviously have moral consequences for the gain-seeker. The first regarding justice was treated in the last chapter. The other forthwith.

The Economics of Moderation

The first hard economic fact arguing for moderation, the economy's **production possibilities frontier** has been mentioned several times already. No matter how intense and widespread the desire for gain, the economy today with its present technology, resources, skills and willingness to work can only produce and distribute so much. If people demand more from the economy than its current production possibilities, they will generate not more goods but higher prices. Translated to the world scene, as was experienced in the post-WWII period of serious inflation in most industrialized economies and run-away inflation in most developing economies is testimony, as Katona points out, that "The simultaneous rise of appetites throughout the world was a major fact in demand exceeding supply and a major explanation of worldwide inflation."[21] Inflation, to be sure, has a monetary dimension reflecting financial community activities and Federal Reserve policy, but ultimately these respond to aggregate pressure for more income and more consumption.

The result in many developed economies was stagflation, a condition of high inflation and low growth, contradicting the conventional wisdom at the time that inflation was growth stimulating. Stagflation by increasing prices, incomes, taxes, book profits and the rest actually inhibits production and employment. In fact it is the mirror image of John Maynard Keynes' (1883-1946) Paradox of Thrift which argued that in depressed times a high rate of savings decreased spending and thus depressed production and decreased incomes, investment and eventually saving itself.[22] **Stagflation, therefore, made clear that the economy must be steered between the Scylla of too much saving and the Charybdis of excessive spending.**

Besides helping to cool inflation, saving is requisite for economic growth. Given reasonably full employment and rising income, an economy can expand only by increasing its capital structure, researching advanced technology, improving managerial and labor skills, opening new markets and responding to changing demands, all of which require huge investments. These in turn require that other sectors of the economy curtail their current wants in order to save. This they are persuaded to do, hoping to gain future income by lending through financial institutions ultimately to investors who go into debt also expecting to reap profits. Gain-seeking, therefore, motivates both savers and investors, shifting expectations of gain from the present to the future. The hope for economic growth means that more cannot be had tomorrow if all current production is consumed today.

Economic moderation, therefore, imposes an obligation on most individuals and families to save and to restrain their credit buying within reasonable expectations of future income. It requires businesses to return a percentage of profits to renew or modernize the plant's productivity, to shore up the business' markets and to maintain its work force. It also makes incumbent on elected officials to administer public monies for the general welfare and to manage spending within reasonable fiscal possibilities and not so as to garner personal prestige or to appease popular appetites. At no time is such moderation needed more than during periods of prosperity. The tendency, when income increases, for wanting and spending to increase faster can generate a culture of euphoria which begets a vicious cycle of price increases urging buying which causes more inflation, stimulating more buying and further inflation. When the good times end and the bubble bursts, the recession is deeper and the gloom replacing euphoria blacker.

All these economic reasons for moderating gain-seeking are confirmed by moral reasons and in turn confirm them.

The Morality of Moderation

Gain-seeking as an appetite with two functions requires two sets of moderating controls. As the appetite seeking income and wealth as means to acquire what the other appetites, especially the vital and acquisitive ones, propose, gain-seeking often paves the way toward an excessive sensuality and vanity. Affluence in particular permits cultivating a variety of sensual pleasures and encourages carrying them to extremes. People will spend billions annually to avoid inconvenience, to mask body odors and blemishes, to flaunt their sexuality and to follow the fashions and foibles of the rich and glamorous. Undisciplined wanting like this can become a cancerous consumption, never fulfilled and constantly goading a person to seek more income and wealth. The Values such sensualists espouse are fleeting and need to be constantly restimulated with more intense or bizarre sensations. Life on that merry-go-round becomes just a string of experiences, lacking real purpose or continuity.

On the other hand, as the appetite for wealth itself, gain-seeking tends to go to extremes in simply piling up paper wealth as symbol of security or superiority, as ego-stroking reward for acuity and competitiveness beyond the ordinary, and as source of economic power. All such frequently manifest a greed which is careless of the rights of others, which tempts to flaunt the law and often jeopardizes careers in reaching for one more bribe or seeking one more crooked deal. Greed in turn begets others' envy which is greed's poor but acidulous relation with all its meanness but without its drive or ability to gain.

Some, applying Mandeville's sophism that private vices are public virtues to contemporary times, will excuse both prodigal spending and greedy gain-seeking as keeping the economy going. The kernel of truth in this must be balanced by the economy's greater need for saving from today's output for tomorrow's growth and for sharing as an essentially social and cooperative effort. Thus a gain-seeking run amuck cannot only indulge the pleasures and superficialities of prodigal spending and feed avarice's promise of power and prestige, but it can subvert the collaboration and cooperation inherent in economic actions, causing not progress but stagnation.

Despite the harm self-interested gain-seeking can do, no one can advance a reasonable argument for suppressing it. Communism tried to eliminate private gain-seeking and failed egregiously. Controls on it can be set by government, by individuals themselves or by a combination of both. Social controls, both laws and customs, help by setting clear and universal conditions for conduct, but they can stifle initiative and are inflexible in application. Self-control, on the other hand, besides respecting laws and customs, directs income, wealth, gain and the rest to ends and purposes beyond the merely sensate and egoistic to more social, spiritual and absolute needs and Values. So described, the virtue sought is what Aristotle defined over 2000 years ago and called Liberality. He is worth quoting at length:

> Therefore, the liberal man, like other virtuous men, will give for the sake of the noble, and rightly; for he will give to the right people, the right amounts, and at the right time;... and that too with pleasure or without pain.... But no more will the liberal man take from wrong sources; for such taking is not characteristic of the man who sets no store by wealth. Nor will he be a ready asker; for it is not characteristic of a man who confers benefits to accept them lightly. But he will take from right sources, e.g. from his own possessions; not as something noble but as a necessity, that he may have something to give. Nor will he neglect his own property, since he wishes by means of this to help others.[23]

Translated to the contemporary scene, Aristotle's liberal persons would not be averse to gain-seeking. Rather they would work their properties and exploit their skills to optimize gain, observing justice all the while. But their emphasis would shift toward dispensing benefactions in ways to do the most good, taking care first of their own and their families' needs and development and then that of others, bestowing their assistance according to their obligations and the benefits to be achieved. Gain-seeking, therefore, plays a necessary role in both liberal persons' getting and giving of wealth.

In particular, liberality breaks the pattern of conformism, substituting personal or family Value aspirations, which differ from the majority's. For business leaders it means hewing to reasonable expectations, ignoring quick-riches schemes to seek profits in the ways they know how, by producing efficiently, rewarding their employees justly and servicing their customers honestly. Further, the moderation liberality imposes steers a course between puritanically suppressing and indulging the appetites. It counters materialism's downward drag by raising a person's Value sights from the sensual, superficial and selfish to the more spiritual and sacred and especially to concern for others' needs. For the very wealthy it reveals Value vistas, both personal and social, which will absorb their surplus ambition, energy and wealth. For the vast majority such moderation does not forbid seeking higher income but rather directs them toward using it well. All of this suggests that moderation is more than just good will but combines economic rationality with a keen sense of obligation to use wealth to foster one's personal and family's well-being and to help those less- and dis-advantaged.

In this respect people are not without help for ways to use their surplus income and wealth well. A large industry is at hand to apprise the generous of the vast array of physical, social, cultural and moral needs and to help them respond according to their preferences and resources. In a world where every nation's poverty is known, the scope of liberality is unlimited. Indeed the Lazarus of human need is begging at every gate, and the obligation to respond falls on just about everyone, even the modestly circumstanced.

Personal gain-seeking thus becomes a help toward espousing Values which relate to lasting Goods, the alleviation of others' needs, and such cultural, spiritual and moral Values which are lasting contributions to society, education, culture and religion. Consequently, the moderate live life not at a sensual, materialistic and egoistic level but where they experience all its aspects, tasting the bitterness of the suffering and the joy of the felicitous, sharing their own and others' successes as well as failures. **Just as their gain-seeking in this way gains a fuller measure of moral meaning and functions at a deeper level of personal interaction, so all combine to yield a more complete contentment.**

ENDNOTES

1. Aristotle, *Nichomachean Ethics, op. cit.*, bk. X, ch. 5.
2. Plato, *Laws, op. cit.*, V, 740-6.
3. Aristotle, *Politics, op. cit.*, bk. 1, ch. 9.
4. Aristotle, *Nicomachean Ethics, op. cit.*, bk. 4, ch. 3.
5. Augustine, *On Christian Doctrine, op. cit.*, bk. 1, chs. 3-4.
6. Aquinas, *op. cit.*, I-II, q. 84 a.1.
7. *ibid.*, II-II, q. 77 a.4.
8. Calvin, John, *Institutes of the Christian Religion*, ed. J.T. McNeill, tr. F.L. Battles. *Library of Christian Classics*, v. 20, Philadelphia: The Westminster Press, p. 798.

9. Calvin, pp. 719-725.
10. Montesquieu, *The Spirit of the Laws*, tr. T. Nugent, rev. J.V. Prichard, London: G.Bell & Sons, bk v, ch. 7, sec. 6.
11. See any history of economics. A recommended short study is *A History of Economic Thought* by Eric Roll, London: Faber and Faber, 1961, chs. II and III.
12. Mandeville, Bernard, *Fable of the Bees*, 2d ed. London, 1723.
13. Schumpeter, *op. cit.*, pp. 233-43.
14. Hume, *op.cit., A Treatise on Human Nature*, p. 452 and *Of Interest*, p. 53.
15. Smith, Adam, *The Theory of Moral Sentiments, op. cit.*, p. 154 and *Wealth of Nations, op. cit.*, bks. 1 and 2.
16. Roll, *op.cit.*, ch. VI.
17. Hofstadter, Richard, *Social Darwinism in American Thought*, Boston: The Beacon Press, 1955.
18. Tawney, R. H., *The Acquisitive Society*, London: G. Bell & Sons, 1921.
19. Mill, J. S., *On Liberty*, Chicago: Encyclopaedia Britannica, 1955, v. 43, pp.304-12.
20. Hegel, G. W. F., *The Philosophy of Right*, tr. T.M. Knox, London: Oxford University Press, 1967, III, par. 240.
21. Katona, George, *Psychological Economics*, New York: Elsivier, 1975, p.400.
22. Keynes, John Maynard, *The General Theory of Employment, Interest and Money*, London: Macmillan & Co., Ltd., 1936.
23. Aristotle, *Nicomachean Ethics, op. cit.*, Bk. 4, ch. 1.

GLOSSARY

agent—Here understood as the person who performs and is responsible for a given act.

Calvinism—The doctrine preached by John Calvin, emphasizing human depravity, God's sovereignty and human predestination, and characterized by an austere moral code.

concupiscence—A tendency toward inordinate or illicit appetites or desires, especially the carnal, sensual and sexual kinds.

connaturality—The innate characteristics of a thing which relates it as similar in nature to another.

de-moralization—The process of progressive erosion of a certain kind of acts' moral implications.

featherbedding—The deliberate slowing down of work in order to generate more employment than necessary.

Invisible Hand—The contention made famous by Adam Smith that free market competition produces more socially beneficial results, unintentionally of the desires of the participants, than by intentional public policy.

liberality—Aristotle's conception includes not only the contemporary notion of generosity but the more general idea of using surplus wealth and money in such wise as to help others, e.g. by investing in a business, thus creating jobs.

make-work—Work which is not really necessary, which an employer generates to keep workers employed.

Milquetoast—Originally a cartoon character but now anyone who is excessively cautious or timid.

reciprocity—The state existing between two parties by which one returns in due but not equal measure the charity or kindness of another.

Scylla and Charybdis—A rock opposite a whirlpool which made for a hazardous passage for Ulysses; therefore, any course of action between two unfavorable consequences, either of which is difficult to avoid without incurring the other.

sinecure—Any office, job or position which pays compensation but entails little or no responsibility or work.

stagflation—A condition of the economy characterized by both stagnant or declining production and inflation.

utility preference—Ranking an economic object on the basis of its perceived usefulness.

theocracy—A form of government in which a priest class rules by religious norms and principles.

volunteerism—A willingness to perform valuable services for another without compensation.

TOPICS FOR FURTHER DISCUSSION OR RESEARCH

1. Demonstrate that prodigality in spending for sensual pleasures and for glamor almost inevitably (in view of scarcity) results in courses of action which transgress social justice.

2. Read Mandeville's *Fable of the Bees* (only the poem itself). In what sense and to what degree is it valid in application to today's industrial economies? In what way does it fall short as a complete theory of economic growth?

3. Reread "Gain-seeking's Economic Role" specifically that part distinguishing between self-interest and self-benefit. Then cite specific examples which illustrate each of the three sets of exchange relationships. Don't search for exotic examples but use homely ones from everyday life, e.g. selling fertilized eggs advertised as fresh.

ADDITIONAL SUGGESTED READING

1. Eric Roll, *A History of Economic Thought*, London: Faber and Faber, Ltd., 1961, chs. II, III and IV.
2. Willhelm Roepke, *Economics of a Free Society*, Chicago: Henry Regnery Company, 1963, chs. I-III, V and VI, excluding the notes.
3. R.H. Tawney, *The Acquisitive Society*, New York: Harcourt, and Company, 1948, chs. 1-4, 9 and 11.
4. Bernard Mandeville, *The Fable of the Bees: or Private Vices, Publick Benefits*, Oxford: Clarendon Press, 1924. (Read the poem, "The Grumbling Hive: or Knaves Turned Honest," and "An Inquiry into the Origin of Virtue and Remarks," pp. 21-153) ed. by Irwin Primer, New York: Capricorn Books, 1962.

CHAPTER SEVEN

SPIRITUAL POVERTY: A THEOLOGY OF WEALTH

All the elements of **economic morality**, with one exception, have now been spelled out. 1) It reflects the complexity and intentionality of the human person. 2) It accepts the basic fact of economic scarcity as well as self-interested gain-seeking, competition, collaboration and the cultural constructs, prices, profits, gain, wealth and the rest, as necessary for the economic process. 3) It relates the formation and espousal of Values to moral development and regards economic actions as valid means toward constructing one's Value hierarchy, being especially wary that the economic appetite tends to favor lower over higher Values. 4) It realizes that a sense of justice is needed to respect others' (especially economic) rights. 5) Finally, it controls the materialistic proclivities of economic aspirations by redirecting them toward higher Values.

The study, therefore, has now blended moral and economic principles into an operational moral attitude except for one all important component, its ultimate end and purpose. **That is, the question remains whether this weighty and complex moral effort has a religious dimension.** While all religions and philosophies have wrestled with the problem of finding some final meaning for business and commercial activities, the most developed theology of wealth is found in the Judeo-Christian tradition. Paradoxically it is expressed as the **Spirit of Poverty**. The skepticism this statement often provokes requires examining that spirit's implications for conduct and economic rationality's compatibility with it. Prior to this, however, some clarification about what religion means in this study's context would be helpful.

THE RELIGIOUS DIMENSION

Religion today, unlike in most earlier civilizations, fits uncomfortably into modern living. Since it relates to an after life, many consider it irrelevant to this or, at best, advert to it only in moments of fear, grief and sometimes joy. A few deny it dogmatically. Nevertheless, religion answers the basic questions which surface even in the most sensate life: Who and Why am I? Does this life have any meaning and what comes after it? **Religion insists that life has meaning by affirming that all finite beings are dependent upon an Infinite Being.**

Life's Origin and End

In contemplating their essential realities men and women are faced with two mind-boggling facts: l) every human life is but a spark of self-awareness between two impenetrable silences, eons prior to coming into being and probably eons after its present existence ends; and 2) the possibility is infinitesimal that any particular individual would ever come into existence. All the fortuities of ancestral mating considered, the chance that this sperm of this man would fertilize this ovum of this woman becomes minuscule to the vanishing point. (When mother in frustration exclaims, "This kid is simply impossible!", she is, mathematically speaking, absolutely correct.) Religion resolves this difficulty by affirming that every creature's coming into and going out of existence is determined by an Infinite Being. Judeo-Christianity adds that only an Infinite Love could will every creature's individual existence and maintain it in being. This answer in turn answers the first question: **every life and every aspect of it has infinite meaning and a destiny which surpasses finite understanding.**

Granted that none of religion's answers yields absolute certitude, agnosticism or outright atheism gives no greater certainty. Moreover, denying religious meaning and purpose to human life denies ultimate meaning and purpose to everything.

With no reason for being nor goal to seek, human existence makes no sense at all. Relationships, however perceived, are purely fortuitous and a-rational. **Things happen because they do: no one is responsible for anything and no one can claim anything as his or her own.** Law, Science, Love, Life and Death are ultimately meaningless, as is this assertion. Thus neither the deist nor atheist can claim certified certitude. But the former is at least logical in asserting that actions and relationships may denote causality, purpose and meaning. From this the atheist is precluded because to assert meaning is to say that something is a means to an end, which in turn will ultimately require a Final Reason and a Reality which simply exists of itself.

Religion and the Economic Process

Applying this logic of ultimate meaning to the economic process forces one to conclude that, for this vast complex of activities and relationships to make sense, it must have a religious meaning. This logic, nevertheless, is resisted by those who would remove economic striving from the religious (even the moral) sphere and seemingly by religion itself, which generally lauds poverty as the better way to union with the divine and the poor as God's special clients. The Judeo-Christian tradition of **poverty of spirit** especially presents three precepts seemingly contrary to that spirit of gain which drives the free economy.

1. Religious Values are the sacred, the most absolute, Values; gain-seeking of all appetites pursues the most fleeting and unsubstantial objects and the least relevant aid to union with the Divine.

2. But in fact the spirit of poverty goes beyond indifference to riches to encouraging effective poverty, real need, whose possible elimination is perhaps the only moral and social justification of economic abundance; and

3. The spirit of doing without for the sake of a higher Good seems to contradict the fundamental drive of gain-seeking and the desire to satisfy ever more wants.

Yet the paradox that the **spirit of poverty** may actually be the basis for a theology of wealth is no more inconceivable than that abundance increases scarcity and generates poverty. The Judeo-Christian postulate of a loving God certainly does not suggest that the divine plan for people is that they live out their lives here in abject destitution. Indeed, spiritual poverty was preached and practiced most sincerely in that civilization which created the blueprint for abundance and promoted it worldwide into cultures more ancient and advanced than its own. All this encourages pursuing the paradox wherever it leads and requires considering and then relating two precepts of conduct: 1) religion has always preached that how a person seeks, uses and shares material goods is important for achieving one's ultimate destiny and 2) the principles which govern the production, pricing and distribution of commodities and wealth are valid and presumably, therefore, compatible with religious aspirations. **Together they suggest that economic aspirations can be infused with the spirit of poverty**

THE SPIRIT OF POVERTY

The Judeo-Christian religious tradition is not unique in warning of materialism's spiritual dangers, of the duty to help others and even of the preferability of poverty to riches in seeking spiritual well-being. All religions and moral philosophies have some version of these mandates. But they are more elaborated in the Judeo-Christian tradition. There the spirit of poverty is integral to that religion's dual thrust, that to love God requires loving and serving one's neighbor. The economic implication of this mandates not only being provident of scarce material goods but showing gratitude for God's gifts by sharing them with others and by helping bear their burdens.

In that tradition the **spirit of poverty** has passed through many deaths and revivals. Like the olive tree it has roots which tap the deepest springs and like it has endured for millennia, surviving several civilizations and many cycles of growth and decline, at each revival acquiring renewed strength and revealing new facets of its riches. **Spiritual poverty**, therefore, cannot be defined: as an organic principle it must be lived to be understood and even then escapes full comprehension. Some sketch of its growth from embryo in primitive Judaism, as Grelot explains,[1] to its internalization as a principal theme in Jewish life and to its full manifestation in Christ and subsequent flowering in Christian practice will give some idea of its informing and transforming power.

Its Biblical Manifestations

Spiritual poverty, according to Gelin, is one of the seminal concepts of the Old Testament, organically linked to the alliance and justice as 'nuances' of the faith of Israel. As the covenantal people, Israel is chosen to witness to Yahweh's faithfulness, who, fulfilling his promises to Abraham, freed them from slavery in Egypt and led them for a generation through the wilderness to a land of their own, promising material plenty. Their being faithful in turn meant living upright and irreroachable lives, dependent on Yahweh as clients, open to and humble before Him, trusting Him and sharing their goods with others. In short, they were the poor of Yahweh.[2]

Biblical poverty is never really defined. Rather the concept plays upon several related themes. Sometimes it implies destitution, often the lower classes, occasionally the afflicted or depressed and always the humble and lowly. Sometimes poverty is called an infliction for sin or more frequently divine retribution for Israel's faithlessness or the scandal of the rich and powerful neglecting or wronging the poor. Most often poverty implies a middle state between abundance and penury as the state most conducive for virtuous living. Out of this mix and ferment of ideas, poverty acquired its religious aura: the poor were the clients of Yahweh, not only depending on Him but doing His will.[3] The emphasis on the obligation to share was, therefore, both a warning against the seductiveness of wealth and an affirmation that the desired standard and benchmark for all was the mean between extravagance and destitution. This was spelled out in Mosaic law as recorded in Deuteronomy.[4]

Much of the Mosaic moral code, scholars now confirm, reflects earlier Babylonian, Egyptian, Hittite and Middle Eastern thought. What differentiates it is its clarity and its unique perception of God, while transcending all powers and principalities, as intimate to the lives and well-being of the people. The Deuteronomic prescriptions are not derived from mandates of the common Good or public order, but they are from God, speaking to and for His people. **Doing the divine will, therefore, requires necessarily loving others and serving their needs.**

God reminds the Israelites that he took delight in giving them prosperity and increase,[5] but warns them not to become proud of heart, since it was he who brought them out of Egypt, "out of the house of slavery."[6] Thus he commands them always to be open-handed with their countrymen, indeed with anyone in need and poor.[7] Do not harvest the fields and vineyards to the last bit, but leave some for the gleaners, for strangers, orphans and widows.[8] In the 3rd year tithe the produce, giving it to strangers, Levites, widows and orphans.[9] Pay wages owed promptly.[10] Slaves are to be freed after six years and dismissed with generous help.[11] Do not take away another's livelihood as pledge for debt.[12] Above all do not pervert justice in dealing especially with the poor.[13] In sum, all are admonished to respect the dignity of the poor as persons and warned not to use power to exploit them. Quite the opposite, Deuteronomy's prescriptions engendered an attitude of generosity, imitating Yahweh's bounteousness and flowing from a deep trust in Divine Providence. This trust was to be severely tested in adversity.

Israel seldom played a noteworthy role in the flux of empire in the Middle East during the two millennia before Christ, being for most of that time either subject to or client of more powerful nations. That they survived as a people over centuries of living under alien rule owes much to their internalizing the spirit of poverty whose practice, far from being minimized, was intensified and raised to a higher and more demanding level. The catastrophe visited on Samaria (721 B.C.) and then on Judah (586 B.C.) contributed much to this change in attitude, as the Remnant of Israel accepted the chastisement which the prophets proclaimed as punishment for forsaking Yahweh. The same period of suffering and subjection produced some of the most powerful literary works, two of which are of prime importance in internalizing poverty: the dramatic poem *Job* and *Isaiah*, especially Second Isaiah's four "Songs of the Servant of Yahweh."

These two works dramatize the spiritual struggle to internalize poverty. *Job*, the story of the just man struck down by disasters, presents two lessons: physical evil is not punishment for sin and calls not for people's reprobation but their sympathy, because, this being the other all-important lesson, God's ways transcend human understanding, challenging humble assent whatever they entail. Implicitly, if people must accept God's inscrutable directions, all the more so they must honor his clear commands, including especially loving and helping others. This is the point of take-off for Isaiah's Servant of Yahweh or Suffering Servant, who not only bears others' burdens but suffers humiliation and harm in assuming the faults, failings and, in a sense, the sins of others, thereby freeing them of the consequences of their mistakes and misdeeds. **Internalizing spiritual poverty elevates its practice to the heroic level.**

The Remnant of Israel, in experiencing persecution, subjugation and exile and forced to accept real poverty, realized that the Divine promises would come in God's good time, and, accepting persecution, humbly awaited God's assistance. So doing, they drew closer together as a people, succoring each other in their needs and encouraging them in faithfulness to God and in awaiting their redeeming Messiah. Internalized poverty, while emphasizing more relying on Divine Providence and awaiting the will of God, nevertheless, was still a theology of wealth in that it strongly encouraged the practice of social justice and social charity both of which are decisive not only in helping people stick together but in promoting their economic well-being.

Christian Poverty: The Final Revelation

In Christian beliefs Christ, as the Servant of Yahweh incarnate, is the final revelation of the **spirit of poverty**. The dimension he adds is what he lived: preferring poverty to riches, he worked most of his life as a village craftsman; during his short public mission, he and his disciples survived on hand outs; despite ambitions to convert the world, he made no plans to fund the effort. While Christ's life was a paean of praise of poverty, he never condemned wealth, numbering many well-to-do among his friends and was not above enjoying the goods things of this life. He warns, however, in an uncompromising way of the seductiveness of wealth and the obligation to share with the needy. Luke's four maledictions, "Woe to you rich.... Woe to you who have your fill now" and so forth,[14] echo repeatedly in his parables and comments about the rich and their undoing.

In all this Christ shows his preference for and identification with the poor, the sick and the outcast. Whatever is done for them in his name is done for him, such acts being the way to salvation. Indeed those followers he especially calls must sell all and give it to the poor. For such detachment from wealth he urges complete trust in the Father, who knows everyone's shortcomings, both personal and economic, and will provide what is necessary. Prefer instead poverty to riches and spiritual to material wealth, shouldering whatever burden life imposes and following Christ. For Christians, therefore, spiritual poverty requires four elements: complete commitment to God's will; freedom, though not divorce, from reliance on material riches; preferring poverty to wealth as evidence of complete trust in Divine Providence; and seeing the sacramental nature of the poor since in serving them one encounters Christ and thus God. To these Yonick perceives a fifth element: the spirit of poverty's all-embracing creativity as revealed in Christian practices through the centuries.[15]

The apostolic Christians took Christ's teaching as applying to all and not just to the chosen few.[16] Paul's advice to Timothy outlines the Christian attitude to wealth and its uses: Warn those who are rich in this world's goods that they are not to look down on other people; and not to set

> their hopes on money, which is untrustworthy, but on God who, out of his riches, gives us all we need for

our happiness. Tell them they are to do good, and to
be generous and willing to share.[17]

Christian communities were probably typical socio-economically of urban society at that time. They differed in holding to the ideal of detachment from wealth, using wealth as means to unite their communities so that all could develop into full humanity and Christianity. The vigor of Christian life, therefore, can often be gauged by how fervently the spirit of poverty is practiced. Languishing at times, it always revives freshly vigorous and creatively contemporary in meeting the needs of its age, each flowering revealing another facet of poverty's appeal.[18]

Detachment from material goods and trust in God were the strengths of both the Christian martyrs whose heroism vanquished Rome and the desert hermits whose strenuous self-denial preached against urban decadence. Monasticism, especially that based on the rule of Benedict of Nursia (480-543), drew much of its spiritual power from the monk's vow of poverty. Blending communal prayer and worship, cooperative labor and social charity, most monasteries provided hospitality to travelers, charity to the needy, while promoting learning, the arts and architecture. Attracting both members and benefaction, they dotted Europe from Ireland to Mesopotamia, some housing but a handful of women or men, others rivaling cities in the number of members, retainers and serfs. Many accumulated vast wealth, resulting often in increasing worldliness and mandating reform. Cluny, Citeaux, La Trappe, each renewal of the Benedictine spirit, rekindled the zeal for the common life and service to others; each illuminated another facet of **spiritual poverty**.

But Francis of Assisi (1188-1226) really revolutionized monasticism by making his followers beg for subsistence, all the while serving the poor and preaching the love of Christ and joy in all God's creatures. Although freed of the management and feudal entanglements of endowed estates, Franciscan and Dominican friars were soon teaching at universities, founding hospices and small-loan shops for the urban poor. Jesuit poverty, as stringent as Franciscan in that the monk owned nothing, was more practical. Ignatius of Loyola (1491-1556) wanted his followers to live and to use material goods according to what their work required, as a missionary or university professor or brother porter. Such pragmatic poverty produced both the mission cooperatives among native peoples and spurred an educational revolution in Europe.

Through these changes the laity's spirit of poverty waxed and waned with that of the hierarchy, clergy and monks. Luther, Calvin, Wesley and other Reformers were more explicit in presenting **spiritual poverty**, as a practical guide for lay living. Much of the zeal driving the Reformation paradoxically both blessed privation and sanctioned prosperity. The doctrine of the Layman's Vocation—to work diligently, to live soberly, and to await the Lord's coming—proved to be a formula for modest economic success, but it also supplied moral meaning to accumulating wealth at a time when fortunes could be made and lost.

However the Protestant Ethic is often maligned as cant, it has sparked real concern for the poor. Despite the disruption of people's lives and the creation of the urban proletariat, which the Industrial Revolution caused, the modern era has seen a vast expansion of social services, largely through the efforts of people from all Christian denominations who were inspired by the spirit of poverty. Don Bosco brought education to the poor; Vincent de Paul and Florence Nightingale revolutionized hospital care; John Howard and Elizabeth Frye did much to temper the brutal treatment of prisoners and debtors; and Thomas Clarkson and William Wilberforce worked to abolish the heinous slave trade. These and many others began the private efforts to assist the less fortunate, from which most of modern welfare programs are derived.

On the other hand, the fact that responsibility for the poor and impaired has passed to the state and that the spirit of poverty has faded into a secular humanitarianism owes much to the decline of the spirit of poverty amongst both Protestants and Catholics. Puritan and Jansenistic tendencies turn virtues into bleak behavior and often regard the real deprivations the poor suffer as blessings, since they are seen, if born submissively, as evidencing the spirit of poverty. This view of spiritual poverty, in becoming an excuse for disregarding others' needs, played into the hands of a secular ethics which, contrasting wealth as a good with poverty as evil, turned social charity into a civic obligation. Marx went further, making the increasing immizeration of the proletariat the necessary stage in the inevitable transformation of capitalism into communism.

However Marx is discredited today, his tenet that the unmitigated evil of poverty is produced by economic abundance, has taken deep root in public consciousness. Consequently, many, imbued with the spirit of poverty, will agree with secularists that government must wipe out sociological and economic poverty by whatever means, even to violating the poor's dignity as human persons. Even more paradoxically secular states find it necessary in this effort to enlist the aid of social service institutions motivated by religious convictions and supported by church groups. Thus submerged under and confused with the secular state's sysiphean agenda to wipe out sociological poverty, the spirit of poverty is set for refurbishing and rebirth. **Recalling its features will help to redeem, fulfill and give meaning to the gain-seeking which drives the modern economy.**

Far from being harsh, joyless and despairing, the spirit of poverty as a theology of wealth celebrates dependence on a bountiful God and emulates divine generosity by sharing with those in need. It urges its devotees to assume others' burdens even to sacrificing their own well-being, doing for the lowliest as if for Christ. Such is the detachment from material goods required by the spirit of poverty which, neither spurning riches as evil nor seduced by their spurious guarantees of happiness, simply uses wealth as a means to develop as a person and to help others. While demanding effort to become habitual, the spirit of poverty will bless its practitioners with strength in adversity, freedom from worldly cares and inner peace and stability. Joyful yet practical in doing good, it maps a way both laity and professed religious can live. Indeed spiritual poverty has been a creative force in rooting out the brutality which used to mar many social institutions and in inspiring a vast array of social helps for the poor, the impaired and the unfortunate. **This same creativity can do much to clarify the ambiguities and ambivalence of contemporary abundance and to fill up the emptiness which seems to lie at its heart.**

THE POVERTY OF ABUNDANCE

That effort really responds to the perhaps unasked question whether abundance needs a theology of wealth. As a force freeing people from penury, as a civilizing agent and self-fueling dynamism does abundance need goal or purpose transcending this material world? On the other hand, without an ultimate goal and purpose, would its freedom tend to self-destruction, its progress create discord, and its dynamism generate insecurity? That little worm of doubt advises looking further.

The Freedom of Abundance

All are aware that affluent people have been freed of many of the natural constraints of the past. As with youths off to college or getting a first job, the larger scope of freedom is a heady experience which at the same time brings the sobering and often terrifying facts of personal responsibility. Rahner sees the present age as a watershed in the history of the human race in being freed in so many ways from the constraints of nature:

> The God of history is entrusting man to an increasing degree to himself, whereas he used to protect him much more from himself by confining him within the necessity of nature . . . Much that was essentially right in his life, much of his morality, was the effect, not of his freedom responsibly exercised, but of the salutary compulsion practiced by Mother Nature on her still infantile offspring, man, allowing him only relatively narrow scope for acts of freedom.
>
> Today it is different. Man is beginning to carry out the task, laid on him in paradise, of subduing the earth, on a hitherto unimaginable scale. There is

> nowhere he cannot go. He can control his own breeding processes, he can make artificial materials that are better than those provided by nature; he can plan himself; he is even thinking of leaving behind this earth which God created as man's home . . . . He has been largely successful in protecting himself against nature, which he sees as cruel and heartless towards man . . . And behold, in protecting himself against nature he has lost the protection which she afforded him against himself, and man is delivered defenseless into his own hands, to all the errant possibilities of his freedom, to his own hubris, to his everlasting temptation to be as God, i.e., to be someone bound by no reality outside himself, no law higher than himself... **Man escaped from nature—protective, nurturing, limiting, formative nature—is handed over to himself, to his destructive intemperance and lack of intellectual bounds.** [19]

Applied to the economy, Rahner's words describe what the Abundance Revolution has wrought. Economic self-interest, by exploiting contemporary science, technology and industry, has not only freed people from a myriad of natural restraints, but has alleviated much of the world's destitution, pauperism, drudgery and hardship. But it can also spell disaster when not controlled by justice and moderation. Greed can destroy political and professional careers, bankrupt families, ruin banks and businesses, cause senseless industrial strife and send people to jail. But even if restrained by justice and moderation, economic self-interest by itself provides no real goal or purpose: the pleasures it promises are ephemeral and the contentment it predicts illusionary. **The freedom abundance bestows is freedom *from* restraints but not freedom *for* a lasting Good.**

Abundance as Civilizing Agent

The Abundance Revolution has not only ameliorated living and humanized working conditions generally for common folk but has spread western civilization over the globe. Western dress, business practice, architecture, communication and transportation have dramatically changed peoples' structure of living worldwide. Western literature, art, music, films and television are available not only in the hinterlands of industrialized nations but widely in other developed and developing countries. Western medicine has wiped out diseases which have plagued peoples for centuries. Western science has mapped the earth, explored the universe, traced the development of *homo sapiens,* explored lost civilizations and recovered more history in the last 200 years than in all prior ages. Abundance has colonized vast, largely empty lands: Siberia, Australia, North and much of South America. It has imported much of the culture of ancient civilizations, both the Atlantic and the Pacific ceasing to be barriers to the movement of peoples and goods.

All in all, Abundance has created a world economy and in so doing made world conflict, such as has plagued the West for centuries, unthinkable. Finally, economic abundance holds the best promise of wiping out destitution in the developing world, given the help of affluent countries and the common sense and public decency of Third World leaders in using their aid.

For all that, many people believe that economic abundance has more failed than fulfilled the promises made in its name. It has turned the United States into a neurotic multi-trillionaire, jittery at every decline of the leading indicators even after years of unprecedented prosperity. It looks apprehensively at the more rapid growth and trading strengths of friendly nations, wearies of its international responsibilities and is becoming paranoid at possible inflation, a staggering national debt, deteriorating environment and competitive disadvantages.

Abundance has not brought the affluent peace of mind, generating instead the competitive rat-race, the pressure for social conformity and the strain of keeping expenses and debts within income. More and more people have been "marginalized," have dropped out of the main economic stream or barely subsist on its edges. The number of homeless and hungry, whatever the causes, is a source of embarrassment. Divorce in destroying families often plunges children into poverty. Large city school systems are failing egregiously to educate especially the poor: in addition to drop-outs, they graduate a large percentage of unemployables and functionally illiterates. Even their graduates are disenchanted, the brightest often determined to get all they can and the idealists turned off by the rampant materialism.

The social environment is chaotic. Taxes mount, while services decline. Travel is a hassle. Petty stealing is all but ignored and public order seems at the mercy of any group which chooses to disrupt it for whatever purpose. Drug and alcohol addiction is pandemic. Crime clogs the courts and jails, while confirmed homicides, rapists and thieves are paroled to the streets. Corrupt and rapacious officials are often rewarded and the honest dismissed. While minorities, public employees, lobbyists, bureaucrats and like are fighting for government tid-bits, taxpayers are up in arms, renters and landlords polarized, welfare-recipients aggrieved, and business leaders complaining. But such domestic discord pales by contrast with the unending string of political coups, revolutions, ethnic and class warfare throughout the world, all usually with an economic component.

Accentuating personal distress is the feeling that modern technology has diminished the human person. Caught in vast webs of production, financial and marketing processes which seem to run on abstract formulae and appear immune from personal influences, people often must yield to computers' making decisions and determining action. More frustrating are the bureaucracies, especially governmental, which will often entangle a person in endless red-tape before anyone accepts responsibility to address the problem. Things do happen but the gears mesh tediously. In sum, the positive cultural benefits abundance provides must be balanced against technocracy's tendency to diminish the human person and against people's disenchantment with the quality of life and the social disorders abundance produces. **Above all neither praise for benefits nor blame for evils imply an ultimate meaning and purpose for economic abundance.**

The Dynamism of Abundance

Abundance requires change and change means insecurity and the feeling that life is transient and unstable. Change of any kind or at any stage in the economic process sets off chain reactions which affect production patterns, employment relations, investment opportunities, consumption behavior and price levels. All these, because change is never totally predictable, involve risk. By upsetting previous calculations and the decisions based on them, they imperil corporate profits, stockholders' dividends and stock values, employees' earnings and jobs and product sales. The larger the firm, the more the whole economy is affected. While such change is endemic to business, it increases exponentially when a general spirit of gain-seeking is striving to increase incomes, profits and wages by inciting consumers to want more and different goods and services. Discretionary income itself permits highly volatile spending; capital is very fluid, moving from one industry to another as profits beckon; professionals, managers and highly skilled workers can usually change employment but not always readily. New **demands, new products, new technology keep the economy in continuous ferment, a ferment itself varying unpredictably.**

Such dynamism necessitates planning for change. Analyzing shifting markets, researching new products, devising new techniques, upgrading labor skills, finding better suppliers, building prototypes and testing the market become more important than producing for current demand. Survival requires going beyond serving today's market to anticipating tomorrow's by responding to changes others generate and by updating one's own product line, techniques and marketing methods. A business must be especially alert to scientific advances coming from corporate, university and government laboratories and try to translate them into products, technologies and sales. **Change, truly, makes for a zestful struggle to stay abreast, a triumph to gain an inch.**

But change is not without its trauma. It makes economic predictions frustratingly uncertain, which, while embarrassing to economic gurus, has serious consequences for government budgetary policy and for business decisions to invest or not, to expand or contract, to hire or lay off and the like. All such, of course, reverberates through the economy, sales reacting to buying, incomes to production, production in turn to sales and investment to overall business conditions. This web of interdependence means that when one strand is plucked the whole system vibrates. Change itself changes because it produces permanent differences in the economic landscape. New markets, new management, new technologies can kill or revive a business, millions of which are born and die every year. Even the giants are not immune from the ravages of change. Recalling the names of corporations, which dominated decades ago but are now dwarfs of what they were, A&P, U.S. Steel, Montgomery Ward, New York Central and the like, confirms the fact of industrial instability.

People skilled in reading economic signs may be psychologically forearmed against the vagaries of change. But the vast majority of people drift uncertain and confused on the sea of economic fluctuations and get in a fret over the latest business news or office rumor. But change is a fact of life for most: markets dry up, techniques change, jobs run out, Such changes means that different jobs, neighborhoods, friends, social status and levels of living are forced on people and there is little they can do about it. **Such is the uncertainty, insecurity and trauma abundance can cause in this life, all of which is often reflected in perplexity about the next.**

An Ontological Poverty

Beyond the cupidity, discord and insecurity abundance often entails, it is most often faulted by social critics because it does not mitigate but exacerbates poverty. Such criticism both hits true and is wide of the mark. In abundant and dynamic economies the wealth of the most affluent will increase faster than that of the poorest. Even if increases in the nation's income were distributed proportionately, everyone's income increasing at the same rate, the absolute increase of the wealthiest would be much greater than that of the poorest. Hence, while the poor would enjoy more income and the well-being it would bring, they would still be falling behind everyone else. On the other hand, all the evidence indicates that, except for a small percentage of the very poor and of the very rich, the life-cycles of most people show movement up and down the economic scale.[20]

Criticism of this kind, while justified in pointing out that poverty is real in developed economies because the poor do experience real deprivation, nevertheless, honesty insists that the **poverty amid abundance** is far from the mass destitution prevailing in economies which for whatever reason—war, climate, resource depletion, primitive technology, political tyranny—cannot produce enough food, clothing, shelter, health care and other necessities for decent living. Secondly, the most hard core and unyielding poverty is not due to structural weaknesses in the economy but is more specific to persons and individual families: health, mental problems, addictions, poor education, divorce, discrimination and the like. Even a vigorous economy cannot resolve such problems. Rather they must be addressed one by one. Almost always also there are innocent people involved, children usually, who are salvageable as persons and as useful participants in the economy, if helped in time. Critics, careless in confusing economic and behavioral causes of poverty, will compound, not find solutions to, the problems.

Critics are on surer ground when warning against ontological rather than socio-economic poverty at the heart of abundance. The drive for more, more profits and more wealth, can result in crowding one's life with sense experiences, each more engaging than the other. Such questing means that no material good and no experience can be fully savored nor seen in relation to an ultimate end. Glutted with goods, the affluent may forget what life is all about. By contrast and without romanticizing poverty, the poor may get greater pleasure from the little they have and greater joy from every day events, good fellowship and the beauties of nature. Being inured to deprivations, they may be spared the trauma of change, illness, unemployment, bankruptcy, which may beset the affluent. Having little, the poor may clearly perceive that little as relating to their final destiny.

All of this forces the inescapable conclusion that abundance needs a goal beyond itself for people to be able to weather the ambivalence and ambiguities of modern life and to fill the emptiness, the **ontological poverty**, at its heart. This encourages the hope that the facets of the spirit of poverty, commitment to God's will, concern for others' needs, effective poverty, a spirit of detachment from riches and a creative and all-embracing charity, are precisely those features which will reorient the affluent away from a narrow concern for material well-being to the larger and more lasting purposes of life. Reconciling the drive for more with the spirit of poverty is treated next.

RECONCILIATION

This concluding section of the chapter will demonstrate that the complex activities of getting and spending can be blended into and governed by the guidelines expressed in the spirit of poverty. It will confirm the rationale and justice of sharing one's worldly goods with others and by doing so crown one's Value aspirations with commitment to an all-provident God. **Integrating the two will not just resolve their seeming contradiction but confirm their mutual corroboration.**

But such blending is not realized automatically and effortlessly. Although the spirit of poverty and one's economic drive are both concerned with producing, sharing and using material goods and services, they impact on these actions quite disparately. First, they look on material goods very differently: the economic mind considers them in secular terms, how people can live better; the religious attitude looks on them as means to an ultimate destiny. Second, they develop differently: in abundant economies the former matures almost spontaneously and unconsciously, often becoming operational and motivating before adulthood; the spirit of poverty, on the other hand, must be more consciously cultivated, usually becoming effective only after much effort. Nevertheless, since religion does not denigrate this life but considers it prelude and preparation for the next, reconciling these two impulses will require showing their theoretical compatibility, making practice possible. More concetely it must demonstrate how the spirit of poverty fits with and can temper the salient features of economic rationality: that material abundance is generated by social productivity; that economic dynamics requires gain-seeking and thereby accelerates change and aggravates scarcity.

Abundance and Productivity

Where economic rationality and practice prevail plenty has replaced privation for the largest part of the population. In fact all peoples can for the first time in human history contemplate the possibility that destitution can be wiped out. The spirit of poverty has no qualms about celebrating abundance as a great human achievement. Spiritual poverty does not perceive God as niggardly or envious of human well-being. The provident Father, who endowed the material world with all its marvelous powers including life and intelligent life, certainly encourages people to master those forces to mitigate the harshness of existence on earth. Like a nurturing Mother God surely is appalled, when human folly, greed and injustice prevents these gifts from being fully utilized or shared equitably.

Destitution, however it was spiritualized or born stoically in the past, is no longer acceptable in affluent and increasingly rebelled against in developing economies. Certainly where produced by war, ideology or greed, the destitution of the masses not only contravenes the wishes of a bountiful and benevolent God, but evinces incredible economic stupidity. Against the plenty which is possible, mass impoverishment generates more brutality than love, more selfishness than generosity, more violence than peace. Furthermore, in view of the obvious fact that this earth's goods are meant for all, the individual can only claim that share of the economy's output necessary for developing as a person and providing for one's family and others to whom one is obligated, the standard still being the mean between penury and extravagance. **In sum, the spirit of poverty affirms the goodness of material goods and wants them shared equitably. It applauds economic abundance, provided all and not just the selfish benefit from it.**

Implicitly, therefore, it approves the work, skills, techniques and management which produce abundance and endorses the principles and motives which guide and propel the economic process. Moreover, as a social system, the freer the collaboration of those involved and the more they share in its benefits, the more productive an economy will, as a general rule, be. Conversely, economies where the masses barely survive while the few live luxuriously are usually marked by labor which is as grudging and coerced as the pay is niggardly. **In short, social productivity requires social sharing.**

The social sharing required here, what is usually called income distribution, is not charity nor is based on need but on a rough proportionality to economic contribution: those who contribute more, get more. Nor does this sharing require an unreal altruism but a hard-headed realism which recognizes that people will cooperate in an enterprise either through force or reward, the latter being much more effective. Briefly put, the success of an economic enterprise is owing in large measure to societal factors and especially the combined contributions of many. Here the collegiality rooted in the spirit of poverty fits neatly with the social productivity the economic mind sees as requisite for economic abundance. The spirit of poverty also, in urging the well-off to share God's bounty with the less fortunate, coincides with the worldly wisdom that an economy, partly rich and mostly poor, where the work of the masses is not rewarded comparably to their contribution, is headed for disaster.

Affluent people, whether they like it or not, are burdened with the obligation to respond to the revolution of rising expectations both in this country and throughout the world. A sense of justice as well as geopolitical prudence will realize that rich nations cannot sail through a sea of destitution without arousing the envy and hatred of poorer nations. Economic rationality will realize that economic abundance cannot turn in on itself but must be expansive: to grow it must invest at home and abroad, developing new markets and products, increasing labor forces and improving skills. All of this requires thawing the economic hopelessness of the people of poor nations and bringing them into the major currents of the world economy.

Thus just as economic rationality mandates both social productivity and equitable distribution, so the spirit of poverty accepts the obligation to emulate divine generosity by helping those in need. In so confirming economic rationality and justice with a true love of the poor and a sense of fellowship with those Christ identifies with himself, affluent peoples can implement God's creative benevolence.

The Dynamics of Gain-seeking

Self-interested gain-seeking presents a greater challenge to reconciliation. Harmonizing the drive for more income, goods and wealth with that spirit which actually prefers poverty to wealth seems a hopeless proposition. But several previous clarifications should be recalled: first, self-interest is a universal requirement for any kind of human action and does not imply selfishness; second, economic self-interest does not mean economic self-benefit, as is evident when parents work to provide a good life for their children. Most necessary, however, is to recall what gain-seeking in modern economies actually seeks. Gain is nothing physical, useful or enjoyable: it consists in those economic constructs, prices, profits, wealth and the like which simply are means for carrying on business. Relatively modest living, therefore, is entirely compatible with great wealth and large income. **Gain, therefore, can be simply accumulated as misers do, used lavishly for one's own benefit or be devoted to the good of others.**

Thus it is possible that a person keen for gain may out of sense of justice acknowledge the right of sharing good fortune with those who contributed to it, from a sense of moderation to direct wealth to achieve higher Values, and finally from a sense of spiritual poverty be willing to bestow much of the gain on others and in this sense to prefer poverty to riches. Further the spirit of poverty in the form of taking less of the gain and glory to give more to others would grease the wheels of collaboration and oil the gears of cooperation for the benefit of the business as a whole. Conversely, milking a company at the expense of capital investment, bullying underlings, niggardliness in rewarding subordinates, intolerance of innovation, skimping on customer service, all evidence of greed and selfishness, are hallmarks of a business on the skid. The spirit of poverty will not substitute for risk-taking, skillful management and the other components of business success, but in itself it is not bad for business.

Of greater benefit, the spirit of poverty will relax people on the treadmill of affluence, slow the rate of acquisition and purge the frenzy of getting. While economic growth requires gain-seeking, the pace need not be frenetic. People can still take time to derive more pleasure from the things they already have, to savor the joy of helping others, and to realize the satisfaction of greater participation in family, neighborhood, church, alma mater and the civic and cultural life of the city. **The spirit of poverty can bring the calming realization that there is many a material good one can do without and still lead a fuller life.**

Gain-seeking, growth, change, risk, these four are bound in an inexorable logic. Growth changes economies, industries, companies, work-places and offices, thus changing incomes, jobs, living standards and the rest. No one and no business is guaranteed a fixed place. All, even the most insulated, are subject to change and thus to risks. The tale of risks in modern living is told by the proliferation of insurance, which, even so, only mitigates the worst financial losses. Chance and fortune continue to play a large role in affluent economies: jobs are lost, markets vanish, businesses fail all by events beyond one's control. The poor in spirit, while nonetheless alert to vocational opportunities, property maintenance and financial planning, will locate their ultimate trust not in the economy or personal ability but in divine providence, judging everything in the light of their transcendent well-being and take what God gives in this life gratefully, confidently and calmly.

The dynamics of change also offer daily opportunities to bear the role of the "servant of Yahweh." Events or circumstances beyond one's control may drastically change one's life and work. A person may be forced to make hard decisions affecting others' well-being. Crises arise which require putting one's Values on the line and calling up reserves of spiritual poverty: quiet acceptance of responsibility, calm confidence to find the means and willingness to make sacrifices to help others. While not muddling hard decisions with maudlin or pollyannish sentimentality, the spirit of poverty is not callously unconcerned but sensitive how to mitigate the harm and let time alleviate the hurt.

In short, the spirit of poverty is effective in the rough and tumble of ordinary life. In survival economies, where the masses daily face economic disaster, trust in divine providence may be their only hope. But the frustrations of the affluent, their sense of insecurity and feelings of life's transitoriness, call for the same humble trust. **A candid analysis of spiritual poverty as both a sense of dependence on God and willingness to bear others' burdens will repay with salt to savor economic abundance.**

Aggravating Scarcity

Where economic rationality and the spirit of poverty are most easily linked is at the paradox that economic abundance does not reduce scarcity but heightens it. A worldly prudence itself acknowledges there is a limit to everything: government handouts, sales, profits, wages, dividends and even the contributions of the generous. It will counsel patience in getting, that nothing worth having is without sacrifice, that there is no free lunch. It will accept the inevitability of poverty in the richest countries because shares in prosperity will always be unequal and, even if all gained proportionately, the rich would acquire absolutely more. Even more paradoxical, a hard-headed realism will favor economic growth in other parts of the country and other nations in the world, even at the cost of increased competition. A tough-minded understanding will concede that overall business is better when there are more and better-heeled customers. All of this fits like hand to glove with the fundamental religious conviction that an effective poverty, some doing without, is essential to dependence on and consequent commitment to divine providence.

Here a person may draw from the deepest well of spiritual poverty by following Christ's example of preferring poverty, that having less is actually having more. The spirit of poverty knows the ontological poverty at the heart of abundance, that material goods can never satisfy completely and their proliferation only increases dissatisfaction. Rather it seeks to relish those goods one has than to yearn for more. This most generous sentiment goes beyond personal concerns to rejoice in others' good fortune and in the role of suffering servant willingly takes on others' burden. In putting one's affluence to the service of those in need, as one would do to Christ himself, everyone in a really unique, though undramatic way, adds his or her special accent to the spirit of poverty.

Far from being the bleak specter painted by secular humanism or the opiate of mass misery depicted by Marx, it should be abundantly clear that the **spirit of poverty is really a theology of wealth.** It does not glorify sociological poverty. Rather it would share the benefits of abundance, thus emulating a bountiful and loving God who set this earth and universe as a home and habitat for all people and all creatures. It goes beyond this roseate dream to the hard realities of daily living, wary that abundance can set forces at work which generate intemperance, frustration, discontent, fear and disillusion. Above all it prevents abundance' luring one into a sybaritic search for pleasure and warns against exploiting wealth just for its power over others, for the animal joy of economic success or for the most senseless purpose of accumulation for its own sake. In the day to day job of living it will give direction to the search for higher Values, strength in observing the mandates of justice and an openness and concern for others. By directing one's consideration to the ultimate purpose of life, the spirit of poverty alone can tolerate increasing material abundance by giving it meaning and a teleology.

ENDNOTES

1. Grelot, Pierre, "La Pauvrete' Dans L'Ecriture Sainte," *Christus*, 8, 1961.
2. Gelin, Albert, *Les Pauvres de Yahve*, Paris: Les Editions du Cerf, 1955, p. 13-28.
3. *ibid.*, p. 10.
4. All biblical references are to *The Jerusalem Bible*, Garden City, New York: 1966.
5. Dt. 28:3
6. Dt. 8:14
7. Dt. 12:24
8. Dt. 24:19-21
9. Dt. 26:12-13
10. Dt. 24:15
11. Dt. 16:12-13
12. Dt. 24:10-13
13. Dt. 24:22
14. Luke 6: 24-26.
15. Yonick, Stephen, OFM, introduction to *Covenant with God's Poor* by Auspicius van Corstanji, OFM, tr. G. Reidy, Chicago: Franciscan Herald Press, 1966, pp. 51-2.
16. Humbert, Alphonse, CSSR, "L'Attitude des Premiers Chretiens Devant Les Biens Temporels", *Studia Moralia* IV, 1966.
17. 1 Tim 6: 17-19.
18. Mulhern, Philip, O.P., *Dedicated Poverty*, New York: Alba House, 1970. Mulhern recounts spiritual poverty's cyclical history of morbidity and vigor during the Christian period. See also his interpretation of it in the light of Vatican II in his chapter VI.
19. Rahner, *op.cit.*, pp. 23-6. Emphasis added.
20. Sawhill, Isabel and Condon, Mark, "Is U.S. Income Inequality Really Growing," Table 1, The Urban Institute, June, 1992.

GLOSSARY

Cluny, Citeaux, La Trappe—All three are locations of Benedictine monasteries where significant reforms began.

collegiality—A manner of exercising authority by eliciting the opinions of one's immediate subordinates.

covenantal—Referring here to Yahweh's promise of a savior to the Hebrews if they remained faithful.

exponentially—A rate of growth by multiples, thus, a very rapid increase.

functional illiterate—One who can read and write but inadequately for contemporary living and participation in a complex economy and political system.

guru—An Hindu religious leader, hence, anyone who exercise great moral or intellectual leadership over others, especially the young.

hubris—An intellectual pride which tends to scorn warnings of danger or misjudgment.

immizeration—A Marxian term referring to the inevitable decline in the living standards of the working class, resulting from wealth accumulation by the capitalist class.

Jansenism—A movement in 17th Century French Catholic Church, which emphasizing human depravity applied moral principles in a straight-laced and rigid manner.

marginalized—As applied to people, their sinking out of the economic and/or social mainstream.

nuance—A delicate or subtle difference of a particular object from the general class.

ontological poverty—Refers to an object's or an action's lack of an ultimate purpose or meaning.

organic principle—The essential or characteristic constituent of an organization in the manner of a living being.

proletariat—The lower working and often indigent classes in society.

Puritanism—The religious and moral doctrine and practices of extreme austerity and scrupulousness.

Remnant of Israel—The group of Jews who returned from captivity in Babylon. Applied often to those who remained faithful to the covenant.

secular humanitarianism—An attitude of care for the needs of other people not from religious motives but from human sympathy and concern only.

servant of Yahweh—A person who accepts the will of God even to the extent of bearing others' problems and sufferings.

sysiphean—Any task requiring great effort but yielding little success.

sybaritic—Pertaining to or characterized by love of luxury and pleasure.

teleology—Pertaining to a person's final end and purpose.

Utilitarianism—The philosophic system which asserts that the final criterion of goodness is usefulness.

TOPICS FOR FURTHER DISCUSSION OR RESEARCH

1. If the excesses generated by affluent living—sensuality, glamour-beguilement and the lust for power—can and have eroded the Spirit of Poverty, as the history of dedicated poverty so amply demonstrates, how is it possible for the Spirit of Poverty to control affluent tendencies and bend their drives toward achieving higher Values and the person's ultimate good?

2. Which movie, *It's a Wonderful Life* or *Death of a Salesman*, in your opinion, paints a more realistic picture of business life? Defend your opinion on the basis of your understanding of this chapter.

SUGGESTED ADDITIONAL READING

1. Philip F. Mulhern, *Dedicated Poverty*, New York: Alba House, 1973, chs.
2. Albert Gelin, *The Poor of Yahve* Trans. by Mother Kathryn Sullivan, Collegeville: The Liturgical Press, 1964, chs. 1-5.
3. Robert Hughes, *The Fatal Shore*, London: Collins Harvill, 1987. Read a few of the early chapters for a graphic picture of the cruelty with which prisoners were treated in the 19th Century.

CHAPTER EIGHT

THE ECONOMORAL SYNERGY

"Synergy", while somewhat pretentious, does describe the effort so far to fashion canons of behavior which blend moral convictions and economic rationality as not only compatible but mutually confirming. Such an attempt at integration recalls that even the most commonplace human act like eating combines many principles of action: biological, social, economic, political and, for many, religious. Synergy, therefore, recollects the book's first theme, the essential complexity of the human person: material yet spiritual, individual yet social, limited yet free, bound to the here and now yet transcendent.

Economoral synergy, more specifically, refers to the actual weaving into a consistent and operational attitude of mind the other major themes of the work. 1) That attitude must accept the basic facts of economic life: scarcity, competition, gain seeking, cooperation and the quantitative constructs necessary for economic activity, price, gain, profit, wealth and the rest. 2) It must be aware that the experience of economic growth and abundance will impact on affluent living by intensifying scarcity, accelerating change and proliferating risks. 3) While Value formation and espousal influence pricing processes, economic aspirations accent the human tendency to sensuality, superficiality and self-aggrandizement, all catering to lower Values. 4) Of the contraposing virtues justice obliges a person to respect the rights of others, especially the least advantaged, to share in the economic common good and to have the opportunity to play rewarding roles in the economy. 5) Moderation looks more to controlling economic self-interest's excesses by directing it toward the higher Values and addressing others' needs. 6) The spirit of poverty provides ultimate meaning to economic ambitions by counseling trust in God amid the uncertainties of affluent living and by emulating Divine generosity in care and concern for the poor.

Even this bare recital of the strands, which form economic morality, promises that multi-dimensional attitude can not be formulated and put into practice without effort. It further suggests that the struggle to achieve it, as with much which is of Value in this life, may be more significant than actually succeeding.

THE MORAL AND ECONOMIC EFFORTS AS ENTERPRISES

"Enterprise" better describes this effort than other words like "pilgrimage" and "quest" for several reasons. Enterprise is more appropriate in discussions with a business context. Pilgrimage and quest emphasize the moral and economic efforts as personal accomplishments, circumstances and other people often being presented as difficulties to overcome or dangers to avoid, while enterprise views them more frequently as resources and collaborators. Pilgrimage and quest also imply missions to be accomplished; enterprise an on-going process with no defined end and ever new risks, endeavors and rewards.

Further Implications of Enterprise

Enterprise presupposes, rather obviously, some get up and go, assuming responsibility for one's life, pondering the principles which should guide it, putting them into practice and reviewing performance and re-evaluating goals. Enterprise implies sacrifice in the usual sense of giving up the inconsequential for the important but also as designating some Values and Goods as inviolate, which cannot be surrendered at any cost.

The **moral enterprise,** for sure, is no pollyannish business. Even the most callous, the most insensitive to others, the most egregious moral failure will preserve some cherished Values and some vestiges of virtue. The moral effort, however, as part of philosophy, seeks answers to the basic questions: What is life? What is a good life? Is life worth living? As enterprise it goes beyond ideas and good intentions to testing one's courage by adhering to duty and confirming one's principles by decisions made affecting complex relationships and in circumstances when answers are not clear-cut. Such hewing to principles, of course, makes a person vulnerable to bigots and zealots, the selfish and prejudiced. Principled people are seldom aware of their moral strength, nor do others recognize it except by increasing reliance on their judgment and firmness in action.

The **economic enterprise** involves no less struggle and effort. The problem of making ends meet is real, universal and on-going: the U.S. deficit problem is just the most glaring example of the struggle with scarcity. The daily worry about paying bills, seeking a raise, complaining about taxes, cutting expenses, meeting payrolls and fulfilling sales quotas are all elements of the same problem of wanting more than income can afford. The exertion people expend to get ahead and the expedients they employ to beat the competition underscores that the economics of life challenges people's skills, capabilities, and psychological resources. Whether successful or failed, people's economic endeavors like their moral efforts will color all of their lives. **Given the universality of scarcity and the continuous downward pull of human nature, both the economic and the moral enterprises are necessarily on-going and life-long.**

As on-going and life-long moral, and economic concerns are dynamisms which pervade all of life. Neither virtues nor vices can be compartmentalized but spill over so as to color every thing one does. Uncontrolled anger or business ruthlessness can destroy friendships, families and lives. Virtues no less can transform one's life and relationships with others, as many a recovering alcoholic has discovered. The economic struggle also touches everything we do. To quote Adam Smith, "In the whole interval which separates those two moments [birth and death], there is scarce perhaps a single instant in which any man is so perfectly and completely satisfied with his situation, as to be without any wish of alteration or improvement of any kind."[1] A person need not be on tenterhooks to wring gain out of every transaction to accept the basic idea that economics plays a role in practically every thing people do and that money, prices, income, wealth and values intrude into even the most private and sacred relations in families, schools, churches, politics and the like. Thus a person must conclude that economics is an aspect of all human action **because all involve scarce material resources and human effort.**

Indeed so much does scarcity pervade all relations and every thing a person does that people are not aware how, like the air they breathe, scarcity is part of the human condition and must be taken into account always and in every way. In this sense, the economic enterprise pervades all human life. Even the seeming exceptions confirm this rule. The wastrel who gaily dissipates his property will eventually be reduced to borrowing, begging, stealing or, worse, working. The person dedicated to helping others is limited to his or her own wealth or what others will give. **Scarcity, therefore, while more overt in some acts than others and more easily seen in some circumstances than others, and the drive to overcome it, while stronger in some people than in others, are factors of every act and no more so than in the life and actions of the affluent.**

The Conflict

Being life-long and all pervasive, the moral and economic enterprises conflict because they impact at different levels of people's well-being and, therefore, pull in different directions. Morality seeks spiritual well-being, truth, goodness and beauty; economics seeks material well-being, the means to satisfy physical wants. Thus the potential is there for disintegrating, tearing apart, the person, governing some actions by moral standards and others by business and economic criteria. Integrity requires that all actions be governed by both.

The moral effort is mainly spiritual, its essence being intentional and transcendental, proposing how a person can develop organically into full personality. As such, however, it cannot be divorced from every day life but rather guides the person in his or her environment and circumstances, family and social ties, psychological make-up, physical abilities and spiritual capacity. While programmed to a pattern of physical growth, aging and death, the human person can, nevertheless, aspire to goals and espouse Values, which motivate action and conduct at a level of existence above the merely physical, sensual and secular. **That is, moral growth is intentional and transcendent.**

Economic aspirations, on the other hand, are secular, concerned with and bound to this life. As a this-worldly wisdom, concerned with the this-worldly condition of scarcity, the economic enterprise in striving to use material resources and limited human effort more efficiently, is never satisfied with the *status quo* but always suggests producing more, producing better and distributing income and output more efficiently. **The economic enterprise knows no surcease in concern for overcoming scarcity and satisfying material wants.**

Economic and moral action differ in two other respects. Economic action always involves **trade-off**, the less desired is surrendered for the more desired, now or later. Moral action, being spiritually oriented, involves an excelling beyond, choosing a **greater Good without repudiating the lesser.** A couple, by sacrificing a night out together for the sake of some charity, may actually draw closer together in love and mutual respect. This suggests the second difference, the goal or good each proposes. The economic goal is satisfying some want, while the moral purpose is the development of the person to his or her absolute best and the Good sought is absolute, something wanted in and for itself. The economic good, conversely, is always relative, an empty basket to be filled by whatever is desired, spiritual or material, moral or immoral and the means used, price, income, wealth and the like, are simply surrogates for what is really desired. Put succinctly, the moral Good is teleologic; the economic good instrumental. **Here especially the moral and economic enterprises diverge: morality is on the high road of intentions, ends and purposes, while economics deals solely with means. While an obvious source**

of conflict, it also hints at the way of reconciliation.

That then sets the theme of this chapter which in a way is the purpose of the book, that both moral convictions and economic common sense must and can be brought to bear on the same human acts. Divergence does not mean contradiction or negation. Quite to the contrary, the differences between the moral and economic enterprises can be blended so as to complement and confirm each other. Just as the force of gravity and the thrust of the jet engine are both necessary for an airplane to fly, one to lift it off the ground and the other to bring it back to earth, so a moral code which is not grounded in the facts of life becomes irrelevant, and economic behavior which feeds no aspirations higher than material gain becomes bogged in purposeless activity. This analogy, suggesting reconciliation, allows looking separately and in turn at both the moral and economic enterprise.

THE MORAL ENTERPRISE

Principles of moral behavior are a practical wisdom grounded in a more speculative wisdom called moral philosophy, that branch of philosophy treating of questions concerning the Good, Values and the Good Life. Frequently today, it is called axiology and as such is part of the philosophic enterprise.

The Philosophic Enterprise

Most people would not think of philosophizing as enterprise in the sense just explained, even if they struggled through a course or two in college. Few people are aware of its claim as the perennial search for understanding. Yet in the grief of a beloved's death, a dark night of despair, the agony of failure or just the calm of a sunset questions arise about the meaning and purpose of living. These are questions which set us apart from the animal, "our meta-animal strivings", according to Daniel Villey.[2] Karl Jasper calls them the basic questions, those asked by children.[3] People philosophize, therefore, because they seek answers to the ultimate reality about themselves, about life and the visible and invisible world. Even though no final answers are possible this side of the grave, **people philosophize because they have to.**

Philosophy asks the three most fundamental questions: what is being? what is truth? and what is goodness? What does it mean to exist in any way, infinitely, contingently, materially, accidentally? How valid is one's knowledge of self, of others, of the physical world, of a spiritual world, of the world of mental constructs, symbols, language, numbers and the like? What is the measure of people, their acts, their relations to others and to the universe? What is their worth, their purpose, their good? These three branches of Philosophy, Ontology, Epistemology and Axiology are not compartmentalized but interpenetrate each other. Ultimately what is, is true and is good. As these questions relate to me, I can affirm that I am, that this self-knowledge is true and that some ultimate Reality and Good is the standard and purpose of my goodness and thus the criterion by which I guide my thoughts and conduct.

In Classical and Medieval times Philosophy, as the quest for wisdom, was *the* intellectual enterprise *par excellence*. There were impressive bodies of practical sciences in medicine, law, astronomy, hydraulics, architecture, husbandry and mathematics. Theology as a systematic interpretation of divine revelation was for believers a comprehensive and uniquely different kind of wisdom. But up until the knowledge explosion of the modern era Philosophy included primitive versions of the physical and social sciences. In breaking out of their philosophic integument and dividing and sub-dividing into independent disciplines, the sciences had to map out their respective fields of inquiry and to discover their particular principles: their approaches to reality, the validity of their knowledge and methodologies, and the cogency of their conclusions for human conduct and behavior.

The formation of a moral attitude, even by many who have little philosophic interest and no training, is in a real sense an encounter with one's self, ideally a self-knowing stripped of illusion, bias and hypocrisy. More often than people realize, it reflects the insights and advice of parents, teachers, pastors, counsellors, authors and others offering a practical moral wisdom. Haphazard, their moral conviction will often bear the scars of moral failures and their rationalizations of those failures. Above all they will evidence the need to strive toward espousing some spiritual and sacred Values to which to fix one's behavioral convictions. The moral effort, therefore, to control one's baser inclinations and to seek higher Values is a life-long enterprise in the sense described earlier. **It is not simply speculative knowledge, not just formulating an ideal, but a praxis, a putting into habitual practice.**

The Elements of the Moral Enterprise

The subject of this moral praxis is, of course, the self-knowing "I" as he or she is here and now, individuated from all others by gender, age, size, genetic, social and economic heritage and so forth. As absolutely unique, whose innermost sanctuary of being is inviolate, everyone must answer for his or her own life. However men and women may shirk this responsibility by drowning it in a swamp of incoherent and random activity or by allowing another or others to dominate their lives, the distinguishing mark of personality is self-responsibility.

From the same fact of personhood, everyone is also social, since all are inherently and necessarily related to others, not simply physically and genetically but as fellow self-regarding beings. Because reclusive self-knowledge is subject to illusion and stagnation, knowing others as persons means comparing one's self-knowledge to and contrasting it with one's experiences of other men and women. Thus in knowing them as persons an individual sees him- or herself as limited person and thereby capable of change and further growth. **Human fulfillment, therefore, can be realized only in commerce with and contemplation of other people.** Besides showing how people differ, communion with them teaches tolerance and sympathy, not only for others but for self. Everyone is seen following a singular path to fulfillment, each needing to fashion his or her own moral attitudes and growth but within a context of openness to and relation with others. **Such is the radical dialectic of knowledge and inspiration which is essential to forming a moral vision.**

Subjective moral responsibility, therefore, does not lead to moral relativism, if a person constantly compares his or her moral standards against others' good qualities. People, however, seldom set out consciously to formulate their moral visions, those Values, human qualities and features of the good life they hold important and in which they believe. Usually a person's moral vision grows haphazardly, reflecting family, neighborhood and school Values acquired almost osmotically rather than consciously. Men and women one loves and respects, parents, teachers, friends, are the obvious sources of moral ideals. Lives and tales of people one admires are ready sources of moral inspiration. Literature, poetry, essays and especially fiction, almost always has a strong moral motive and content, portraying men and women in crises weighing enticements to sensuality, materialism or self-aggrandizement against their moral principles.

Formal analysis of the qualities of the good person and the essence of good conduct has absorbed more effort of philosophers from Plato to the present than any other branch of Philosophy. While differing in points of views and particulars, the good person Aristotle describes would be acknowledged by Aquinas, Hume and Rawls. The models of morality they propose, though differing in emphases and settings, may reflect an almost universal and natural feeling that the good person is **just** in dealing with others, **moderate** in desires and appetites, **prudent** in judgments and **courageous** in actions. Thus everyone can idealize, form a vision, of the kind of good person he or she would like to be, truly unique and individual but reflecting universal standards.

All so far says that the moral enterprise does not consist simply in formulating high ideals but in putting them to work. There inevitably they will be battered and muddied in the give and take of social intercourse and will need to be recast when found inadequate and renewed when transgressed. This effort, furthermore, implies change: a growing into what one should be, as a child grows into an adult, with no loss of continuity or self-awareness. Morality is a knowing but more so it is a doing and a becoming, a dialectic in which knowing directs doing and doing clarifies knowing.

The dialectic is not a blind, haphazard process but one involving mind and will. It implies a vision which, however hazy and incomplete, must be realistic of what a person would like to become. Though taking into account a person's present state and circumstances, the vision is not static: moral ideals become an horizon, always receding but beckoning, urging another step, another mile, another push. **The dialectic, in short, is a process of effort, evaluation and refinement by which a person's moral potentiality is progressively realized.**

Failure is very much a part of this dialectic, not the total failure of moral indifference, despair or surrender, but the daily foibles and shortcomings or even the serious wrongdoing and yielding to passion of people trying to live righteously. Such failings and falls are not defeats, if acknowledged and efforts made to amend. Rather repenting them affirms one's moral vision by testifying to the will to renew the struggle. (By contrast the morally indifferent or callous may seem to possess an equanimity which those striving against their shortcomings do not.) Since moral growth is never really measurable, patience with one's stumblings as well as tolerance of others', is a must. But spiritual progress is evidenced more by effort and intention than by success, because **persistence manifests an efficacious moral vision and striving to fulfill one's nature and potentiality as a person and social being, that is, some ultimate standard and imperative.**

Most moralists would agree that the moral vision, which this dialectical interplay brings progressively into focus, produces a conversion, a turning toward objective, though perhaps unarticulated, moral standards, as the sunflower turns toward the sun, rather than an introversion, a turning into oneself, to the distorted and deviant principles of purely subjective rationalizing. Furthermore, this vision of the ideal is not fantasy but reflects ordinary social intercourse and can be practiced in daily life. What motivates and guides this effort is the basic *should* underlying all moral action, the ultimate reason for doing, what philosophers call and have always labored over, *the moral imperative.*

The Moral Imperative

The moral imperative, as a milder form of the blunt imperative, always implies a reason and an obligation that the person commanded should know. Thus: You *ought* to love your wife because you *owe* repaying all her kindness to you. "Obligation" from the Latin *obligere,* "to bind," implies an indebtedness to another, again from the Latin *dehabere* "to have from" another, that is, "to owe" something, "ought" itself being the past participle of "to owe." In short, the moral imperative always implies some form of debt, arising from a gift, grant, kindness or just the dignity of the person, which imposes a moral obligation on the debtor. Some philosophers, therefore, insist that the moral imperative requires an Infinite Good, the source of all being and goodness, to whom all finite beings are indebted for existence and sustainment. Acknowledging this debt is always depicted as a conversion, a turning toward the Ultimate Good. Opposed to this, ascribing one's goodness to one's self is an inversion, a turning into one's self, a denying of any bond to another being. Thus people with a strong sense of religion, even when misguided, display a stronger and more effective moral imperative than the a-religious.

But moral obligation flows from several sources: the Latin words, *mos, jus, lex* and *fas,* each rooted in the original Indo-European language, express various layers of moral obligation. *Mos* is social custom; *jus* is respecting the natures of people and things; *lex* is a civil ordinance or law; *fas* is the divine will imposing an obligation which, however resisted, is inevitable. Thus moral obligation arises from the many facets of the human condition, from social intercourse, the natures of people and things, the needs of the general welfare and public order, and from religious convictions.

Three other terms, "Good," "Right" and "Value," all met previously, bear on the meaning of the moral imperative. "Good" indicates that a person or a thing lives up to its nature and achieves its purpose for being: a bat is good for hitting base balls; a good person acts and develops as a human being. Every thing's goodness is, of course, relative to the Absolute Good, and as such relates to the moral imperative as the object and measure of what and to what extent anything should be sought. "Right" relates to Good as way to or means for achieving an obligated Good. Rights, therefore, always imply a duty to perform, an obligation to honor or a Good to pursue. To claim a right is to imply a moral imperative. The relation of Value espousals to the moral imperative is obvious in that Values are perceived preferences[4] of the Good of a person, thing or relation and as such ought to be pursued as purpose or goal. **In sum, Good, Right and Value are all elements of the moral imperative.**

Further, the Schelerian analysis of how a person's Value hierarchy develops[5] suggests a similar dynamics in clarifying the moral imperative. For example, when a man's attraction to a woman goes beyond the physical to esteeming her moral qualities, the spiritual Values precede but do not purge the vital Values. In fact, he may find her even more physically attractive. Just so the moral imperative is not achieved in one blinding insight but ideally develops from a deepening perception of the many sources of obligation and their interrelationships which bind a person to others and to an Absolute Good. Just a cursory review of philosophers' efforts[6] to formulate a theory of the moral imperative will repay in a deeper appreciation of the many elements which constitute the imperative as a principle of moral action as self-interested gain-seeking is of the economic.

Plato is always a good beginning. He translates the Socratic "Know thyself" into the spiritual effort to pierce the appearances of things to their eternal forms and in turn to perceive these in the light of the immutable and transcendent Good. While only the elite will ascend to this height, everyone should strive as far as he or she can go. Furthermore, peoples' roles and their power and authority in the social order should reflect their moral superiority, at the top the philosopher kings down to the lowest slave.. Aristotle was more pragmatic, seeing the Good in all persons and things as the source of human happiness and the goal of human striving. But the Good, hence happiness, is multifaceted, including virtue as the mean between the extremes of vice as well as a moderate use and enjoyment of pleasure. Ultimately, Aristotle locates a person's highest happiness in exercising one's highest faculty, contemplation, on the highest object, the absolute Good, the Unmoved Mover from which all reality takes its motion.

In effect, therefore, the ultimate moral precepts Plato and Aristotle prescribe complement rather than contradict each other. Certainly Stoicism and Epicureanism, reflecting respectively Platonic and Aristotelian modes and the most widely practiced ethics of the Classical era, develop codes of conduct which were easily reconciled, as for example, in the worldly wisdom of someone like Cicero. Christian philosophers, like Augustine and Aquinas, reconcile them on a higher plane: Plato's Absolute Good and its reflection in all particular goods and Aristotle's Unmoved Mover and also its effects on all contingent reality are incorporated into the Christian God, who is Ultimate Being and the Highest Good, the source of every creatures' Goodness. Thus the Good, the nature of each person and each thing, becomes the criterion by which each must be treated. This natural law and its reasoned specifications, all infused by the Christian law of love, determine a person's nature and potentiality and, therefore, how he or she should act.

This delicate balance between Faith and Reason was upset in the Modern era. Martin Luther (1485-1546) in his distrust of that "whore reason" fixed the moral imperative on the literal but faith-inspired understanding of God's word, denying the need and validity of any human authority to interpret it for another. Renaissance individualism drew the obvious conclusion that religious faith pertained to private morality only and that reason was sufficient to devise rules for secular conduct. This split was further widened by the wedge Descartes drove between empirical and speculative reason.

While they generally accepted Judeo-Christian moral principles as guides in private matters, philosophers as diverse as

Hobbes, Spinoza, Rousseau, Locke and Henry More (1614-1687), formulated a doctrine of natural law respecting the person's rights of self-preservation, property, association, expression and the like. These rights were perceived as original endowments fundamental to political freedom and self-government. As such they were unlimited except in tacit or explicit contract to respect the rights of others. From them, therefore, are derived codes of public morality which now possess the clarity and cogency of mathematical propositions. The Sentimentalists, Shaftesbury (1621-1683), Hutcheson (1694-1746), Smith and Hume, went a more empirical route, basing the moral code on people's basic instincts and feelings as to what conduct was morally acceptable and what was not in given situations. Sentimentalism, in thus preserving a radical individualism which, nevertheless, worked both efficiently and for the social benefit, shaded inevitably into Utilitarianism. This in turn, cast as a social ethics by Bentham (1748-1832) and the Philosophic Radicals, developed an agenda for many needed social reforms.

Shocked from his dogmatic slumbers by the chaos of a Humean ethics derived from feelings and sense experiences, Immanuel Kant (1724-1804) set modern ethical theory on an entirely new course. In seeking a fixed center of reference, he discovered a categorical imperative, which, being innate, is a *should* which is both more universal and absolute than a conditional imperative. His moral imperative has the force of a simple imperative because he postulates a sense of obligation or duty, preceding all moral motives whether of pleasure, happiness, self-esteem or even the love of God. Thus duty becomes for some a personal conviction, impervious to reason, laws and customs and for others a moral obligation defined by a particular moral, social or political system. Kant's categorical imperative, therefore, can lead to both moral relativism and moral totalitarianism.

Attempts to resolve the Kantian dichotomy produced almost as many solutions as there were philosophers. Hegel locates the individual's moral imperative "in the norms of the free and rational society."[7] Marx fixes human perfection in species man, the solidarity an individual has with fellow humans in a socio-economic order transformed by Communism. Kierkegaard (1813-55), affirming a person's absolute moral autonomy, concludes that a person achieves fulfillment only in a blind and "irrational" leap into Christianity. Equally Existentialistic but totally atheistic, Nietzsche (1844-1900) places the personal imperative which over-rides all traditional moral restraints in the individual's will to power. In the more empirical Anglo-Saxon tradition G.E. Moore (1873-1958) held that people intuitively feel the Good and that the infallible guide is to follow that course of action which produces more Good than any alternative. By contrast, Dewey's Pragmatism (1859-1952) invests the reason for acting with good intention. Thus the Good, even though lacking an ultimate standard, is realized in achieving one's purpose.

While in contrast to the overriding unity of Classical and Medieval philosophizing the Modern seems to dissolve into a welter of conflicting views, some unity can be perceived in moral imperative theory. The *summum bonum* of Classical/Medieval theory has been enriched by the insights of Modern thinkers: the moral imperative reflects personal, civil and economic rights; personal autonomy and freedom; sensitivity to others' reactions to one's conduct; and human solidarity. It implies a fundamental duty which overall tests one's abilities; requires doing what is useful and good in the social order; fulfills the purpose of one's life and thus yields happiness. No one probably incorporates all these facets into his or her moral imperative and thus has plenty of scope for a deeper understanding as revealed in putting into practice one's moral principles.

Complex as the moral enterprise may seem from this analysis it can be reduced to the simple principle of seeking the Good in all actions and in all relations with others. That implies living physically in harmony with nature and socially at peace with others, personally, politically and economically. This last, the economic enterprise, must now be studied and analyzed, preparatory to showing how it and the moral enterprise work together in daily living.

THE ECONOMIC ENTERPRISE

That economic principles can merge with moral convictions in everyday life and actions is suggested by the fact that the first and primitive economic ideas were broached as elements in ethical analysis. In fact, economics continued as a branch of moral philosophy right up to and into the 19th Century. Even today, while most economists think of their science as empirical and positivistic, many, including this writer, consider it more as a behavioral science and thus related to the moral sciences. Finally, economist engage in continuous discussion of questions about the science's subject matter, the validity of its methodology and the force of its prescriptions for conduct, all basically philosophical questions. Together these reasons argue strongly that moral and economic aspirations can be blended into a consistent and coherent attitude.

Preliminary to this effort, however, a short review of the make-up of the economic enterprise will help show how it can mesh into the moral enterprise. Few, of course, would deny that the job of acquiring the material means for living is a universal, life-long and all pervasive effort, an enterprise as defined earlier. A quick look at the content of the economic enterprise will preface explaining how the economoral synergy works.

The Elements of the Economic Enterprise

While the economy is often conceived as a kind of machine, it is actually a complex, multi-dimensional and diversified network of **people**, whose efforts, property and aspirations mutually interact. Individual persons, each with his or her talents, training and education, with different ambitions, work/leisure preferences, adroitness in seizing opportunities and willingness to assume risks, are, therefore, the *subjects* of the economic enterprise and their aspirations determine its goals. Aside from the chance of unavoidable calamities or unanticipated wind falls, people on the whole achieve the level of material well-being in a given economy to which they aspire and try to attain.

At the same time, economic success has a *social dimension* in requiring both using and benefiting others: that is, all economic acts involve some form of cooperation, first, in producing goods and services and then in satisfying others' wants. Consequently, in affluent economies where workers and owners are skilled, technically advanced and ambitious, success spells abundance and large incomes; in survival economies even the successful, however their effort, creativity or good fortune gives them an edge, will live meagerly. Only the rarest person will aspire to riches far above or much less than the average. But within the prevailing parameters in a free economy people's self-interests and abilities will generate innumerable combination of income aspirations and patterns of wanting and spending.

A person's Value hierarchy, though often ignored, importantly influences patterns of producing and spending income. While all Values require effort and the use of economic goods, rarely do people spend excessively on the spiritual and sacred Values but can and do waste resources on the lower sensual and vital Values, which are especially fed by sensuality, vanity, pride, greed, envy and other baser tendencies. Here two economic principles, both derived from human psychology, apply. The first states that, since the person is multi-faceted, all wants are in some sense complementary: they complete each other and, conversely, one want satisfied to excess harms the others, as any addiction testifies. The other is a practical and empirical one called diminishing marginal utility, expressing the generally verifiable fact that as more of a particular good is had, the desire for additional amounts decreases. Together they affirm that economic rationality imposes a constraint on satisfying any particular want and thus on wanting as a whole. Even the most sanguine economic aspiration must be limited. This is further determined by the economic contexts in which individuals are set and within which they must exercise their expectations.

That context, while always multi-dimensional, can be viewed as local, regional, national or global in scope. Obviously the narrower the range, the more individual conduct will affect the whole, though usually trifling, and the more the condition of the whole will impact on the success or failure of personal or business plans and programs. Public policies, at their respective levels, while influenced by and responding to private activity, should be especially alert to overall and general conditions and the factors which shape them, like the money supply, credit market, fiscal policy, employment, work safety, welfare and the like. Public policies, therefore, because they affect the whole economy, must reflect consistently the common sense of achieving the highest ratio of benefit gained to cost incurred.

Finally, two other conditions must be mentioned even if space does not permit adequate discussion. First, all economic acts have time constraints: they must be done immediately, very shortly or over a longer time. The time available, of course, determines what analysis, planning and performance is possible. It also influences the degree of competition a course of action will encounter. In general the longer the time span the greater and more sophisticated the competition. (This, of course, does not change the nature of economic competition which is unique in that competitors contend for business by offering customers more or giving better terms than do their rivals.) **In sum, all economic acts, even those as simple as buying a loaf of bread, are multi-dimensional: individual, collaborative, public, time-bound and competitive.**

Administering this system is a vast array of institutions: banks, savings and loans, investment houses, security and commodity markets, accounting firms, compilers and analyzers of data, legislatures to formulate and courts to administer laws governing rights not only to property, land and material goods but also to ideas, formulas, names, words, and information. All these and others performing like services do nothing to feed, shelter, clothe, move, teach or entertain people directly. But by administering those economic artifacts mentioned several times now, money, prices, wealth, gain, costs, profits and the like, they organize the process and synchronize the signals by which resources and human ideas and effort become the goods which do satisfy the needs, wants and desires of people. In primitive economies all this is done in simple ways; modern economies need a set of sophisticated institutions to produce and market out-put, to gather and invest savings and to finance the mammoth operations of government and business. But in all of these complex matters it is still the individual economic agent who makes decisions and acts. Thus it is important to examine what drives him or her to act.

The Economic Imperative

None of this wilderness of institutions and ceaseless activity makes sense except for the fact that people who already have much want more. It is easy enough to call this madness and greed except that the critics, already enjoying abundance themselves, want more. In fact were it not that throughout history people's economic aspirations always exceeded their abilities, a scattering of primitive peoples would still be eking out short and miserable lives in caves. These observations bring the analysis back to the beginning, **the problem of economic scarcity**, the problem of making ends meet, wants exceeding income, and its implications for behavior.

Prices, of course, are evidence of economic scarcity. Abundance, therefore, by generating both more goods and more wanting does not lessen but increases scarcity. Indeed, because humans are creatures of increasing wants in a finite and limited world, scarcity is inherent in the human condition. To have more of any economic good something else must be foregone. This becomes obvious in the following absurd example. Suppose everybody could have everything he or she would ever want, all at the same time: all the furnished houses, cars, yachts, clothes, food and every thing else in such amounts that no one need give up anything to have more of something else. What a mess this would be! There would not be enough room on earth to store the goods, let alone produce or enjoy them. Even the superrich would be more prisoners than possessors of their opulence.

Economic scarcity, of course, does not mean dearth or lacking, nor imply destitution or a want of basic necessities. It does not mandate a clutching self-interest or stinginess in caring for others. Nor does it require that people devote all their efforts to making a living and acquiring material riches. Least of all, does it deny that a bountiful Providence has endowed this world with sufficient powers and resources that all may live decently. To the contrary, economic scarcity is entirely compatible with plenty. Indeed its study implies that more sharing generates more, and people, who order their priorities to espouse higher Values and to help the needy, both enrich their lives and stimulate the economy. **What economic scarcity does affirm is that, because of people's continuing and increasing wants, limited resources as well as human time and energy, must be used *efficiently*, that is, to satisfy the most and most desired wants.**

The rational alternative, therefore, to a world glutted and clogged with goods is a system of producing for exchange. The basic rationale of every economic act, therefore, involves **choice and trade-off**, everyone getting what he or she wants by working or using property to produce what other people want. Ideally then commodities should be produced currently in such amounts that all, while getting enough regularly for decent living, would only have and keep enough for present or near future use. **All this translates to the economic imperative: the mandate imposed by economic scarcity on every individual, family, business, government agency, and non-profit institution to strive for economic efficiency, to choose that which promises more net satisfaction or gain over that which promises less.**

While this maxim can be reduced to the universal proposition, that an economic agent in every act should make gainful trade-offs, it must, of course, be done morally and, more to the immediate point, put into practice in a complex and changing real world and made specific to the multi-dimensional context of economic actions. In the simple acts of buying/selling commodities, negotiating employment and producing for profit, a person should choose that course which gives the highest satisfaction relative to what must be given in exchange, each party consulting not only his or her self-interest but what the other party wants. The same principle applies in collaborative action. Here the entrepreneur must consult the self-interests of employees, suppliers and investors in such wise as to pay all (incur costs) proportionately to their contributions to the product's expected market value and thus to profits, whose generation is the firm's purpose for being. Thus the mandate of efficiency, the imperative of gain-seeking drives the economic enterprise with all its multi-dimensional relations with others and through a maze of institutions, administering those economic constructs which both constrain and enable economic action.

Progress from Failure

Given the economic act's many dimensions and its complex setting, doing it expeditiously and with finesse is quite a trick. Despite the help of private institutions and government agencies, people do make mistakes: some constantly, others occasionally; some willfully, others rashly; some in minor matters, others disastrously. Even the experts will disagree, advocating and pursuing courses of action at cross-purposes. As a result the economy is always marked with a constant seething, a continuous process of reactive adjustment. To some it always seems teetering on the edge of the precipice.

Rather obviously, therefore, all economic decisions and activities are fraught with the possibility of failure or of falling short of expectations. Getting anything requires giving up something else. Even so no commodity will live up to anticipations. Since choosing is of the uncertain future, risk is endemic. Timing constrains analyzing all the factors involved, so that one can hope not for maximum gain but only the best under the circumstances. The market itself is a restraint, imposing prices and, thereby, impacting on goals and Values to the extent economic means are essential to achieving them. Prices are more annoying when they seem to cater to wants and tastes of which a person disapproves. They are most oppressive when protected by monopoly power of corporations, unions or, worst of all, governments, especially when they exclude from buying those whose needs are greatest.

Besides these pitfalls people most frequently fail by forgetting complementarity in their wanting and in their gaining. No want can be satisfied in isolation but must be balanced with gratifying other wants, some necessary for satisfying it, some enhancing and others diminishing it. Also in producing for sale success is dependent on others' collaboration and, consequently, acknowledging their functional complementarity by sharing in the gain is essential. More egregious failures results from not seeing economic ambitions in terms of life goals and fitting one's standard of living, income generation and wealth accumulation to these higher ends. Indeed some levels of opulence may endanger callings, professions and vocations and even pervert the goal of pursuing spiritual Values, of helping others or of engaging in public service. The moral collapses and career shipwrecks of many professionals, public officials and clerics bear sad witness to this. On the other hand, idealistic aspirations cannot ignore the precepts of economic scarcity. Indeed heeding its precepts may contribute to, while disregarding them impede, realizing one's ideals.

All the preceding confirms that economic rationality is a hard practical wisdom and that economic progress, like moral growth, comes not from never making mistakes but from acknowledging, analyzing and correcting them. Submitting to this discipline is the way to improve methods, to anticipate risks and to submit to market demands. This is how failures create new businesses, generate new values and realize gain for themselves and others. This is how conscientious workers learn their crafts and homemakers salvage family finances. **Economic progress has never been failure-free.** When moral failures result in economic failure as, for examples, when an employer's niggardly wage policy constantly loses competent employees or doctored expense accounts result in being fired, the need to blend economic aspirations into the larger moral picture becomes painfully clear. Indeed, if one can find in almost every business failure either blatant vice or moral shortcomings, it should be just as evident that moral integrity buttresses good economic practice.

In short, moral aspirations and economic rationality, though at distinct levels of human effort, can be directed toward an ultimate purpose for living. This is the meaning of synergy and is, in fact, the theme of the book. What remains is to combine conclusions already affirmed into a working synthesis and thus by blending moral convictions with economic rationality to fashion a functioning code of economic morality.

The Economoral Blend

Such blending, of course, mandates setting up an overarching purpose or destination for life. Teleological integrity, even for those who consciously strive for it, is very fragile because the multi-faceted human person has not only different but conflicting goals, most obviously so in his or her effort to combine the moral and economic enterprises. Prerequisite is mutual acceptance and tolerance of the validity of each discipline's principles of action and honoring their respective areas of competence. A science of scarcity cannot be gotten from the Bible or philosophic analysis nor an ersatz ethics derived from economic principles and analysis of the free market. On the other hand, the point was made repeatedly that economic common sense fits well with moral convictions. Certainly, economic rationality is a kind of ***prudence*** and making decisions about the uncertain future requires a form of ***courage,*** called risk-taking. Justice and respecting others' rights is essential for economic and business collaboration, and scarcity requires ***moderation.*** **Virtue, as a general rule, makes good economic sense.**

Boulding makes the converse point that disordered affections can foul up good economic practice:

> It would be interesting to go through the seven deadly sins and to see them as critique of unhealthy preferences: pride preventing learning and feed-back, anger preventing cool and rational judgment, lust involving inordinate desire which destroys rational choice, envy involving malevolence at the welfare of another, greed or covetousness involving not only

> inordinate desire but lack of benevolence and a crippling of identity, gluttony likewise involving a loss of restraint and rational choice, and sloth involving the decay of the decision-making power itself.[8]

How morality and economics, both equally valid sciences of human behavior, can fit together is the problem. A frequent solution tries to balance efforts to make a living with concerns for the spirit by allotting time for each. Too frequently this tends to split one's life, the larger part given to economic ruthlessness and the lesser to good intentions and reconciliation. Most usually, the struggle for economic means swamps concern for moral ends. Tawney is to the point: "Men will always confuse means with ends, if they are without any clear conception that it is the ends, not the means, which matter."[9]

Comparing the economoral synergy to a marriage is also off the mark. Here two equally valid and necessary but different principles, the masculine and feminine, are joined together in a common endeavor and manner of living. The analogy correctly demonstrates that two diverse principles can be blended together. It fails, however, in that moral and economic principles, while both valid and necessary for living, contribute unequally as canons of conduct. **Morality relates to the ultimate purpose and end of life, including using material goods to achieve them. Economics schools people in the efficient use of material means toward material well-being in this life.**

A more apt analogy is that of short-run tactics and long-run strategy. A person's moral goal and ultimate end is fulfillment as person and encompasses all the acts and means to attain it. This is a person's long-run strategy. Short-run tactics would be the daily acts, each with its particular purpose and manner of doing. For example, an economic act would be to use scarce material good so as to satisfy some want in the most efficient way. The two, an over-arching purpose and the flow of activity, occur simultaneously but the moral is the definitive guide and coalescing agent tying disparate and seemingly contradictory actions into some sort of consistency. Despite, indeed because of, these functional differences, economic and moral principles can blend in appraising the same actions and attitudes. Moral criteria must take into account practical considerations or they lose credibility; economic acts must aim beyond themselves or they becomes meaningless. **Together they fashion a more coherent and purposeful life. Moral goals can endow the daily struggles, anxieties and even failures with transcendent meaning. Economic efforts, whether successful or not, in challenging moral purpose both clarify and harden it.**

In principle, therefore, the two enterprises, the economic struggle with proliferating scarcity to gain material well-being and moral striving for self-fulfillment by combatting the human tendency to baser Values, can be so integrated that they are mutually corroborating. For both the many-faceted individual person, constantly wanting more in a limited world, set in a web of human relations and in a many-layered context of cultural and economic institutions, is subject and agent. Failings in such complexities are inevitable, but people can clarify and firm up both their economic aspirations and moral efforts by acknowledging mistakes and reaffirming goals. In all this the moral imperative, to seek one's highest Good as person in every act, and the economic imperative, to seek gain by striving for efficiency in every transaction, can work together to enhance a person's manner of and purpose for living.

Most especially the light of a person's moral vision, even though flickering sporadically on daily activities, will reveal them as consistent or not with one's moral goals. Such sensitivity to and awareness of moral principles in all facets of economic life will alert one to the all too human dispositions to sensuality, superficiality and self-aggrandizement; to self-interest's easy slide into selfishness and greed; and to the peddler principle which weighs every human action, relation and Value solely as a gain/cost ratio. Such a moral attitude will by itself encourage a person to find some moral meaning in daily economic and business activity. A person may even remember some of the themes of this book: the value of value-thinking over price-thinking; the need to raise, refine and clarify one's Value hierarchy to grow as persons; moderation as an internal control on self-benefit and the affluent tendency to want more; social justice as sensitivity to the rights of others especially in collaborative activity; and, finally, using one's abundance as a way of emulating a bountiful Providence by sharing with others less fortunate.

In all of this moral intentionality, as the grand strategy of one's life, has primacy. In every conscious act people commit themselves in some small way to realizing or failing to realize their ideals. Where the vision lacks specificity or is blurred in the flux of events, a person may even with the best intentions waste income, time and effort in pursuing haphazardly goals at cross-purposes with each other, all adding up to frustration and disillusion. This more than the moral shipwreck of the willfully evil, the materialism of the spiritually indifferent or the bitterness of the self-righteous is the real tragedy of economic abundance.

This then brings the book back to where it started. Beyond economic ethics and its techniques for solving issues of conscience in business, economic morality develops a healthy attitude to economic principles and endeavors, seeing in economic self-interest, competition, gain-seeking and the rest in all their variations and configurations as necessary responses to scarcity. Economic morality, therefore, keeps its equanimity when viewing lives and vocations devoted to exercising such principles in the course of generating a material abundance undreamed of just a generation or two ago. On the other hand, economic morality asserts that the spiritual principles, which guide moral development, define rightful relations with others, govern Value aspirations and give an ultimate meaning to this life's striving, are not only compatible with economic purposes but are essential for their functioning well.

Wauwatosa, Wisconsin
May 13, 1993

ENDNOTES

1. Smith, Adam, *The Wealth of Nations, op.cit.*, pp. 24-25.
2. Villey, Daniel, "Prologomenes a L'Enseignment de la Philosophie Economique," *Revue d'Economie Politique*, v.59, p. 377.
3. Jaspers, Karl, *Introduction a la Philosophie*, Paris: Aubier, 1951, p. 4.

4. Scheler, Max, *op. cit.*, pp. 105-10.
5. *ibid*
6. MacIntyre, Alasdair, *A Short History of Ethics*, New York: Macmillan, 1966. The following section is largely owing to MacIntyre's treatment.
7. *ibid*, p. 209.
8. Boulding, Kenneth, "Ethics of the Critique of Preferences," in *Limited Resources and Social Policy*, eds. W.M. Finnin, Jr. and G.A. Smith, Baton Rouge: Louisiana State University Press, 1979, pp. 9-10.
9. Tawney, R.H., *op.cit.*, p. 46.

GLOSSARY

canon—Any rule or principle which is generally accepted as true and as criterion of good conduct or usage.

categorical imperative—An absolute, unqualified and obligatory command. Kant's principle that one must act on those maxims, whether public laws or personal convictions, which one would will to become universal laws.

ersatz ethics—An ethics not derived from philosophic and psychological principles but from another discipline, e.g. from economics.

existentialistic—A keen awareness of one's being, contingency and freedom, thus, individual responsibility for becoming the person one has become.

integument—An external coating of skin or covering, thus a confinement, restraint or limitation.

moral relativism—The denial of absolute moral principles and affirmation that an act's morality depends on the agent and circumstances of the act.

moral totalitarianism—The condition of a people for whom the state or a community has determined the moral principles and precepts which govern them.

natural law—Moral principles derived from the nature of the human person and the natures of other things and animals in the universe.

osmotically—The diffusion of one thing into another by osmosis, hence, the blending of one mode of acting into another by a spontaneous process.

Sentimentalism—The moral system which asserts that the goodness and evil of one's own and others' acts are perceived by an internal moral sense or sentiment.

species man—Marx's conception of the ideal moral state of the individual in becoming perfectly in tune with the nature of the human species and thus to all other human beings.

synergy—The combined and mutually reinforcing action of two or more forces.

TOPICS FOR FURTHER DISCUSSION OR RESEARCH

1. Defend the proposition that the ancient concepts, lex (law), mos (custom), jus (justice) and fas (the Divine word), are still relevant as elements in one's moral imperative.

2. In your opinion is it necessary for Mother Theresa and her Missionaries of Charity in their desire to alleviate destitution and physical need wherever they may be in the world to heed such economic facts and principles as scarcity, competition, gain-seeking, diminishing marginal utility etc. If you think so, explain why so. If not, why not?

3. In your judgment which process is more economically efficient in terms of costs and benefits: a welfare program administered by a government agency or a private charity such as above, both addressing the same human needs. Give strictly economic reasons for your judgment.

SUGGESTED ADDITIONAL READING

1. Alasdair MacIntyre, *A Short History of Ethics,* New York: Macmillan, 1966.

INDEX